Manchester's Victorian Art Scene

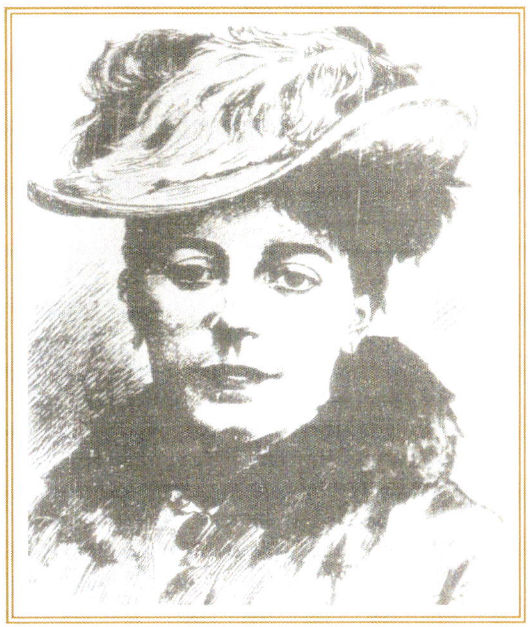

And Its Unrecognised Artists

First published in 2007
by Manchester Art Press,
Warrington WA1 1JW.

Designed by Susan Thomson
Printed by Biddles,
King's Lynn PE30 4LS.

Cover illustration:
The Stanfield Catalogue, 1895, Manchester Art Gallery.
Left to right – Artists, F.J. Shields, J.H.E. Partington,
E.G. Thomson, Manchester Central Library.
Frontispiece:
E.G. Thomson, Manchester Central Library.

ISBN 978-0-9554619-0-3

To Chris and all our boys and girls

CONTENTS

ACKNOWLEDGEMENTS
Very special thanks to Christopher J. Thomson
Special thanks to Melva Croal, Curator of Fine Arts, Manchester Art Gallery who opened the door and made me so welcome.

I should like to thank the following for being so generous over reproduction rights:
Blanche Peter E.
Central Library, Manchester Archives and Local Studies, Kevin Bolton
Cheltenham Ladies' College, Anna Parker, Rachel Roberts
Columbian University Press, New York, Zoe Arey
Eton College, Nick Baker, L. Connor, P. Hatfield
Gallery Oldham, Dinah Winch, Stephen Whittle, Peter Fox
Honourable Michael McLaren Q.C., Bodnant Hall, Conwy
Lady Aberconway of Bodnant Hall, Conwy
Lord and Lady Ashbrook and Charles and Jane Foster of Arley Hall, Cheshire
Manchester Academy of Fine Arts, Sheila Dewsbury
Manchester Art Gallery, Tracey Walker, Picture Library Manager
Northwich Library, all the staff
Pankhurst Centre, all the staff
Reverend Canon Hill, St. Ann's Church, Manchester
Stockport Art Gallery Andy Firth and Katie Cavanagh

I should also like to thank the following for their kind help:
Bury Art Gallery, Richard Burns
Courtauld Institute of Art, Witt Librarian, Barbara Thompson
Hodder Education, Nick Wetton
John Rylands University Library,
John Rylands Library, Deansgate, Manchester
Local Heritage Library, Stockport, Carole A Perry
Manchester Art Gallery, all in the fine arts
Manchester Metropolitan University Library
Musee de Pont-Aven, Catherine Puget
National Portrait Gallery, Caroline Molyneux
Oldham Local Studies and Archives, T. Berry
Pearson Education Limited, Nikki Bannister
Platt Hall Costume Gallery, Manchester, Miles Lambert
Tate Gallery Picture Library, London
Warrington Library, Museum and Archives Service, Michelle Kay
Whitworth Art Gallery, Manchester, Charles Nugent

I have made every effort to contact copyright holders: if there are any errors or omissions I apologise.

PICTURE ILLUSTRATIONS

INTRODUCTION

"So Mr. Shields will remain unrecognised
except by those who seek him out."
Charles Rowley.

This small but very significant statement, made by a leading member of Manchester's Victorian Art Scene, really does sum up the complete contents of this book. In fact, just three words taken from this quotation actually suffice: seek out, unrecognised. Its chapters do exactly this. They seek out Manchester's unrecognised Victorian artists and then gleefully smother them in history.

CHAPTERS

Chapter 1 Joseph Allen - 1769-1839
Portrait Painter

Sets the Manchester Scene before Queen Victoria comes to the throne – biography and techniques – Allen's sitters with snippets of history: Hannah Hatfield: the Peterloo Massacre, Peter Clare: Horologist, Quaker and a leading member of the anti slavery committee. Dr. White: Founder of the Manchester Royal Infirmary and leading surgeon in the North of England, -Sir George Richard Philips: Eton College and M.P. for Horsham 1818.

Chapter 2 Charles Allen Duval - 1805-1872
Portrait Painter and Photographer

Heralds in Queen Victoria's reign – paints the landed gentry: portraits of Rowland Eyles Egerton and his mother at Arley Hall, Cheshire – Duval's extrovert nephew: Charles Henry Duval – Duval's paintings: The Ruined Gamester, The Methodist Centenary, Luther Burning The Pope's Bull – political paintings: Daniel O'Connell, Richard Cobden, John Bright in situ at Bodnant Hall, Denbighshire - Thomas Milner Gibson – Duval the photographer: Sir Joseph Whitworth.

Chapter 3 The Royal Manchester Institution And Warwick Brookes

Formation of the Royal Manchester Institution – life drawing banned – a portrayal of the Manchester artist Warwick Brookes.

Chapter 4 The Manchester Academy Of Fine Arts And The Manchester Society Of Women Painters

The Manchester Academy and some of its objectives – the formation of the Manchester Society of Women Painters – critics and their exhibitions – behind the scenes at the Manchester Academy on Varnishing Day.

CHAPTER 1

JOSEPH ALLEN
1770-1839
PORTRAIT PAINTER

Obviously Joseph Allen was not a true Victorian painter. He had already played an important role within Manchester's art scene before Victoria came to the throne. As a competent artist, he helps to portray the art scene just before Manchester explodes into a vibrant Victorian city full of art and colour to be enjoyed by all its citizens.

With the help of Allen, and by turning the hands back on the clock just a little, it is possible to go back to a time when portraits were very fashionable, but could only be commissioned by wealthy patrons. This form of art was definitely the way forward and Allen was in his prime and ready to take full advantage of this situation.

A good portrait painter was held in high esteem. Allen was an impressive portrait painter with an equally impressive portfolio; in fact it was a unique portfolio containing a vast number of well known Manchester faces. Faces which for a fleeting moment allowed their viewers to drift off and imagine all sorts of things.

Before he came to Manchester Allen studied at the R.A. Schools in London, and then settled for a time in Wrexham, which he used as a base to visit a number of northern towns and gradually build up his impressive portfolio. He was astute enough to realise Manchester had some rich pickings.

So in 1810 Allen established himself in Manchester taking rooms in a house in King Street. He became well known locally as a top portrait painter and was patronised by some very distinguished Lancashire families. Robert Crozier [1] a well known and respected Manchester painter wrote about Allen in the following manner: **In height about five feet eight inches, and inclining a little to stoutness, though not over much. His hair was grey and he had not much colour. His features were squarish.**

1 Crozier was a founder member of the Manchester Academy of Fine Arts and its President from 1878 until a month before his death in 1891.

His painting room in Manchester was in the house which had been occupied by Dr. White. One large room was a sort of showroom and a smaller one he used for painting in, working by a side light. He was much employed on portraits, and he would have from thirty to forty portraits ranged round his large room at once.

He got about fifteen guineas for a three-quarter and twenty guineas for a kit-cat. 2 **His portraits were excellent in likeness, his handling was of a good square character, and his touch positive.** 3 **His pictures are not luminous, consequently his colour is not great, there being a tendency to blackness. He might not stand so high now as in his own day.**

With fashions persistently evolving it would seem there were doubts about Allen's portraits being too dark at the end of the nineteenth century. How an artist paints is continually reviewed throughout the centuries, fashions come and go, and dark paintings are a personal thing. What is so exciting about Allen's paintings are their historical value. Almost like a spider's web, Allen's portraits have trapped an intricate Mancunian social history between their dark layers over the centuries.

They are brimming with history, a history which makes them glow through the darkness. Seek out this history and they immediately become alive even losing their sombre tones. The following portraits all have some kind of history hidden away between their painted layers.

---

2 Kit Cat (Kitkat). A canvas, size 36 x 28 inches, which is adapted to a portrait showing the head and one hand.

3 A person named Epson wrote in the Manchester City News, 26th October 1878 - Allen was commissioned by Lord Lonsdale, Lowther Castle to paint the full length portraits of his three daughters at four hundred guineas each. Which if true does seem a good deal more compared to Crozier's kit-cat paintings.

"I am the family face;
Flesh perishes, I live on."
Thomas Hardy.

HANNAH HATFIELD - 1754-1827

The following information appears on the back of Hannah's portrait which belongs to the Manchester Art Gallery.

Hannah Hatfield painted at the age of 72, oil on canvas, unmarried, died 1827 Aged 73.

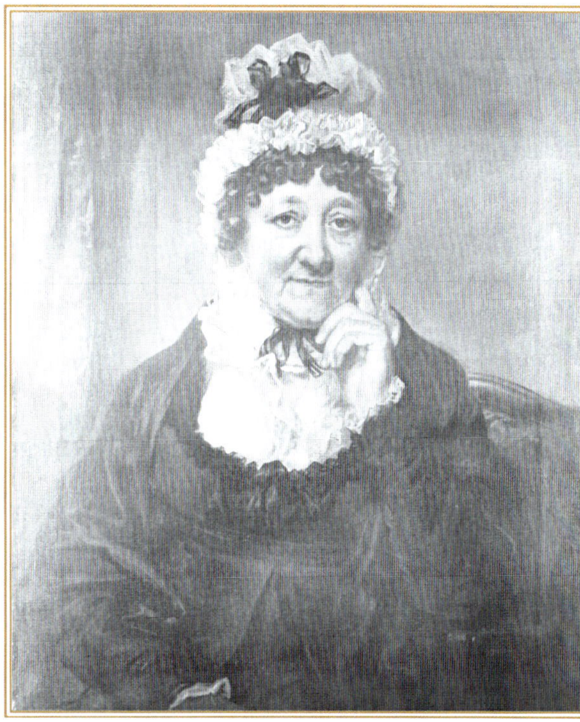

Figure 1. J. Allen, *Hannah Hatfield*
Manchester Art Gallery

Allen has captured and portrayed such a perfect image of this middle class stalwart woman.

Alas Hannah is confined to a dark basement. She is a gem, and could almost be seen as an archetypal Jane Austen character. At a glance she seems very ordinary, but in a similar way to Austen's characters she too has hidden depths.

Her black dress and plain background add a sombre tone to the study. Her lace indoor cap trimmed with ribbon contrasts against her black dress without managing to avert the viewer's eye away from her strong facial features. Allen has captured her eyes. Her direct gaze engages the onlooker and proudly says, "I am Hannah Hatfield an educated woman with a vast amount of knowledge behind these eyes."

Most importantly, Hannah is dressed properly for her sitting. She is a product of her time and has followed etiquette and worn a black silk high waisted dress signifying her age and her station in life - that of an elderly middle class spinster. Her dress is dark, practical and respectable. Her cap is extremely fashionable made of white cotton and lace gathered into a full crown and tied with a ribbon under her chin. It has an abundance of dark curls attached to it.

She has a deep cotton ruff over her long sleeved lace cuffed linen chemise - all are immaculate, snowy white proving she is a prosperous lady. There are no obvious objects of wealth in the picture. She is void of any jewellery and there are no expensive items on show in the background. Her clothing says it all.

At the time Allen painted this portrait both he and Hannah would be extremely class conscious. Hannah shows this in the way she dresses. Allen in the way he paints her. There is a good deal of kudos in this portrait for Allen as he has already painted her father and now paints Hannah, the unmarried daughter of Thomas and Mary Hatfield.

Her father, a self made man, was born in Rotherham around 1725 and came to Manchester as a boy. At the age of twenty eight he went into partnership with a baker, George Bramwall, who at that time was recognised as the leading corn merchant in the town. In 1758 the partnership was dissolved and the business became a family concern. It became a prosperous and thriving business, even though a year earlier, in November 1757, Travis Mills belonging to Messrs Bramwall and Hatfield had been nearly destroyed during the food riots.

Allen has captured Hannah's direct gaze. What is she thinking about? That we will never know. What we do know is Hannah is in her early seventies and has seen history being made around her in the city of Manchester. There are letters in Hannah's own hand writing which allow us a quick glimpse into some of her more disturbing memories of Manchester.

Hannah's letters begin in 1812. A year previous to this the people of Manchester are angry and ready to rebel against the authorities. They are starving and rebelling against the Corn Laws. They have done this before but this time it is different: they are full of vengeance and their rioting will have far deeper repercussions.

In 1812, at the age of twenty three, Hannah's nephew Thomas has sole charge of the family business and he is feeling very anxious and scared. He had seen the riots coming and wrote as much to his uncle, Thomas Nicholson: [4] **The times are very bad in Manchester and if something is not done to alleviate the distress of the poor, or to relieve the depression of commerce, I fear there may be much calamity created, for which the prudence of future years will not compensate.**

How right he was. Trade was rock bottom, the middle classes sensed something awful was about to happen and the working classes were starving and ready to riot. The authorities had called a meeting to make a loyal address to the Prince Regent. When it was found that the occasion would be taken to actually inform the Prince Regent of the sufferings of the inhabitants the meeting was cancelled. The crowd became furious and the riots began. The Corn Exchange was torn down.

Through her letters Hannah's shrewd character unfolds: **At present we have no reason to be alarmed although there are great disturbances all around.**

She then refers to the angry crowd who had been let down by the authorities: **Such meetings are very improper at such times as the present and in a populous town as Manchester where there are so many suffering for want of bread. They have no idea of any one suffering but the corn dealers.**

They will be more cautious I hope in the future to endeavour to keep peace and not to irritate. It has always been a painful subject for me who has seen and heard so much. To keep still is the best for one cannot help being sorry for many at this time, now every necessary is so high. At the same time Hannah writes to her nephew Thomas Nicholson: Since I last wrote our minds have been very much disturbed. Every day fresh fears upon us.

---

4 All the letters in this section have been taken from: Nicholson Francis, and Axon Ernest, Transactions of Lancashire & Cheshire Antiquarian Society - 1910, The Hatfield Family of Manchester and The Food Riots of 1757 and 1812. Copy Manchester Art Gallery.

My poor nephew is quite unmanned. These are distressing times I pray God we may be supported under them. We are robbed of our soldiers, so many places want them. It is 11'Oclock and we have heard the noise of the cannon twice which is dreadful to hear. From whence we cannot tell.

She apologises for her gloomy letter and states she is anxious for the morning.

Thomas writes to his uncle stating he intended to retire and that: All seems quiet here today. The weaving factory was destroyed at Newton last night and 15,000 pounds worth of property destroyed.

On the 26th April 1812 Hannah informs us that the week has passed without intruders, and three soldiers had attended Travis Mill every night. She states she will not be parting with her guards until things have settled down, and concludes her letter by saying she is in poor spirits.

After a gap of nine months in January 1813 she writes: What a dreadful scene it must be to see fourteen executed in one day. It surely will be a terror to evil doers. There are some hardened wretches still left. I fear we have many doubtful people in this part of the world.

In October 1816 she writes to Thomas James who is filled with foreboding: There is no one now can be divested of thought, they are trying times. It is a public calamity, the winter is dreaded when we see so many out of employ and many unable to work.

A letter written in April 1817 showed how serious the situation had become. She describes Manchester with no prospect of better times. She also comments on the large number of soldiers within the city.

Since Sunday we have had watch and ward every night. In such a place as Manchester any commotion is alarming. So many out of employment and greatly distressed. No prospect of better times. So many soldiers increase the price of provisions.

In February 1819 Thomas writes: We have had a dreadfully tempestuous week with that radical demagogue Hunt. I once saw him and from his white lips which are an invariable sign of meanness I expect he would do mischief before he left us.

This could now be seen as an understatement. All these letters underpin the build up to what became known as the Peterloo Massacre.

This massacre took place around noon on the 16th August 1819 when thousands of people converged on a piece of ground called St. Peter's Field to hear the staunch radical, Henry Hunt speak. Many were reformers carrying banners for their causes. Hunt was to address the crowd. His speech would cost him three years imprisonment. He climbed the scaffolding to speak and within a short time the Yeomanry Cavalry advanced upon the crowd and made their way towards Hunt dragging him off the scaffolding and arrested him.

Having achieved their aim they then turned on the crowd and began to trample them with their horses and hack them down with their sabres. They killed 11 people and injured over 400.

Hannah Hatfield's premonitions had all come true. The Battle of Peterloo plays an extremely prominent role in Manchester's history and Allen's portrait and Hannah's precious letters have allowed the reader a rare glimpse into how it came about.

PETER CLARE - 1781-1851

In the twenty-first century CIS Manchester Gallery - hangs a portrait of Peter Clare painted by Joseph Allen.

In 1927 Elias F. Jesper wrote to the curator of the art gallery asking him if he would be interested in purchasing a portrait of Peter Clare.

Jesper wrote: **Clare was a well known Manchester man – a Horologist, a Quaker and a**

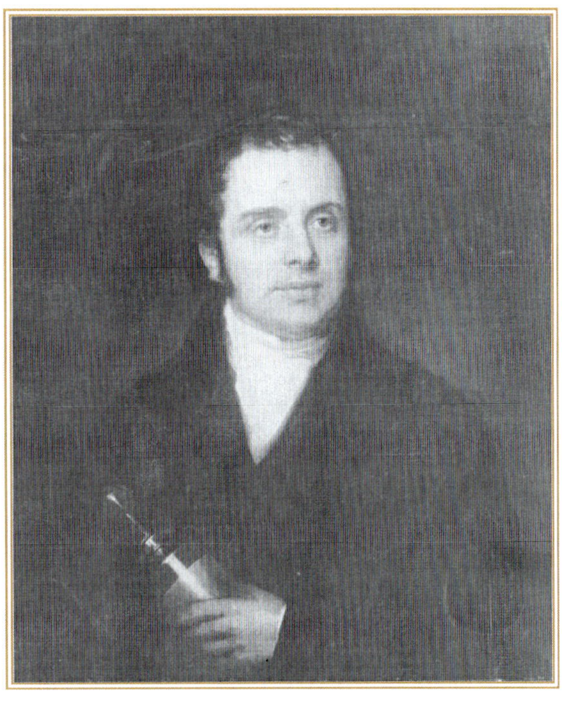

Figure 2. J. Allen, *Peter Clare*
Manchester Art Gallery

leading member of the anti slavery committee. He was also a fellow of the Royal Astronomical Society and Vice President of the Literary and Philosophical Society of Manchester. Clare was a very close friend and executor of the famous Dr. John Dalton - the Atomic Theory man.

These two well known Mancunians were described walking through the streets as follows: **Clare and his friend "the greater Ajax" both wore the garb of a Quaker in cut, not drab, but black, and there was a primness and finish about their broadcloth and spotless linen that one seldom saw. Clare was erect and dignified, and seemingly proud of the burden on his right arm which Dalton's left hand pressed upon it.** [5]

In his portrait Clare is holding a Leyden Jar, the earliest device for storing electric charge, named after the University of Leyden, where it was invented in 1746. A glass jar was coated inside and outside with metal foils, which were connected by a rod passing the insulating stopper. The jar was usually charged from an electrostatic generator, and was an early form of capacitor

In his youth Clare would assist his father, who was in the habit of giving occasional lectures on electricity, and some kindred subjects in natural philosophy, illustrated by experiments. It could be this Leyden Jar was used by his father when experimenting. By placing this in the painting Allen is letting the viewer know Clare had a scientific side to his nature. He was in his later years Vice President of the Literary and Philosophical Society of Manchester.

---

5 T. Swindells, 1906, Manchester Streets and Manchester Men, p.10-11.

DR. CHARLES WHITE -1728 -1813

Manchester Gallery also own a portrait painted by Joseph Allen of the famous Manchester surgeon, Dr. Charles White. In 1752 at the age of twenty four he was responsible for founding the Public Infirmary in Manchester, now the Manchester Royal Infirmary.

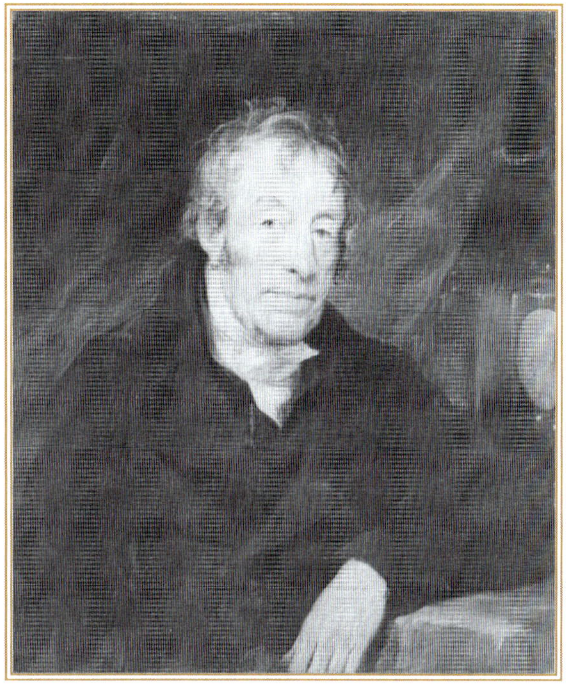

Figure 3. J. Allen, *Dr. Charles White*
Manchester Art Gallery

He resigned at the age of sixty two, and founded the Manchester Lying-In Hospital now known as St. Mary's Hospital.

In 1762 he was elected a Fellow of The Royal Society and in the same year he was admitted a member of the Corporation of Surgeons. By the time he was forty he was recognised as the leading Surgeon in the North of England. In 1772 he published a revolutionary work on midwifery which introduced modern methods of strict hygiene into a branch of medicine previously dominated by semi-barbarism. As a result many lives were saved which formerly would have been lost through puerperal fever. [6]

White bordered on being a medical genius, but he also had another side to his character. He had a house at the corner of Cross Street and King Street now the site of Lloyd's Bank, where he taught medical students and housed his medical museum. At first it housed professional objects, but later furnished attractions to an unusually large variety of tastes.

6 Talk by Dr. W. Brockbank given to Sale Medical Society in the early 1960's.

In the "humanities" there were two items of particular interest. A mummy and a skeleton. The mummy was a Miss Hannah Beswick of Hollinwood who when alive had a great dread of being buried alive. Charles White had attended Miss Beswick medically for some years. She therefore left him by will a bequest of not less than £250, but with one condition annexed: that she should be embalmed, and that once a year White with two witnesses of credit should withdraw the veil from her face.

The lady was placed in a common clock case, having the usual glass face; but a veil of white velvet obscured from all profane eyes the silent features behind. Visitors described it as a repulsive looking object, swathed in ticking and standing upright in a wooden case.

Over the years the mummy was kept in several places. White left it to his friend Dr. Ollier, of King Street; afterwards it was put in the Museum of the Natural History Society. On July 22 1868 the hundred years having more than expired, it was finally buried at Harpurhey Cemetery.

The skeleton had quite a provenance. According to the writer, Thomas de Quincey,[7] the skeleton was that of the infamous Edward Highwayman Higgins, who lived in Knutsford. By day he was a well respected gentleman, but by night he was a highway robber. He was finally caught for his crimes and sent to the gallows in 1767.

In his own time Allen's working techniques were respected and his portraits still hang in some very prestigious buildings: for example Eton College, Windsor.

---

7 David Marson, 1889, Thomas de Quincey, Autobiography: Collected writings of Thomas de Quincey, p.35.

SIR GEORGE RICHARD PHILIPS - 1789 -1883

Allen's portrait of Sir George Richard Philips hangs on the stairwell wall of the Provost's Lodge.

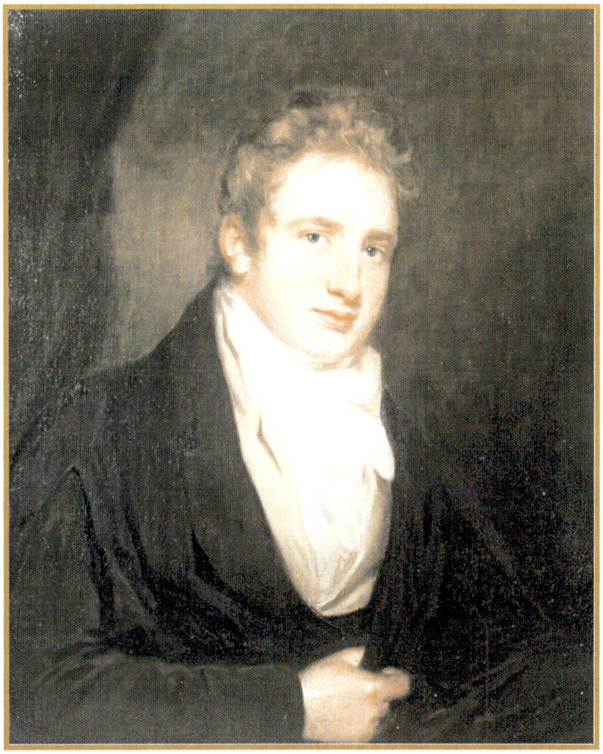

Figure 4. J. Allen, *Sir George Richard Philips*
Reproduced by permission of the Provost and Fellows of Eton College

The college Archivist, Penny Hatfield, states: **Sir George came to Eton in September 1803, giving his age as 13 years. He left Eton in summer 1808 by which time he had reached the Sixth Form, the top 20 boys in the school. He went on to Trinity College Cambridge and started his parliamentary career as MP for Horsham in 1818.**

Sir George's grandfather was a successful Manchester cotton manufacturer, Thomas Philips of Sedgeley. His father sat in Parliament from 1812-1834 as a member of the Whig Party and was created a baronet in 1828.

Allen went on to paint many more portraits all with extremely interesting life styles. He proved portrait painting, as in committing people's likenesses to canvas for posterity, could be a lucrative profession in Manchester during the early part of the nineteenth century.

His Manchester sitters are valuable pieces of a jig-saw puzzle pushing history ever onward. Time marches on, and there is an air of great excitement in Manchester, Victoria now has the throne and there is much celebration. At the same time there is an air of anticipation circling the city's ever evolving art scene, the word "photography" keeps being bandied around.

CHAPTER 2

CHARLES ALLEN DUVAL 1808-1872 PORTRAIT PAINTER AND PHOTOGRAPHER

"That distinguished looking man just entered the room, with the Scotch plaid around him, and in the act of removing his black sombrero, is C. A. Duval the artist and fashionable portrait painter of the period." A. Darbyshire. 1

Portraits were now a very lucrative way to use one's paints. With this in mind, similarly to Joseph Allen, Charles Duval2 settled in Manchester with a view to creating himself an impressive portfolio. When building up this portfolio he not only used his paints but chalks too, and he became personally endeared to many families by his exquisite chalk portraits of their children.

At first he specialised in painting the rich and famous, but with an eye on the future he realised that paint and chalks were not going to be enough. The not so rich and famous wanted their portraits taken too and he began to realise this was possible through the art of photography. Photography was definitely the way forward and Duval opened his own studio/gallery in Manchester. Times were moving on and he was determined to move with them.

But not so fast, Duval had quite a painting history before he decided to try his hand at photography. He painted a splendid portrait of Rowland Eyles Egerton-Warburton, who was responsible for building the present Hall at Arley between 1832 and 1845. This Hall is an extremely impressive building with a plethora of exciting architectural features. It is surrounded by acres of Cheshire countryside and exquisite formal gardens. What a fabulous setting for Duval's painting.

Rowland's portrait hangs above the fireplace in an elegant Drawing Room which boasts the most gorgeous ceiling and cornice depicting birds eating grapes, designed by George Latham.

---

1 A.Darbyshire, 1892, "A Chronicle of the Brasenose Club, Manchester." a book based upon the memories of "The Lion," edited by The Jackal (Manchester Guardian Printing), p. 16.

2 Duval is sometimes spelt Du Val.

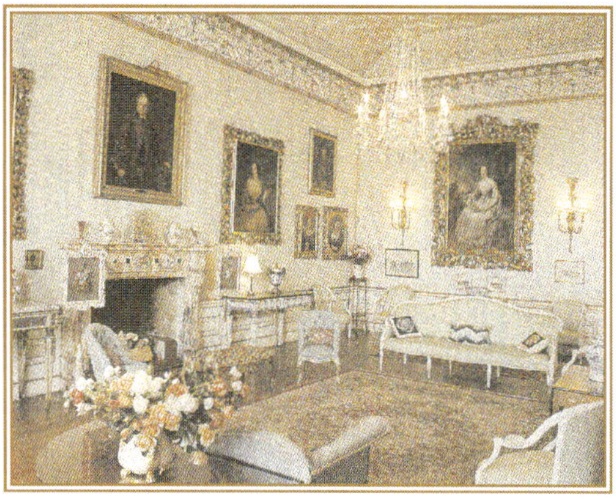

Figure 5. ***The Drawing Room at Arley Hall, Cheshire***

This elegant room is devoted to the memory of Rowland and his wife Mary Brooke. Mary has her own full length portrait on one of the walls. She looks out into the room and she and Rowland make a handsome pair.

The room is brimming with family portraits and amongst this array there is another Duval painting.

It is Rowland's mother at the age of eighty-seven. She lived to be ninety nine. Duval has captured the likeness between mother and son perfectly.

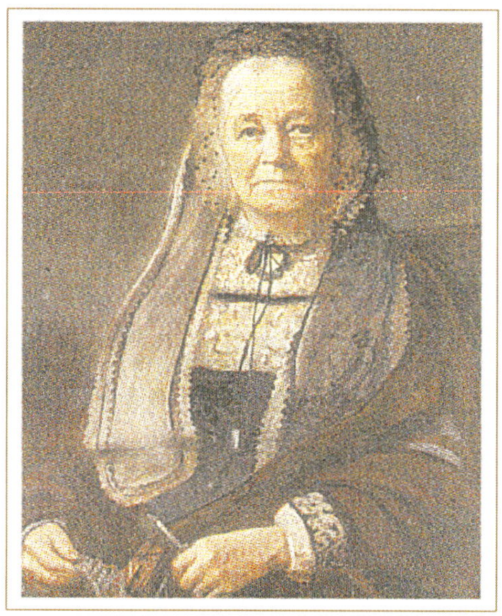

Figure 6. C. A. Duval, ***Mrs. Rowland Egerton,***
Arley Hall, Cheshire

In the Arley Hall Guide Book, Charles Foster writes: To Rowland Egerton-Warburton we owe most of what can be seen at Arley today.

His long period in control of the estate from 1825-91 coincided with Victorian prosperity.

He was concerned to carry out to the full the duties of a Christian landed gentleman. Lord Halifax once referred to him as "a perfect combination, a good churchman, a good landlord, a keen sportsman and a man of literary tastes." 3

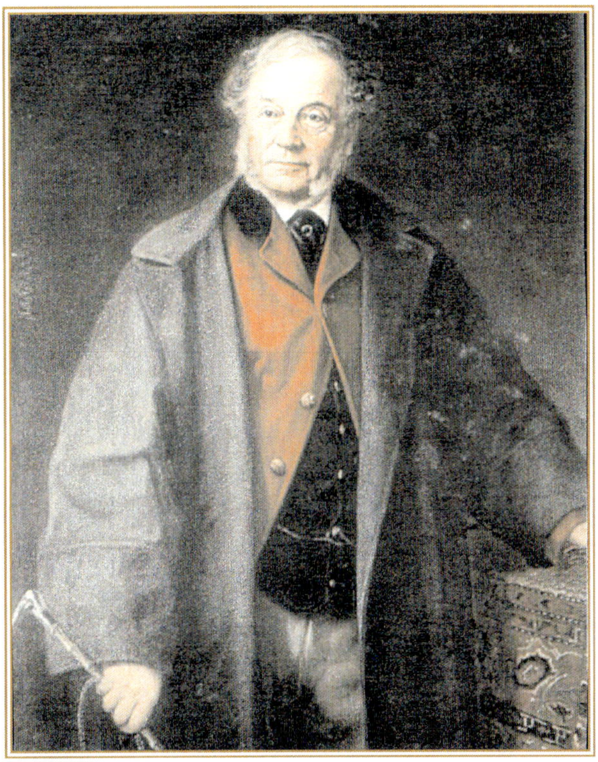

Figure 7. C. A. Duval, *Rowland Eyles Egerton-Warburton*
Arley Hall, Cheshire

This is exactly the image Duval has captured in his painting. This strong confident man has honest eyes showing just a hint of gentleness and even a sparkle of humour. He has mutton chop sideboards and almost untidy hair. He is not a fop. He gets things done. The picture's

3 Arley Hall and Gardens, Cheshire, The Family, p.20.

background is sombre, no tell tale books, expensive animals or vast acres of land - he has nothing to prove.

His silver topped whip and outfit are a statement - he is interested in horses and all their rhetoric. He was indeed a great lover of horses and was Secretary of the Cheshire Hunt for thirty five years. Duval's portrait confirms Rowland was just as Lord Halifax described him. However, the paint goes a bit deeper than this. Bubbling away under this portrait's coded messages is the important fact, Rowland Eyles Egerton-Warburton, the landed gentry owner of Arley Hall, Cheshire, commissioned a Manchester artist to paint his portrait.

But then Duval was no ordinary artist. Even though he was never famous: he was a very accomplished painter. He exhibited for thirty six years at the Royal Academy, London (1836-1872). As a portrait painter he had connections all over the British Isles and he frequently visited London. Obviously Duval was able to live very comfortably in Manchester - unlike many of his colleagues who moved to London. The competition was very high on the London scene and for any artist to succeed they would have to spend most of their time in the capital promoting their works.

In the summer of 1881, before Duval moved to Greenheys, Manchester, he and his wife spent the summer on the Isle of Man. The author Vivien Allen 4 states: **After his marriage he also took to spending part of each summer in the Isle of Man, advertising his arrival in 1831 thus:**

Mr C. A. Du Val, Portrait and Miniature painter, begs to inform the Nobility and Gentry of the Isle of Man, that he has arrived from Dublin, and intends following his Profession here for a short time. Those who are anxious of possessing a memorial of one that is dear, have now their wishes in their own power.

Allen gives us an amazing insight into the Duval family - describing them as close-knit, affectionate, extrovert, artistic and on the whole a hard-working lot. Extrovert is putting it lightly. She writes: **Charles Allen Du Val had a nephew, Charles Henry Du Val who was of**

4 Vivien Allen, Du Val Tonight! The Story Of A Showman, 1990, (Worcester: Square One Publications). p.p.3,4.

Irish descent and born in Manchester in 1846. He travelled the world with his one-man show "Odds and Ends."

He was commanded to appear before royalty and could fill a large London theatre for more than four hundred consecutive performances. He danced, sang and acted his way through twenty characters in an evening holding the stage alone for two hours.

His characters were male and female, from the lisping dandy to the voluble Irish washerwoman. One of his acts was based upon his uncle - Mr. Palette Brush.

Charles Henry was indeed an extrovert. His uncle may have been seen as the artistic member of the family, but he too had a gregarious side to his character, unveiled by the Manchester Evening Times:

After a somewhat roving life Mr. Duval settled in Manchester in 1833. Some years previously, after vacillating for a period between the attractions of art and literature, in which he had made early essays, he suddenly cast both aside, and went to sea, but was soon disgusted with a seafaring life by the hardships attending a stormy voyage to St. Petersburg.

He appears to have begun his profession of an artist in Liverpool, but when still a young man he came to Manchester, where it seemed to him the chances of a career appeared brighter. [5]

Duval gave up his somewhat precarious seafaring life to become an artist and arrived on the Manchester scene in 1833. He soon settled in Manchester and quickly became a well respected member of its ever increasing artistic circle.

5 Manchester Examiner and Times, 17th June, 1872.

The following letter dated 1835 sent to T.W. Winstanly Esq., gives some insight into the way Duval was painting and his charges around this time.

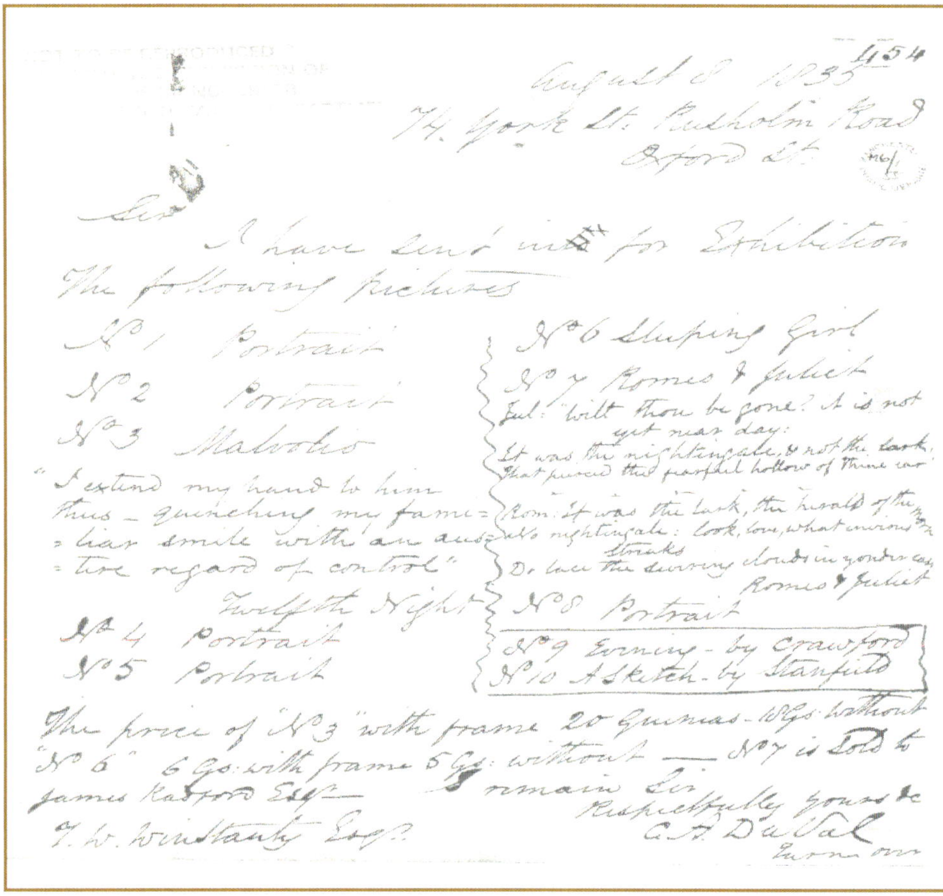

454

August 8 1835
74 York St. Rusholme Road
Oxford St.

Sir

I have sent in for Exhibition
The following Pictures

No 1 Portrait
No 2 Portrait
No 3 Malvolio
"I extend my hand to him thus – quenching my familiar smile with an austere regard of control"
Twelfth Night
No 4 Portrait
No 5 Portrait
No 6 Sleeping Girl
No 7 Romeo & Juliet
Jul: "Wilt thou be gone? it is not yet near day:
It was the nightingale, & not the lark,
That pierced the fearful hollow of thine ear"
Rom: It was the lark, the herald of the morn,
No nightingale: look, love, what envious streaks
Do lace the severing clouds in yonder east
Romeo & Juliet
No 8 Portrait
No 9 Evening - by Crawford
No 10 A Sketch - by Stanfield

The price of "No 3" with frame 20 Guineas - 18 Gs without
"No 6" 6 Gs: with frame 5 Gs: without — No 7 is Sold to
James Radford Esqr — I remain Sir
Respectfully yours &c
C.A. Duval
Turn over

T. W. Winstanly Esqr.

Figure 8. ***Letter 1835 from C. A. Duval to T. W. Winstanly***
Manchester Central Library

He was just what the Manchester art scene needed. He was not some provincial drab dauber: he was young, artistic, an extrovert, witty and very eloquent. He became an art and literary critic, an illustrator, and a writer. In 1863 he published five pamphlets on the American Civil War.

One of his more successful earlier works was "The Ruined Gamester"[6] which was purchased and engraved by Mr. Dewhurst a print seller in Market Street. It became so popular that a cartoon in Punch caricaturing Sir Robert Peel was drawn from it.

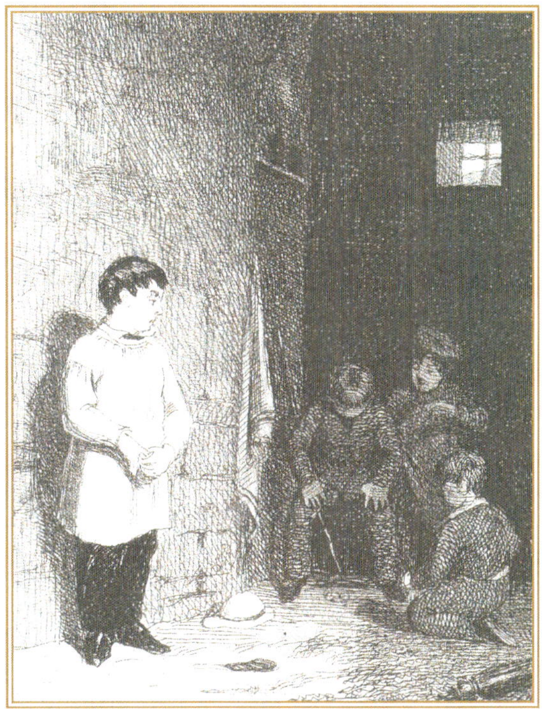

Figure. 9 C. A. Duval, *The Ruined Gamester*
Manchester Central Library

Duval's portraits played an important role within Manchester's history. His major historical painting "The Methodist Centenary," contained a hundred portraits of leading Wesleyans who had assembled in conference in Manchester to celebrate the hundredth anniversary of the institution of Methodism. Unfortunately, this painting has vanished without trace.

He also executed in water colours a series of vignette portraits of the leading members of the Anti-Corn Law League, which were engraved and published, and reproduced on pocket handkerchiefs.

6 The Ruined Gamester see The North of England Magazine, Book 11, Chap 11, p.297.

Another ambitious work, "Luther burning the Pope's Bull," a large historical painting, 10ft by 6ft containing many figures was exhibited at Westminster Hall and afterwards in some of the principal towns throughout the country.

By now, Duval was able to hold his head high within the most elite circles, and was painting some very impressive portraits - in particular a number of prominent politicians. Daniel O'Connell - the Liberator (1775-1847) was one of his earliest portraits. In 1838 he was commissioned by Mr. Daniel Lee to paint a life size picture of the Irish politician Daniel O'Connell. This was quite an accomplishment since O'Connell granted only one sitting of two and a half hours.

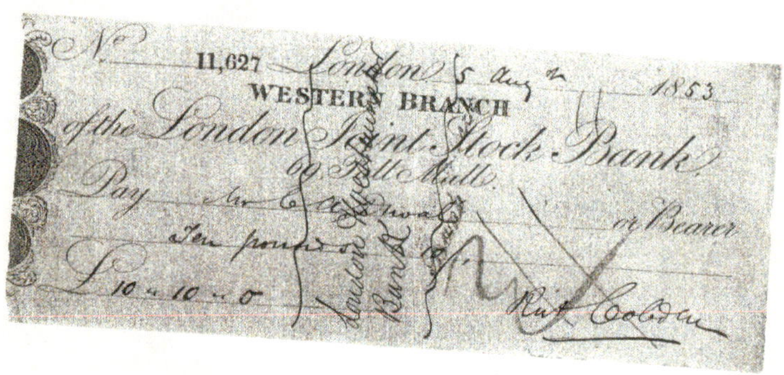

Figure 10. ***R. Cobden's Cheque No: 11,627 5th August 1853***
Manchester Central Library

One of his more prestigious political Manchester clients was Richard Cobden (1804-1865) who commissioned Duval to paint his portrait in 1853 for the price of £10.10.0.

In 1828 Cobden went into partnership with two friends selling calico in London. Three years later they opened a calico printing works in Lancashire. Cobden moved from London and settled in Manchester in 1832. He became profoundly involved in the city's cultural life and its politics, and was one of the first men to be elected as a Manchester Alderman. In 1839 he was one of the seven founding members of the Anti Corn Law. Two years later he became an MP for Stockport.

Another high status political figure Duval painted in 1843 was the British Radical statesman and orator: John Bright (1811-1889)

"As you know, I am neither Roman Catholic, Protestant Episcopalian, nor Presbyterian, nor am I an Irishman." John Bright

Bright was born at Rochdale. His father, Jacob Bright, was a Quaker and self made man, opening a cotton mill at Rochdale in 1809. At the age of sixteen his son entered his mill and later became a partner.

Bright was associated with Richard Cobden in the formation of the Anti-Corn Law League. With similar views they became not only good friends but politically dependent on one another. They were the mainstays of the Manchester School of Economics. They first became acquainted in 1837 when Cobden asked Bright to give a speech at an education meeting in Rochdale. Cobden was impressed by this speech and persuaded Bright to speak against the Corn Laws and join the Manchester Provisional Committee - which in 1839 founded the Anti-Corn League. Bright went on to make a name for himself with his numerous highly successful speeches. Eventually, he became a member of Parliament for Manchester. (1847-57).

Over the years Bright had his portrait painted by some very influential painters.

The following portrait was painted by Duval and exhibited in the R.A. Exhibition in 1843.

It now hangs very comfortably amongst splendid surroundings in Bodnant Hall, Denbighshire. Its present owner, the Hon. Michael Duncan McLaren QC., is a direct descendant of John Bright's sister. The painting has been in the family since 1949 when Sir Henry Duncan McLaren, 2nd Baron Aberconway (1879-1953) was alive.

This picture sits very well on a wall surrounded by a number of other fine works of art.

The figure has a presence. There is no eye contact, Bright looks far into the distance. His face is relaxed but full of determination, perhaps his thoughts are somewhere else while he is being painted. His clothes are dark and sombre. The tell tale landscape in the background gives some clue to his being one of the landed gentry.

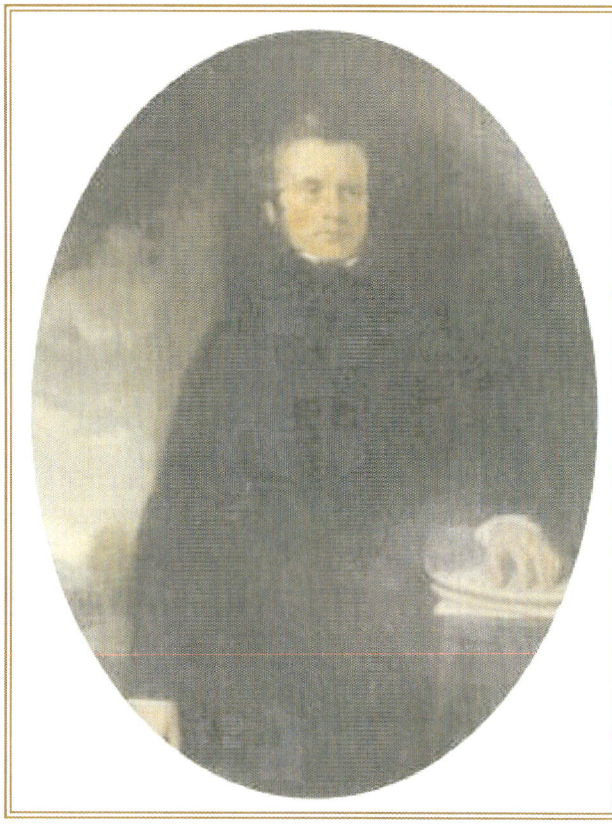

Figure 11. C. A. Duval, *John Bright*
Bodnant Hall

In this picture Bright's hand plays a very important role in guiding the viewer's eye towards a stack of papers. Without knowing the owner of the hand it is obvious that he is some sort of academic. Knowing whose hand it is the painting becomes very exciting.

This is a study of John Bright, the famous radical statesman and orator, and the large sheets of paper he rests his hand upon are more than likely one of his famous imposing speeches used in the House of Commons.

With great expertise Duval has captured a piece of important history and saved it for posterity.

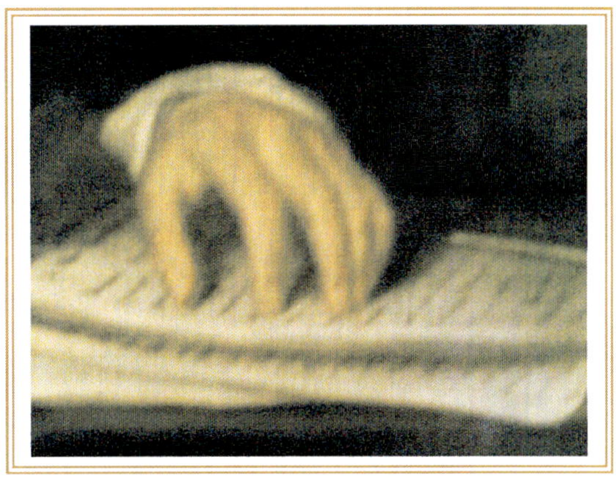

Figure 12. C. A. Duval, *John Bright's Hand*
Bodnant Hall

It is to Duval's credit that a number of engravers copied his originals. Duval's portrait of John Bright was engraved by J. W. Reynolds and published by Thomas Agnew in 1843.

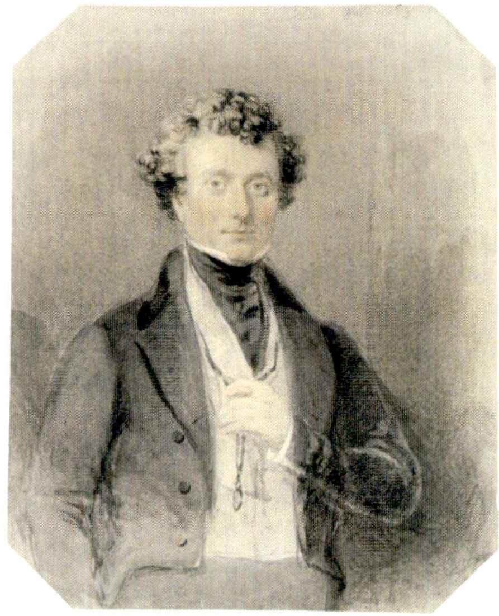

Figure 13. C. A. Duval,
Thomas Milner Gibson
National Portrait Gallery

Not all Duval's political portraits were in oil, he also used watercolour as a medium. This portrait of Thomas Milner Gibson (1806-1884) was painted in 1843. It consists of water colour and gum with touches of Chinese white on paper. It was bequeathed to the National Portrait Gallery by G. Milner Gibson-Cullum in 1922.

Gibson was born in Trinidad where his father was serving in the army. He went to Trinity College, Cambridge and in 1837 was elected to parliament as a Conservative member for Ipswich resigning after two years having changed his views.

He became a staunch supporter of the free-trade movement and a close ally of Richard Cobden. He was elected an M.P. for Manchester in 1841, and from 1846-1848 was vice president of the Board of Trade in Lord John Russell's ministry.

The portrait painter was still seen as a cut above other artists. The critic for the Manchester Times made his views clear: **C. A. Duval whose portrait painting has been long and extensively recognised in our good city, has just finished a couple of Cabinet pictures which undoubtedly give him a considerable advance in the estimation of all who possess a knowledge of and a feeling for art.**

Some years ago he painted a small picture called "The Gambler" - a scene of humour that indicated very distinctly the true direction of his genius; but humanity is wayward, and will take rambles occasionally into isolated byways instead of keeping

on the main road to fame, even of what genius may say.

Mr. Duval, we are happy to find, has again returned to the genial atmosphere of that land of promise whence he diverged, and here in a couple of talented and pleasant subjects, has shown that Manchester can boast an artist of high merit. [7]

This Victorian critic, along with a number of others, was still obsessed with what had once been a strict code for all portrait painters, i.e., "They should stick to the rich and famous if they wanted to stay on the main road to fame." This may have worked in the past but times were changing. Some producers were having to look towards the not so famous to make a living. Their patrons were changing. They could no longer get away with painting a portrait for a specific person for a premium price.

More and more Manchester citizens wanted to become part of their city's new exciting art scene. They were waking up to the fact that they too could have their portrait hanging on the wall through the art of Photography. This was confirmed by the Sphinx: **The portrait painters of this generation are verily the most unfortunate of mortals. Besides their struggles against modern innovations on their art (photography) which has taken the bread out of their mouths, it has become quite the fashion for critics to have a fierce lunge at them whenever an opportunity offers.** [8]

From ruling supreme the portrait painter was now struggling hard to make a living. Duval was one jump ahead - he had already had the foresight to set up his own photographic studio. The Examiner and Times ran the following advert on Thursday 23rd October 1862:

---

7 Manchester Times, July 10th 1856, Art In Manchester.

8 Sphinx, September 25th 1869.

Messrs C. A. Duval & Co

Have the honour to announce that on Monday the 3rd November they will open **PHOTOGRAPH AND PORTRAIT GALLERIES** at the premises of Messrs Thomas Agnew & Sons, 14 Exchange Street, Manchester.

They trust that the special training and knowledge of the artist, combined with the skill of the photographer, will ensure results more satisfactory to the public than those hitherto realised by photographing alone.

EVERY DESCRIPTION OF PHOTOGRAPHIC PORTRAITS
MR DUVAL'S MINIATURE PORTRAIT
OIL AND WATER - COLOUR VIGNETTED PORTRAITS
DITTO DITTO DITTO IVORY FINISH

COPIES OF PICTURES AND DRAWINGS REDUCED
OR ENLARGED FROM THE ORIGINAL

CARTE DE VISITES PORTRAITS
ALBUM GROUPS AND PORTRAITS
INSTANTANEOUS PORTRAITS OF CHILDREN

CRAYON AND PASTEL PORTRAITS
LIFE SIZE PORTRAITS IN OIL
MESSRS C A DUVAL & CO WILL NOT EXHIBIT
A PORTRAIT WITHOUT SPECIAL PERMISSION
14 EXCHANGE STREET
MANCHESTER

In 1854 the French photographer, Disderi patented a new process the portrait-card or carte de visite. He perfected the art of making a number of small images which could then be separately glued onto a visiting card.

These cards took a little longer to catch on in England, becoming popular around 1861. When Prince Albert died in 1861 over 70,000 portraits were sold within a week. [9]

In fact, it was Queen Victoria who set the fashion. Duval was indeed right at the forefront where photography was concerned. He supplied his carte de visites to some very influential persons. For example, Sir Joseph Whitworth, 1st Baronet.

Whitworth was an extremely distinguished man.

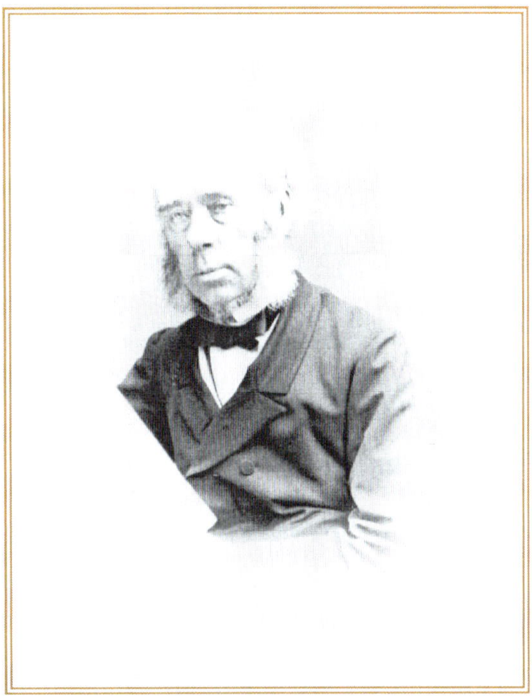

Figure 14. C. A. Duval, *Sir Joseph Whitworth*
National Portrait Gallery

He was born in Stockport in 1803 and died whilst wintering in Monte Carlo in 1887 at the age of 84.

9 Quentin Bajac, 2002, The Invention of Photography: The First Fifty Years.

He became one of the utmost engineering authorities in the world.

In 1856 he was elected President of the Institution of Mechanical Engineers in appreciation for his outstanding contribution to the development of industrialisation and mechanical engineering.

Over his long life time he attained many prestigious awards.[10] On his death he had amassed a fortune of more than one million pounds. Some of this money helped towards the setting up of the Whitworth Art Gallery, Manchester.

Where Duval the photographer was concerned: he did have a large portfolio of influential clients and he certainly looked after them, but at the same time he was shrewd enough to see that Manchester's art scene was definitely changing. He realised that the not so wealthy could also become very significant clients and by using Disderi's techniques he made sure they too could afford several dozen copies of their portrait.

Duval had five children, three of whom were artists. His eldest son Charles was a photographer and partner in the above business. The firm was established in the 1860's and remained in business for around forty years. From having only 17 studios in 1855, Manchester possessed 71 in 1865 and Duval's was one of them. At this time the photographer was seen as a dubious character, even as a failed artist. This is where Duval came into his own: not only had he a brilliant reputation as a portrait painter he was well known and admired throughout the city. He played upon this and when taking photographs he used his studio in the same way he would when painting a portrait, even incorporating some of his special scenic backgrounds. His sitter would be immediately impressed with his great expertise and filled full of confidence.

Duval played an important role within Manchester's art scene and remained very loyal to his artistic surroundings. For nearly forty years his name was held in high esteem within Manchester's art circles. He was not just an artist and photographer he was an innovator. He got things done: he formed an Academy and became president of it before the Manchester Academy of Fine Arts was established in 1859.

---

10 For further details see: Norman Atkinson, 1996, Sir Joseph Whitworth The World's Best Mechanician, Sutton Publishing Limited.

Perhaps it was because Duval was so popular within his own circles a certain person actually took on his identity as an artist, and got away with it.

An Impostor "Artist in Bradford"

On Tuesday last a well dressed foreigner called upon several artists and Drawing Masters in Bradford stating that he was "Mr. C. A. Duval," artist of Greenheys, Manchester and that he had lost the use of his right hand and arm, and as he appeared familiar with all the Manchester artists both by names and works he received several donations. He then left for Leeds. 11

Even though he branched off into photography unlike many other portrait painters Duval continued to receive prestigious commissions right up to his death. He was painting the portraits of a family at Alderley in Cheshire, when he felt faint and decided to leave his painting for a while and go for a ride on his horse. Unfortunately, he had to cut his ride short because he felt so ill. He returned back to his friend's house where he was staying and shortly afterwards died.

Manchester's art scene was being turned around and with the advent of photography certain barriers were now being broken down. The artist (painter) was not quite so elite, and portraiture was no longer the sole domain of the wealthy. Was this the end for Manchester's artists? Not at all, it could be seen as an exciting beginning for most of them, for the city was now buzzing with industrial entrepreneurs greedy for all forms of art.

11 Manchester Guardian, December 29th 1857

CHAPTER 3

THE ROYAL MANCHESTER INSTITUTION AND WARWICK BROOKES

It was no coincidence that Charles Barry's classical monument to Manchester's purveyors of art was erected at exactly the same time the city was booming.

Manchester had now become a world famous icon for cotton. It was a highly lucrative thriving place - stacked to its gunnels with cotton and overcrowded mills spewing out their contents twenty four hours a day.

For some, the privileged few, cotton seemed like a licence to make money, but for others i.e., Manchester's vast populace living within its overcrowded streets, it represented: steam, dirt, noise, smoke, chronic illness, alcoholism, atrocious living conditions and extreme poverty. There were no exceptions children worked as hard and suffered as much as their parents. The privileged few, the new prosperous captains of industry, took a step back, paused for a while and then at break neck speed decided to copy the "extremely" privileged few - the local gentry.

Grand houses began to appear on the outskirts of the city and their opulent owners had grand ideas to match their houses. They decided to decorate their interiors sumptuously and after a while an element of competitiveness crept through the front door and enveloped the house's four walls. What could be more impressive than a self portrait hung over the ornate fireplace? Or a family group with their favourite pets? The surrounding landscape and the family's favourite haunts could now be brought right into the dining room and discussed with one's friends and neighbours over several courses.

These were exciting times: a brand new set of patrons had arrived on the scene - Manchester patrons - impatient to flaunt their status through the fine arts. But were they really interested in Manchester's purveyors of art? These artists were beautifully summed up by Walter Butterworth: [1] **They are not the lofty figures of the great world's art; they are nearer to our own level; they lived in our streets; some of them we knew, chatted with, dined with joked with.**

---

1 See Chapter 11.

It is good to have their drawings and paintings on our walls; to glance at them when the early sun shines into the bedroom; or downstairs at the morning coffee; or when we receive visits from old friends and sit in a warm room, the curtains drawn. The last is the best: to sit at a table, or by the fire, talking of life, of books, of art. Discussing who painted that landscape over the bookcase, the portrait by the window, that bit of jewel-like colour which recalls Morocco, or that quiet, cosy interior which our friend painted while he was so much under the influence of the homely Dutchmen. They open out their hearts to us, in eloquent silence, through their works, enclosed in the gilded frames. [2]

All these Manchester artists could see was a ready market raring to go but with no means to feed it. It became blatantly obvious to a select number of local artists that what they desperately needed was a building in which to exhibit their work. They could then try to woo these new patrons and get them through its splendid front doors to look at their work and subsequently buy it. They were full of confidence, but were these provincial artists being slightly naive? Where did fame, fortune and London fit into the equation?

On the 9th September 1823 "The Associated Artists of Manchester" was established. This was a body of people who were determined to have a building in which to exhibit their art.

A prominent member, Warwick Brookes [3] was an exemplar of the times. He was born in Salford in 1808 and died at Egerton Grove, Stretford New Road, Manchester in 1882.

He was educated at the National Free Schools, Bolton Street, Salford. Leaving school at nine he went into a print-works to act as "tear-boy" to his Uncle Thomas, who was a block printer on calicoes. His duty was to dip a brush in colour and to keep supplied the colour-cloth on which the printer daubed his block before he applied it to the fabric.

This early background within the textile industry led to Brookes becoming a textile designer working for calico printers John Barge &

---

2 Henry Liverseege - The Ancoats Artist by Walter Butterworth - file Manchester Art Gallery

3 The following information on Warwick Brookes - file in Manchester Art Gallery.

Co., of Broughton Bridge and then John Dugdale & Brothers, High Street, Manchester - later known as The Rossendale Printing Co. He was well aware of Manchester's cotton rhetoric and its consequential spin off - its new prosperous artistic patrons.

He, and the other members of the Associated Artists of Manchester knew it was crucial to find a place where they could hold an annual exhibition of art. At a public meeting it was decided to try and raise enough money to buy a building which would promote: literature, science and the arts.

At first a building was purchased on King Street, but when it was realised just how successful their fund raising had been they decided to build a brand new building at the junction of Mosley Street and Princess Street, in a prestigious part of Manchester. This would not be just any building, but a Manchester temple to the arts, bringing credit to the city of Manchester and great kudos to all those involved in its inauguration.

Desperate to place their work on display, and realising it would be some time before they could use the gallery, the artists held their first exhibition in an art shop, 83 Market Street, appropriately named "The Gallery." [4]

Meanwhile the money for the new gallery was raised by a scheme of governor subscriptions, by which contributors of forty guineas were made hereditary governors, of twenty five guineas life governors, and of two guineas annual governors.

A real coup for the Governors was the President of the Royal Academy, Sir Thomas Lawrence asking to be included in their list of subscribers as a Life Governor. This came about when they wrote to Lawrence asking his advice on whether they should apply for Royal Patronage.

With his blessing they went ahead and a letter addressed to The Borough Reeve of Manchester, T. Holdsworth Esq., dated March 11th 1824 confirmed his Majesty was graciously pleased to signify his consent and to express a warm anxiety for the success of the Association.

---

4 According to "Manchester Old and New," it was here in 1827 the first picture exhibition in Manchester took place.

Although the building was not completely finished it was decided to hold the first exhibition of pictures in 1829. At last, everything The Associated Artists of Manchester had striven to achieve was coming true. The display occupied one large room, a smaller room and a corridor. There were many more exhibitions before the building was completed in 1835 and the Royal Manchester Institution for the promotion of Literature Science and the Arts came into being. [5]

In the same year the Manchester Institution came into being Benjamin Arthur Heywood established the Heywood Prize Fund. He presented the Governors of the Manchester Institution with £500 to invest and subsequently use the income yearly for a prize for the best piece of art. A medal was designed and minted by William Wyon of the Royal Mint. Heywood appeared on one side and the Art Gallery was on the other.

And what of Warwick Brookes and his artistic career? It began to take off. In 1837 he was able to attend a series of lectures delivered by the distinguished London artist, Benjamin Robert Haydon at the Royal Mechanics'Institution. The following year he became a pupil at the newly opened School of Design, established in the Nicholas Street wing of the Royal Manchester Institution.

The school was founded on the insistence of Robert Haydon [6] and its head was John Zephania Bell, who earlier in his career had been dissatisfied with the way drawing was taught at the Royal Academy and decided to study in Paris, entering the atelier of M. Le Baron de Gros.

Bell taught the use of French chalk and the stump. He said "that his object was to make his pupils draughtsman and not to break their hearts and destroy their faculties by covering surfaces with faultless but mechanical stipple." He set himself against drawing from flat copies insisting on drawing from the round, to which end he had models carved in wood. From these the students passed to separate features of the human face, then to limbs and extremities, then to the entire figure, and lastly, to the living model.

---

5 This building now houses the Manchester Art Gallery.

6 Benjamin Robert Haydon (1786-1846) – see his "Autobiography and Memoirs" (first published 1853)

It was in 1837 he accepted Sir David Wilkie's exciting proposal to organise and manage a School of Design in Manchester. Full of enthusiasm he accepted the post but when he was shown the instructions sent for his guidance by the Council of the Head School in London, and the diagrams for the students to copy, he found to his horror it was a scheme to keep as separate as possible Schools of Design from Schools of Art, and that the diagrams would teach nothing.

At Manchester he decided to teach the French way for a certain time, in other words, exactly the same training would be given to the design students as to those for high art, and when the different students had acquired the power of drawing, they could then decide whether to study high art, or ornamental art. He was convinced that it would be of advantage to the ornamentist or pattern drawer to pursue his own studies along with the artists.

At first he had his own way until the Council decided to interfere complaining that too much attention was being paid to art, and that ornamental art was being neglected. Even though members of the London Council visited, and were satisfied with his course, Bell resigned and later set up his own atelier in London.

For Manchester's artists there was yet an even bigger blow to come. The committee decided to discontinue the life class. Furious, but undaunted, its chief members were determined it should be carried on. Warwick Brookes, Francis Chester, Robert Crozier, Edward Benson, George Hayes, Sam Mayson, Fred Tavare, and Thomas Letherbrow set up life drawing classes in an attic room over Rose's China Shop, King Street and became known as "The United Society of Manchester Artists."

In 1843 Benjamin Haydon visited Manchester again to deliver a further series of lectures and gave special praise to the work of Warwick Brookes and Robert Crozier. The highlight for Warwick Brookes and his colleagues was a visit by Haydon to their studio in King Street.

Whilst he was visiting Manchester Haydon wrote to his wife: **Only think of what has happened. I had established here, as you know, a School of Design with the figure as the basis. Some time since, again influenced by those obstinate ignoramuses in London, the Council here allowed itself to be persuaded to abolish the figure.**

The young men behaved admirably well. They met together, subscribed, and continued the figure privately, and waited for my coming down. Now that I have arrived they have brought me their drawings, which are admirable for their accuracy, breadth and finish.

It is pitiable to find such obstinacy and ignorance, wilful, intentional ignorance of what is for this great Country's good in high places. But if the young men only remain sound, and continue to draw the figure, those gentlemen in London will one day be brought to acknowledge their error.

These councils and pupils are doing here what is being done by councils and pupils in many of the great towns in which I have lectured. Such is the baneful and mischievous influence of that blot of centralized ignorance in London. The moment my back is turned they seek to undo all the good I have done.

Haydon fought hard to bring the live model back. He even opened his own art school, The Society for Promoting Practical Design which, of course, advocated drawing from a live model.

The Manchester born artist, Mark Anthony (1817-1886), joined the battle. He had an axe to grind with the Royal Academy, who seemed to him to be sitting on the fence whilst trying to placate the Government with regard to their stance on drawing from a live model. He wanted to know why the Royal Academy did not lead the way and adopt the French method of teaching i.e., using a live model right from the beginning of the course and not spending weeks drawing from casts.

He had experienced first hand the French way of working. He went to study art in Paris and the Hague, becoming a pupil of Delaroche and Vernet at the Beaux-Arts, and Atelier de Nuit. In the 1830's he met the artists Corot and Dupre at Fontainebleau. Anthony had a distinguished artistic background and he and a large number of similar artists were furious at this bureaucratic interference.

Eventually the powers that be gave in and advocated drawing from a live model should be continued throughout all the institutions in the country. This meant in 1849 Warwick Brookes and his cronies were able to rejoin the school on its removal to Brown Street under J. A. Hammersley.

Brookes was now becoming well known in Manchester for his wood-engravings, etchings, and illustrations for children's books. He illustrated some of the many books of Dr. John Brown, author of "Rab and His Friends," and the cover and six lithos for "Little Tales for Tiny Tots."

His forte was definitely his beautiful pencil drawings of children: those beautiful babies that Dante Gabriel Rossetti pronounced: "triumphs, every one of them."

On advice from three of his colleagues, Dr. Crompton, Mr. Nesmith and Mr. Shields, his pencil drawings were photographed and published in a series. [7]

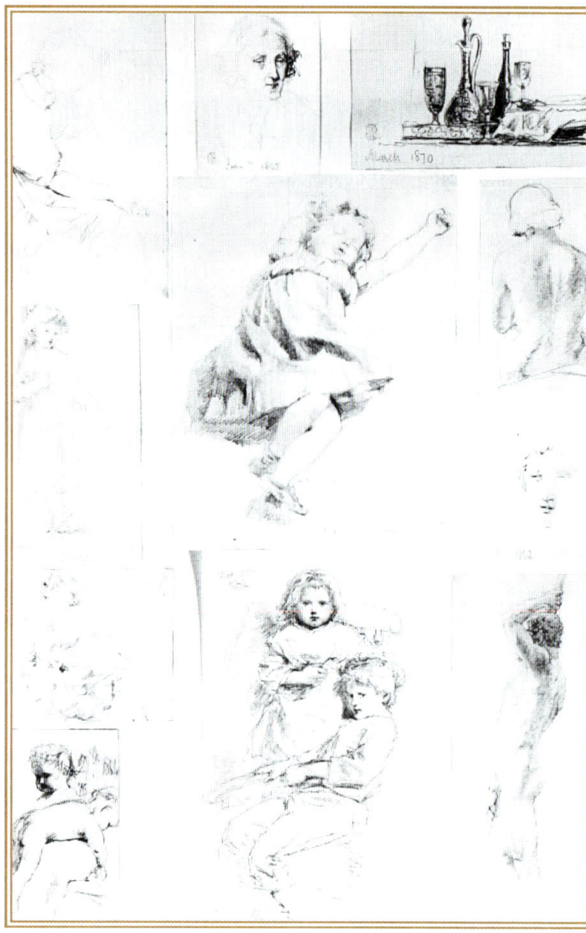

Figure 15. Warwick Brookes, *Pencil Drawings*
Manchester Art Gallery

7 Thirty one photographs of Brookes's original sketches were published by Brookes. Copies are held by The Royal Academy Library, The V & A (Forster Collection), Manchester Central Library.

This turned out to be extremely good advice. His work became well known and was admired by a number of intellectual leaders of London Society, who in turn invited him to their town and country houses and liberally bought his drawings.

The president of the Royal Academy, Sir Francis Grant, and other eminent artists such as Millais, Rossetti and Watts, marvelled at the fine quality of his art. He became a good friend of his influential patron Lord Northbourne.

In 1871 the Queen in the course of a letter to Mr. Gladstone comments: "Mr Warwick Brookes' drawings are really charming." She purchased four and so did her daughter the Princess Louise.

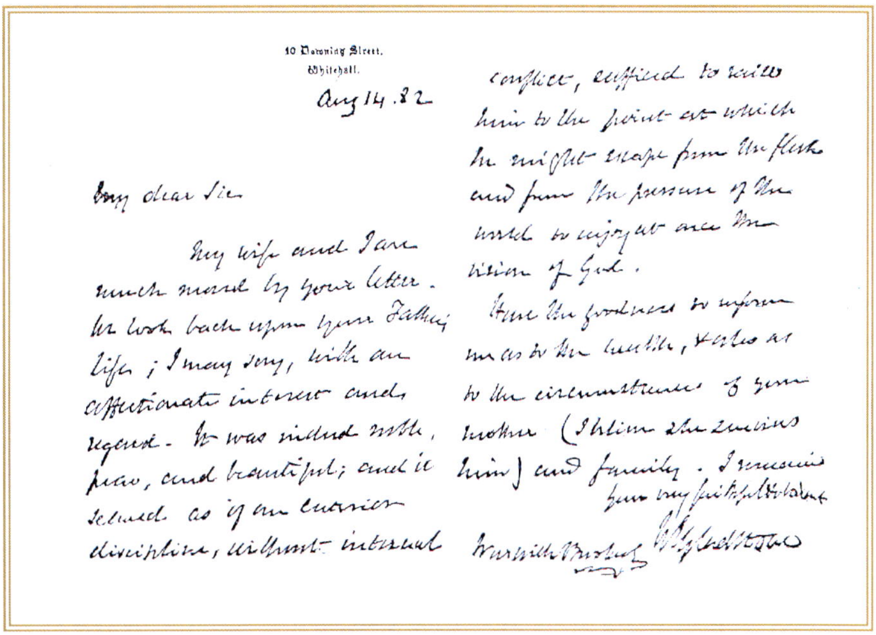

10 Downing Street,
Whitehall.

Aug 14. 82

My dear Sir

My wife and I are much moved by your letter. We look back upon your Father's life; I may say, with an affectionate interest and regard. It was indeed noble, pure, and beautiful; and it seemed as if an earlier discipline, without internal conflict, sufficed to raise him to the point at which he might escape from the flesh and from the pressure of the world to enjoy at once the vision of God.

Have the goodness to inform me as to the health, & also as to the circumstances of your mother (I believe she survives him) and family. I remain

Your very faithful servant

W. Gladstone

Warwick Brookes

Figure 16. ***Letter written by W. Gladstone***

Manchester Central Library

In the same year Brookes was awarded a Civil List Pension of £100 a year, and on hearing of his death the Prime Minister immediately wrote a letter of condolence and forwarded a donation from the Queen's Bounty of a hundred pounds. [8]

Warwick Brookes was just one of many of the Institution's successful members. He was an unknown Manchester artist striving for recognition - which he managed to attain through hard work, sheer determination and helping to set up the Manchester Institution for the Promotion of Literature, Science and the Arts.

The city's art market was getting stronger. Local artists were at last showing what they were made of. Their works became collectable. It was, therefore, agreed the time was right to promote Manchester's art scene even further by setting up an Academy of Fine Arts. [9]

1857 was a memorable year in Manchester, because of the Art Treasures Exhibition at Old Trafford. Running concurrently, but not quite on such a par, was an exhibition of the works of local artists at Peel Park, Salford. Why did this smaller exhibition become so memorable? Because it was out of this exhibition the Manchester Academy [10] was born.

---

8 Atalanta, October 1889-Sept 1890, T. Letherbrow, Warwick Brookes And His Pencil-Pictures.

9 A Manchester Academy anterior to the present Institution was founded about the year 1844. It had few if any of the formal surroundings of the present Academy. It was a gathering of artists for the mutual criticism of their work, and it lasted for some ten years. It was so popular artists travelled over fifty miles for the reunions. Its members were: Selim Rothwell, William Percy, George Anthony, Sam Bough,George Hayes, G. Bury, Charles Allen Duval, H. Hadfield, John Bostock, W. K. Keeling, Moris Brebant, Henry Calvert, Michael Calvert, Edward Royle.

10 For further information on the Manchester Academy of Fine Arts see Sheila Dewsbury, The Story So Far: The Manchester Academy of Fine Arts from 1859 to 2003.

CHAPTER 4

THE MANCHESTER ACADEMY OF FINE ARTS AND THE MANCHESTER SOCIETY OF WOMEN PAINTERS

The air was electric, the city was buzzing with rumours, and loud whispers could be heard throughout its artistic circles. Then like a tidal wave the news broke.

Forty artist from the city and its neighbourhood had attended a meeting in the lecture theatre at the Royal Manchester Institution. Mr. J. A. Hammersley was in the chair and he had stated it was agreed by all desirable an "Academy" should be formed. He and nine others were appointed to draw up a constitution.

Some of the Academy's objects were of great interest. For example:

The union of members in furtherance of all art objects in the locality.

The promotion of an Annual Exhibition to demonstrate the condition and prospects of the British School of Fine Arts.

The education of members of the public generally in the history and principles of art.

The formation of an Art Museum.

There shall be academicians, associates and students and honorary members.

The number of academicians and associates to be unlimited, and may be of either sex.

Classes from the antique and life.

Rooms to be supplied by the Institution.

The collecting of pictures for the Exhibitions and their arrangement to be aided by selected members of the Council of the Academy and the members generally to endeavour to promote those exhibitions.

How could it fail?

History was once again being made within Manchester's artistic circles. It was exciting - Manchester was determined to be noticed and appreciated. Not only was it going to bring the arts to the people, it was going to aesthetically educate the people. Well you can take a horse to the water but you can't make it drink it: it seemed the only way the local artists were going to get some people interested in their artistic creations was to give them away.

In 1861, after an abysmal attendance at the Institution's largest and most important water colour drawing exhibition, it was decided to boost numbers for their next exhibition by holding an Art Union. Shares could be bought for 1/- each. The whole amount of the subscription less expenses would be devoted to prizes and each prize holder could choose their own work.

This was very successful and attendance numbers went up, but it was far to soon to celebrate. In fact, the Academy was far from being congratulated. A few years later it came in for a blistering attack from the Sphinx: [1] **Can anyone explain to us the purpose or influence, or define the exact position of the Manchester Academy of Fine Arts? Has it any power, any object, any value whatever; or is it a mere high sounding nullity?**

It criticised the Hanging Committee: in particular its president, Mr. Keeling. The words tardy and apathy were bandied around and amongst a number of things it wanted to know was: Why had only eighteen members out of thirty seven exhibited their work in the exhibition? Also why out of the thirty one works which had been sold during the exhibition: only four were by Manchester Artists - producing around £54 when the aggregate sales amounted to £411?

Outraged they wanted to know why the Academy was not looking after their own members properly? Not just the Sphinx, but a number of local newspapers, in no uncertain terms, told the Academy it had better account for itself. It did.

Articles praising the Academy began to appear in the local newspapers: **That institution, after a period in which it was worse than useless, and another period in which it began to display a wish and a power to do good, has now reached a third stage of**

---

1 Sphinx, September 25th 1869, Local Art at the Royal Institute.

development, and attained a recognised and honourable position in the working world of art. [2]

Manchester may feel proud of the Academy of Arts, and we trust that its members may always receive that countenance and support which they so richly deserve at the hands of her citizens. [3]

The Manchester Academy could once again hold its head high, it was receiving a good press. All its artistic producers sighed with relief. They were being appreciated. People were interested in their work and were making an attempt to come and see it exhibited.

Its numbers had increased. Its members talents were being acknowledged - that is, all its male members talents. But what about all the talented Manchester female artists?

In March 1874 the Manchester Evening News stated: It must have impressed itself upon many of the visitors to the Manchester Academy - nothing which bore witness to the artistic talents of the gentler sex in the whole exhibition. This was a great pity. Manchester has a number of lady artists, and some among them are reported to be possessed of no mean ability.

One of the "rights" of woman which we have always been ready to recognise is her right to enter, upon in equality with man, into the professions for which she is fitted. Why are there no paintings along side the men which express the spirit and illustrate the genius of the woman? Why do not the lady artists of Manchester study in the Academy classes? [4]

This was exactly what a number of Manchester's talented lady artists wanted to know themselves. They petitioned the Council asking to be placed upon an equal footing with students of the other sex. But the Council had misgivings as to whether these ladies should be allowed to work alongside their male colleagues in the Academy's life drawing class. They blatantly hid behind the rule that a person must attend as a student at the Academy before a picture could be sent in.

There was a lot of heated discussion and at one point the question was asked: "Why not run the Manchester Academy on the same lines as a Parisian studio?" In Paris study from the nude model was

2 City Jackdaw, 8th March 1878.
3 Manchester Courier, 14th March 1878.
4 Manchester Evening News, March 1874.

generally permitted for female artists and they could usually study alongside men in Gleyre's Studio. Rooms were reserved for them in the studios of Girodet, Ary Scheffer, Charles Chaplin, Feyen-Perrin and Edouard Krug, and they were also welcomed in separate studios at the Academie Julian at the Academie Delecluse and at Colar-ossis. These three commercial studios particularly welcomed women who paid higher fees than male students.

Married women could undertake professional study abroad without fear of the social discredit that would have ensued at home. Both Annie Swynnerton and Louise Jopling took full advantage of this. Jopling went to study with Monsieur Charles Chaplin and said: "Chaplin had a large following, his was the only atelier at that time where all his students were women." Married with two young sons Jopling declared: **It was glorious having so much opportunity for serious work. Only abroad can a working and domestic life be carried on simultaneously with little effort. In France one is expected to cultivate what little talent one possesses.**

How my relations in England would have stared, fancy entertaining the idea of becoming a professional - I, a married woman! I had sixteen delightful months of study. I was able to see the great man at work and this was my best lesson. [5]

In Manchester there was such a hoo ha about lady artists attending mixed life classes. At one stage the following statement was made: **We hardly think the ladies would care to avail themselves of the full rights of their membership. Their best friends, at least, would not wish them to, unless they studied in classes by themselves.**

Finally, it was suggested that a new form of membership, relieving its holders of the necessity of attending classes for drawing from models, and yielding to them the right of submission to the exhibitions, might be established and this would meet the views of the young ladies who were naturally so anxious to show that males in Manchester had not a monopoly of the artistic faculty.

In 1875 nine women were elected members and were known as "Lady Exhibitors." Ann Crozier, Isabel Dacre, Annie Hasling, Annie Robinson, Emily Robinson, Julia Robinson, Mary Southworth, Emily Gertrude Thomson, and Elinor Wood. Eventually women members of

5 Louise Jopling, Twenty Years Of My Life, 1867-1887.

the academy did have the same rights as male members. For example in 1897 Isabel Dacre was made a member of the council, Emma Magnus literary secretary, and Florence Monkhouse an auditor.

Before this in 1885 the female members of the Manchester Academy received the following accolade: 6 Every visitor must observe that the most ambitious figure paintings exhibited at the Manchester Academy this year are the work of the ladies.

Rosa Bonheur and the painter of the Roll Call long since proved conclusively that the gentle sex is not a disqualification for the effective treatment of masculine subjects: and that the female mind has abundant sympathy with wild activity and material incident.

The ladies who have been admitted as members of the Manchester Academy do not soar as high, but they have fully justified their right to the position they have won.

Miss Robinson's "Through the Orchard" is the best piece of art hitherto exhibited. Miss Dacre's "Passion Flower" which is a study of a female head, so subtle in expression so intense in colour, so finely modelled, and so powerfully painted that we regret that the artist has not enriched the collection with other contributions.

Miss Emma Magnus has made remarkable progress - 'Peaches' is the best bit of fruit in the exhibition. Miss Rose Magnus also displays growing power and gives promise of excellence.

Even though they were receiving excellent press coverage, a number of Manchester's female artists were decidedly fed up with being told what they could and could not do especially with regard to life drawing classes. They took the bull by the horns and in the following manner. The Manchester Society of Women Painters was formed

6 City News, 1885, The Pictures at the Manchester Academy – Figures and Portraits.

MANCHESTER SOCIETY OF WOMEN PAINTERS
MEMBERS

Susan Isabel Dacre	President
Annie L Robinson	Secretary
Emily Robinson	Treasurer

E. Gertrude Thomson - Jane Atkinson - Eleanor Wood
Julia Pollitt

WITH POWER TO ADD TO THEIR NUMBER

The object in forming this society is, firstly, to provide facilities for the members working together and studying from the life - there being now no course open for such advantages, except by leaving Manchester - and secondly, to disseminate the principles of true art among art students generally, who are desirous of more thorough training, wider experience, and high culture.

In order to assist the committee in carrying out the object as set forth in the above, subscriptions are earnestly requested, and those willing to assist the movement will greatly oblige by giving their names with the amount of their donation, upon the form attached, sending said form addressed to the Secretary at No. 11, Barton House, Deansgate. [7]

7 Manchester Academy of Fine Arts Cutting Book.

The Manchester Guardian printed the following article on 3rd September 1879.

MANCHESTER SOCIETY OF WOMEN PAINTERS
MEMBERS
ART CLASSES

In connection with the above Society are now open
THE COURSE OF INSTRUCTION COMPRISES:
PER TERM

Elementary Drawing ...	Wed - 2-4p.m.	15s 6d
Drawing from the Antique ...	Wed & Fri - 1-5p.m.	31s 6d
Drawing and Painting from the Living Model Special class ...	Wed & Fri - 1-5p.m.	52s 6d

FEES PAYABLE IN ADVANCE
Students joining the special class have the privilege of attending the Studio when it is open without the payment of an extra fee.

Their first exhibition took place on 1st December 1880, with eleven artists exhibiting eighty-eight pictures - mostly oils. Portraits and landscapes mainly featured.

The Manchester Guardian reported it as follows: [8] Miss Thomson's clever drawings of child life and fairy land are exhibited by

8 Manchester Guardian, lst December, 1880.

themselves in a second room. The character of the work justifies the existence of the Society.

Miss Dacre and Miss A L Robinson, who exhibit between them no less than thirty three oil paintings, strike the keynote to the show. The work is almost all honest, and we had almost said masculine.

During their second exhibition six artists exhibited eighty three pictures and the following comment was made by the Manchester Guardian. The fact that the number of exhibitors has diminished has rather raised than lowered the general quality of the show.

Fourteen members exhibited during the third exhibition and The City News stated: Of the general impression produced by the exhibition we are bound to say that if some of Miss Isabel Dacre's work were eliminated from it, we should without a catalogue or any other inspiration, have soon divined that the work was mainly the work of a woman.

What with the entire absence of imagination and humour in the very few original subjects the great profusion of fruit and flower pieces, and the capricious colouring by one and the same artist in different pictures, the collection generally suggests a certain want of individuality, strength and self control.

In this brief notice of an interesting exhibition we may observe that it would be a poor compliment to the Society of Women Painters to judge their work by any but the highest standard. Our general verdict is that as artists these ladies are too diffusive or too ambitious, and that each should realize her special gift and be content to develop it slowly, patiently and with the assurance of ultimate and crowning success. [9]

It was all too easy, if not rather patronising, to tell these female painters they should realise their special gift and be content to develop it slowly and patiently. It would be impossible not to be too ambitious. In fact, down right fool hardy.

Their male opponents were shrouded within the safe walls of the Manchester Academy - a predominantly male bastion. Just step behind the scenes for a moment. You can almost smell the male testosterone, turpentine and nicotine.

---

9 City News, 24th November, 1883.

Varnishing Day: 10

The most select day is Varnishing Day when the lambs have been chosen and the goats rejected into utter darkness, and when the pictures have been arranged on the walls, there comes what is known as Varnishing Day, and that is the best time, if you can get in by hook or by crook, for seeing the pictures freely.

The assistants on such occasions are, firstly, the artists, secondly, the critics, and thirdly, the favoured few. The artists, most of them with pipes in their mouths, are either varnishing or going about putting finishing touches to their works.

The light in the studio where the picture was placed upon an easel is one thing, and the light in the exhibition room another. It happens constantly that the painter finds it necessary, when his work is hung in the fierce light that rests on the walls, to modify this effect, or heighten it.

Everyone present is busy in one way or another but there is a free-and-easy air about the whole business. The smoking for instance looks strange, and yet it makes everyone feel at home.

The gifted Toneist, whose transcripts of nature always seems to have been dabbled with blotting paper before the colours were dry is rolling cigarettes as rapidly as Fortuney, and he was the fastest smoker of the Roman Spanish School.

The Josef Israels of Manchester - the painter of 'The Winter Sheep Fold' - inhales his nicotine through the short stem of a modern pipe. The favourite of Pont-Aven, whose landscape exhibit shows such rare combinations of exquisite colour and tender feeling, consoles his soul also with cigarettes.

The Oldham Cox and the Oldham Teniers do not smoke much, but the wild Welshmen, from the convivial hermit of Conwy, or the recluse of Talyeafyn, down to the younger member of the Cymric brotherhood prefer pipes.

All this joviality is part of an exhibition scene, but there is a down side to it. What about the paintings that were not accepted? These are poignantly summed up in an Artist's Anecdote:

---

10 Manchester Academy of Fine Arts Cuttings book, 1857-1878.

The Condemned Cellars

"I know of no spectacle more painful and depressing of its kind than is seen in a walk through these cold whitewashed cellars after the selection is finished. Stack after stack of pictures, many of them 10, 12 and even 18ft in length; their faces turned as if in shame to the wall. Groups of sculpture, statues, busts innumerable looking grim and ghostly in the gloom, what a mass of frustrated, wasted human endeavour do they not represent." 11

Back to the successful. When walking around the Academy's pristine exhibition rooms would anyone guess what had been going on just a couple of days before?

Just who did walk around the Academy's rooms viewing and commenting on the pictures? According to the City Lantern and Free Lance: 12 a certain type of person definitely always attended the Academy's exhibitions: **Everybody that was anybody - in the artistic world at least - was there in full force; artists: young, old, middle-aged, male, female, good looking and the reverse, hair worn long and hair worn short - the extreme in either case, the best artists seemingly the most common place man, and the most artistic - looking creatures undoubtedly the worst painters.**

Everyone went, not with the intention of seeing the pictures, but rather to see and be seen themselves.

The ladies costumes were as a rule, extremely pretty, a great number wore printed calicoes, but some were made in more pretentious materials. Amongst the ladies, I am sorry to say again the artistic element looked the worst, though the late aesthetic craze seems to have run its course in Manchester. Very few disciples of Oscar Wilde appearing on the scene.

The Academy was alive with sound and colour - filled with jostling artistic people and members from the middle and upper classes - it must have been exhilarating for all concerned, but then there does seem to be a large void. What about the vast numbers of so called working class people who were part of this City's scene? There is no

---

11 City News, 13th October, Painters and Pictures - An Artists Anecdotes: The Condemned Cellars.
12 23rd February, 1883.

sign of them. Did none of them like art? Surely some did. Had any been invited?

The Academy and its exhibitions were for all to enjoy. Part of its constitution was: "The Academy should be involved in the education of members of the public generally in the history and principles of art." In other words all members of the public not just a chosen few. Why were the working classes not represented? Probably because they neither had the time, energy or means to attend such an occasion. This did not mean they were not interested in the arts; given half a chance they too would probably have enjoyed a stroll around the rooms.

Certain members of authority had very preconceived ideas. They were quite sure that the working classes never visited the gallery because they did not appreciate good art, and they saw it as their duty to introduce it to them. The burning question was - what was good art? They seemed to presume they could answer this question and in so doing they opened a Pandora's box.

CHAPTER 5

ART FOR ALL MANCHESTER'S CITIZENS

Mr. T. C. Horsfall wrote a paper -

"By What Means Can The Inhabitants Of Large Towns Be Induced To Buy Examples Of Good Art?"

It was aimed directly at the working classes.

According to Mr. Horsfall - photos, photogravings and chrome-lithographs of good pictures were now so cheap that well paid workpeople could afford to buy several such copies every year. "So why was it" he asked "that as a rule, only worthless engravings and coloured prints were found in their houses?"

"Did they not know some copies of good pictures were also cheap?" He decided they did not know enough about the subject matter to care much about them, and they needed a helping hand to appreciate the "noblest kind of pictures."

How was he going to achieve his goal? He suggested that in every town a number of people conversant with art should select such good cheap copies of pictures as they thought could be made interesting to work people by explanation, and that they should have printed on slips of paper, one of which should be sold with each copy, a statement of their reasons for choosing it, a brief criticism of it merits and defects, an explanation of the incident or thing which it represented, and of the connection existing between what it represented and incidents or things known to most work people; the price of the copy and of a simple frame for it.

In the discussion that followed, Mr. W. H. J. Traice said he thought that if the Committee of the Art School were to do as the reader of the paper suggested they would lay themselves open to the charge of being ambitious prigs, of stepping out of their way to assist a commercial matter instead of really promoting art.

He was of the opinion that the excellent art work which appeared in the pages of Punch and other illustrated journals would result in an increased appreciation of the true and the beautiful in art.

The Bishop of Salford expressed his sympathy with the views of Mr. Horsfall, and remarked that the fact that the poorer classes of society delighted in the possession of statuettes and pictures, common though they might be, proved that there was in the people an innate love of art - if they could not have good they would have bad.

Whether the art they liked was good or bad who knows? But, the working classes eventually proved they were interested in seeing Manchester's art when the gallery was opened on a Sunday afternoon - free of charge. It did take a while and a number of experiments to achieve.

In 1879 the Royal Institution decided to open its doors free of charge on a Sunday between 2-5pm in order to avoid interference with Divine Service at the various places of worship. When its doors opened at 2pm there was a large crowd waiting. It grew larger and larger so that towards the end many people were unable to gain admission.

On the final free Sunday 5,350 persons were admitted. During the eleven consecutive Sunday afternoons that the exhibition was open the aggregate number of persons visiting reached 51,682.

Statistically it would seem the Sunday opening had been a great success. So did this prove that ordinary working people were interested in the Manchester art scene and its producers? Not really, as sometimes happens with statistics they were unreal. They did not represent the whole story behind the free Sunday openings.

These were not the only figures causing concern. The Governors of the Royal Institution held their annual meeting on 27th March 1880 and there was some debate as to why the exhibition had been so expensive. Then Mr. Samuel Cotton drew everybody's attention to an item of £54 for Sunday expenses incurred in connection with the Sunday opening of the exhibition. It appeared to him, he protested, that any profit they made out of the exhibition had been swallowed up by the Sunday opening.

Having brought this £54 to all the members attention he then launched an attack on the Council for opening the Institution on a Sunday. Sunday was a day of rest, the Sabbath. Not for viewing exhibitions, and definitely not for drinking alcohol.

He declared the publicans must be deeply indebted to the Council for opening the exhibition on a Sunday, and was quite sure that instead of drawing certain people away from the public house, it attracted them, and that the majority of people who were thus attracted into the city would find it very dry work to gaze at pictures, and consequently would seek refreshment at the public houses before returning home. He, therefore, recommended that the council should be instructed not to repeat the experiment on Sunday opening. A vote was taken and seconded by Mr. G. Gauthorp.

However, Mr. G. S. Darbyshire was not having any of this. He moved as an amendment that the Governors present should congratulate the Council on their Sunday opening and that they should repeat their experiment. This was seconded by Mr. H. J. Leppoc.

There was much heated discussion on the subject. It was mooted that many who attended for free on a Sunday were too mean to pay 3d on a week day and that it was the fact it was free that people came to the exhibition rather than to look at beautiful art. At one stage in the debate it was suggested it was impossible for the thousands of people who came on Sunday to see anything and that it was like having a mob in the place. (It was agreed this last sentence should be removed from the record).

On a show of hands being taken, there were six for the amendment and twelve against it. The resolution was then carried by seventeen votes against four. The working classes were not wanted on a Sunday, art lovers or not. Then a furore broke out with regard to the Sunday closure of the Royal Institution. At a Band of Hope meeting a Mr. Hugh Mason made a speech condemning the Sunday exhibitions at the Royal Institution on religious and alcoholic grounds.

This was counter attacked by a letter in the City News. [1] Its writer pointed out that: **although Mr. Mason was in the midst of admiring and applauding friends on Saturday evening like many others he had met with, both in the ranks of church and dissent, he would persist in ignoring the fact that there were thousands who did not want to join the Band of Hope, and did not want to go to church or chapel.**

Furious he rammed home the point that the Royal Institution's committee had gone out of its way to avoid opening during the ordinary hours of divine service in church or chapel and he had not heard of any diminutions in the Sunday School attendance. As for drunkenness, when the Royal Institution was open the public houses

1 City News, 13th March 1880.

were all closed. Perhaps this letter helped to sway the Governors of the Institution.

They held a special general meeting on the 1st November and decided to re-instate Sunday opening - subject to such restrictions as may be necessary to prevent over-crowding or danger to the works exhibited.

Once again the Institution would be open free of charge on a Sunday afternoon for the working people. Surely, every one concerned in the great debate would now be satisfied. A person signing himself Epsilon in the Manchester Guardian 2 certainly was not, and he did have a fair point. A point that would prove why the statistics previously quoted for the free Sunday openings were incorrect.

He declared it was not the working people who were visiting the exhibition when it was free on a Sunday but members of society who were able to put their hands in their pockets and pay the appropriate entrance fee.

He was so fired up he wrote: **Anyway, I hope during the next few Sundays the exhibition is opened, that we shall see less seal skin jackets, gold chains, and "superfine saxony," and a preponderance of fustian jackets, corduroy trousers, and other habiliments denoting the *bona fide* labouring poor - for whose whole and sole benefit the Council have so kindly thrown open the door of the Institution on Sunday afternoons.**

It would seem the Council were in a no win situation: they had tried to involve all Manchester's citizens within its local art scene, but instead had found themselves entangled in some kind of class war, and it would not go away. In fact it was becoming more vicious with every letter sent to the Manchester Guardian, which incidentally was having a field day reporting all its readers comments.

One writer wanted to know what about the people who could afford to see the exhibition, but whose week day employment gave them no time to enjoy looking at pictures? **I have been surprised that the Council should continue this miserable patronising of the "working man." It is time all this petting of the "working man" was ended.**

2 3rd December 1880.

I am sure it must often disgust the sturdy honest working man to be pampered with unnecessary benevolence. It has been said that in time there is only to be the very poor and the very rich, and the action of the Council very much countenances this option.

"Epsilon" must know very little of the dress of the present working man if he considers that he is to be discerned on Sunday by fustian jackets or corduroy trousers.

He suggested to reach "the labouring poor," it would be more reasonable to get together a small collection of art and place it closer to their homes.

Then the Council had an inspiration: they decided to try and attract the working classes on a Sunday by making a certain number of tickets available every week. These would be distributed through a number of libraries: Central Reference, Cheetham, Rochdale Road, Ancoats, Chorlton, Ardwick and Hulme branches, the Savings Bank, Working Men's Clubs and Coffee Taverns.

It worked: they had managed to reach the working classes at last. **Most of the visitors yesterday were composed of the labouring poor. The two galleries in which the students of the School of Art exhibit their works were thrown open, and a great number of visitors availed themselves of the opportunity.** [3]

What a triumph, the tickets seemed to have worked, most of the Sunday visitors were working people. Statistics showed, although it was the last Sunday, the attendance of the visitors was among the smallest recorded during the present season, being 1,993, the most part (1,699) entering the building between 2 and 4 0'clock. The total number of visitors on the corresponding Sunday after Christmas last year, when no tickets were issued, was 5,350.

There was no doubt that the Institution was now having an effect on all its citizens. But there was no time to bask in success, for there were now plans afoot for Manchester to have its own prestigious City Art Gallery.

---

3 Manchester Guardian, 27th December, 1880.

CHAPTER 6

THE MANCHESTER CITY ART GALLERY

Proposed Art Gallery For Manchester

A meeting of the Council of the Royal Manchester Institution was held to consider the formation of a permanent public Art Gallery for Manchester. Dr. Ainsworth presided: set forth by: Thomas Worthington, George Falkner, W. A. Turner and C. J. Pooley. It was proposed the gallery should be supplied by the Corporation.

With the anticipated removal of the School of Art to its new building it was suggested placing three picture galleries on the south side of the Institution {en suite} with those on the north side, by the formation of a large central hall over the lecture theatre, the adoption of which would enable the Council to possess a series of seven galleries, in addition to the sculpture corridors, the entrance hall, and the numerous rooms on the ground floor available for museum purposes. This would enable the building in Mosley Street to become the natural and historical nucleus of a permanent public gallery worthy of the city of Manchester.

It was then proposed to transfer the entire property as a public gift to the City of Manchester and to the custody of the Corporation, upon trusts to be hereafter formulated. The principal of these would be the endowment on the part of the Corporation, by the investment of £50,000 of the sum of £2,000 annually, to be devoted to the purchase of works of art of the highest character, by which in time, a permanent art gallery for the city would be formed. [1]

On the 10th August 1882 [2] the Manchester Corporation Act received Royal Assent: the old Royal Manchester Institution in Mosley Street became the City Art Gallery of Manchester, and the Corporation took possession of the building and its collections in January 1883. Manchester now had its very own Art Gallery underpinned by a rhetoric of industrial growth, civic pride and determined artists.

In September 1881 the last exhibition to be held in the old established conditions of the Royal Institution took place. The 29th and

1 Facts and figures taken from: Manchester Guardian, 1st March 1880.
2 Timothy Clifford, 1983, A Guide to Manchester Art Galleries.

last Heywood Gold Medal awarded under the old constitution went to Mr. H. Clarence Whaite, for his drawing of a "Stronghold of Edward 1st."

The Mosley Street Galleries were to become the property of the citizens before another autumn, and the Governors of the Royal Institution would have to voluntarily surrender their sovereignty to throw in their efforts with the new Committee of Management.

Its new owners did not hold back: in August 1885 the committee of the Manchester City Council decided, subject to the approval of the Council, to light the Art Gallery by electricity - cost £1,715. It was estimated that the annual cost as compared with that of gas would not be increased by more than £259.10., whilst the advantages would be considerable.

Then disgruntled mumblings could be heard. Certain persons were not happy with the basement of the art gallery. Unbelievably, the basement of the art gallery was being used as a chemical laboratory. "Should it continue to be occupied as a chemical laboratory?" This was the question being asked at a Council meeting in 1890. Apparently the committee had decided, some time ago, that the tenant should have notice to quit in March and then changed their minds. One member said, "It was ridiculous, surely the most unsuitable place in the world for a laboratory would be under a gallery filled with valuable works of art. The Corporation had spent £50,000 on pictures for the Art Gallery since taking it over and the laboratory was being retained for sentimental reasons." The City Surveyor's report with regard to the injurious character of the gaseous fumes which came from the laboratory stated: "Men working on the roof of the gallery could not endure the fumes and ceased work."

It was pointed out that the Council had just added a work to the collection at a cost of £1,200 and that it was absurd these works should be put into a building which is touched with poisonous and corrosive fumes. It was agreed that the basement should be used for storage only.

Manchester City Council were not the only ones having problems with their building. Salford Corporation actually proposed they should cut the legs off the portraits in the municipal collection, in order to economise space.

This statement naturally excited much interest in artistic circles.

The editor of the Evening News wrote: **I am overwhelmed with correspondence on the subject - mostly from indignant artists. One of this class asks whether there are no portraits of Mayors and Councillors in the collection which could be reduced to half size by trimming their robes and other insignia of Bumbledom.**

Somebody else suggested: To complete the Salford collection, a portrait should be added representing the Art Committee without heads - in which condition he is confident that no one could fail to recognise them. Another correspondent advised the Corporation to get over the difficulty by cutting up all their pictures and exhibiting them from time to time in sections. The public could then go and look at the head of a famous character one day, his body the next and his legs on a third.

The Manchester City Art Gallery's committee had not quite reached these tactics, but they were being accused of some pretty tawdry ones of their own. They declared the Autumn Exhibition was no longer a popular one with the public and proposed they should abandon the usual Autumn Exhibition and substitute it for temporary exhibitions open free to the public as an addition to the permanent collections.

The Evening News had an interview with one of the leading members of the Manchester Academy, a gentleman who had been intimately associate with the art life of the city for considerably more that a quarter of a century. In his opinion the unpopularity of the Autumn Exhibition was due to the fact that the Committee would keep ignoring the claims of local artist and its neglect to avail themselves of the trained assistance which would be willingly rendered by any of them. "The exhibitions are not interesting to artists themselves so how could they be expected to be interesting to the general public?" he asked, and continued, "for a number of years the hanging of the Autumn Exhibitions has been left in the hands of one man, and should that man be the representative of a certain school the character of the exhibition will suffer. One opinion is not enough to represent a hanging committee. It is essential to the success of an exhibition that every branch of art should be adequately represented." He also pressed home the fact it was recognised in Manchester that all the principal places were allocated to London Work.

He also wanted to know why the Committee had spoilt two of the finest rooms by introducing unsightly pay stiles? Apparently an important work by one of the leaders of art in the North of England had been placed close to one of the stiles in such a position that the policeman guarding the stile was bound to stand in front of it and obstruct the views of anyone who wished to study it. "This sort of treatment causes our artists of good local position to refrain from contributing any work of importance," [3] and just to emphasise his point he asked the same question once again: "Why is this most crucial and difficult task in connection with the hanging of an exhibition left to people of inferior experience?"

The next Autumn Exhibition was a lot smaller. The Committee decided not to disarrange the permanent collection. This time it was most obvious the local artists had received much fairer treatment from the selection committee and hangers. The critics backed their productions too.

R.G. Somerset - "Falls on the Lledr" - Bit of honest open air work, strongly painted and fine in its sober and harmonious colour.

Elias Bancroft - Represented by an architectural subject in Rothenberg - capably drawn and painted, and is much more pleasant in colour than is sometimes the case with his work.

Byron Cooper - "A Cornish Coombe, Moonrise" - tenderly felt and tenderly painted.

William Stott - There are some fine and subtle passages of colour in Mr. W. Stott's "Memory of an Island." If this eccentric man of talent, who so narrowly misses the dangerous gift of genius, were to devote himself to marine painting, there is no saying what success might not be in store for him.

F.W. Jackson - "In the Orchard, Springtime." Tender apple blossom and half fulfilled foliage, sunlight and dapple shadows, and the background of mist sea far below. The treatment is partly decorative and the colour scheme is delightful, but apart from the merely decorative feeling there is a vein of dreamy reverie running through the picture.

---

3 The Unpopularity of the Autumn Art Exhibition, Evening News, 4th October 1897.

Manchester's male artists were being noticed and praised but not quite to the extent some of its female artists were. It had also come to the eyes of the press that Manchester's female artists had been excelling themselves. One writer had noticed that a preponderance of male artists had devoted themselves almost exclusively to landscapes, and this had led to a somewhat curious development: The lady members of the Academy noticing perhaps, that their male brethren feared, or were disinclined, to attempt portraiture - boldly rushed in and produced a number of paintings which reached a high standard of excellence and importance. M. Breakell, S. Dacre, A.L. Robinson, E. Magnus were amongst those who exhibited the most power, imagination and technical expertise in the nobler form of creative art.

For a time the women in the Academy were commonly spoken of as the "best men" of that association. 4

Despite one or two hiccups Manchester's art scene was going from strength to strength. It not only had a new City Art Gallery, but its Art School was also receiving a great deal of praise especially from the City News: At the opening of the winter session of the Manchester School of Art, of which Mr. Willis is the head master, it is perhaps not out of place to recall the fact that half the entire number of special national prizes offered to the kingdom came to Manchester, including two of the three first prizes; and the Manchester School this year takes the greatest number of national medals ever awarded to any London, local, or provincial school. 5

This was a great triumph for Manchester. The Society of Women Painters could also feel pretty triumphant too. The Manchester Academy had opened their doors fully to female artists i.e., granting them full membership and drawing from the model. They now joined the Manchester Academy on equal terms with its male members.

---

4 A Curious Development, Manchester Weekly, December 1896.
5 City News, 19th September 1885.

CHAPTER 7

A MISHMASH OF ARTS AND COMMERCE

It was 1887 and the city had just hosted the "Manchester Royal Jubilee Exhibition" at Old Trafford, an impressive and extremely successful exhibition with the arts right at its forefront.

The Royal Jubilee was an exhibition of National Arts, Science and Industry celebrating fifty years of Queen Victoria's reign. On one day over a crowd of 74,600 attended this exhibition. During the 166 days it was open over four and a half million people passed through the turnstiles. Even the lowest day's attendance was over 14,000. [1]

This fantastic glass extravaganza was opened by the Prince of Wales and Princess Alexandra. For lovers of art there were no less than thirteen fine art galleries. So far as the arts were concerned the crowning glory was the decoration of the building's dome by the artist, Ford Madox Brown. This was indeed a triumph for Manchester's art scene.

Ford Madox Brown was contacted in November 1886 by a Mr. G. F. Armitage of Altrincham, asking him "if he would undertake the decoration of the dome of the Jubilee Exhibition - then in course of construction at Old Trafford, Manchester."

In the time allowed this would be quite a task for Brown. In his own words: **I was informed that there were eight large spandrels of the four huge arches 72 feet wide supporting the dome, for which I was required to furnish figures, the decorative portion to remain with the committee (Mr. Armitage). These spandrels, of which the shapes were not quite fixed, were each of them 36 feet long by 18 feet deep.**

I decided that the eight spaces should be representative of Wool, Corn, Shipping, Commerce, Coal, Iron, Weaving and Spinning. As soon as I began to study these spaces, charcoal in hand, I found that their eccentric shapes, with one acute angle far extended like the orbit of a comet, would in any case require more than the one

---

1 Bill Norton, Manchester Royal Jubilee Exhibition Old Trafford, 1887.

emblematic figure to fill each of them. So I decided that each distant angle should be filled with a winged, but legless, second figure, a spirit of Lancashire Energy. [2]

Brown reckoned on only having to execute one of the Spandrels himself, and the seven others could be repeated by assistants.

He converted his large stable and carriage house at the end of his garden into a studio, and devoted it entirely to angels and their 12 feet long wings. Here he came against a number of obstacles. To his horror he found that there was no prepared canvas, in London, or in Paris, or anywhere else that he could think of, to be had under three months' delay. After a good deal of research he found a manufacturer of floor cloth in Dundee who was able to supply huge quantities of very rough and open sail cloth, 12 feet wide. This sail cloth a coach painter and decorator of Altrincham undertook to prime and prepare for him. Brown said, "It was rough and heavy at best, but there was no time for rubbing it down or giving it a surface; the heavy rolls were only half dry when they reached my house."

Mr. Bruce Wallis, of the Manchester Academy of Arts and another male assistant - an old pupil and assistant of Rossetti, named Knewstub helped him. Madox Brown wrote: **I also had the assistance of four young ladies, extremely vigorous figure painters, partly of the Manchester Academy, these ladies had also studied in Paris. The young ladies - and they were emphatically such - worked with a skill and energy that nothing could baffle or impair from the top of a ladder to sitting on the floor. Two of them even offered, at last, to take my place when they heard I should have to be hoisted up fifty feet in the air to retouch some parts of the paintings that when upon high looked weak and defective - while we were at work on them the dome was simply that of heaven itself.**

Ten days before the opening, the twenty-four rolls of canvas were placed on the lorry and departed. When they reached the dome, Madox Brown said "they were handled by heroic workmen up in their perilous perches and floating galleries." When the project was finished Brown was ecstatic, "I no longer have to wake at four in the morning and remain sleepless, in the horrid dread of the thing never getting done for

---

2 From an article in the Universal Review on Historic Art written by Brown himself.

the ever nearing 1st May." The dome was a huge success and so too was the Jubilee Exhibition bringing great kudos to the city and its people.

The City News reported: **That the funds, property and effects of the Royal Jubilee Exhibition should be paid over to Mr. J. C. Lee and Messrs. C. J. Galloway, W. Agnew and Oliver Heywood, to be transferred to the Institution - £10,000 to be applied for the extension of the School of Art under the express title of the Royal Jubilee Exhibition Section.** [3]

£20,000 was to be expended in the purchase of works of fine and decorative art of the highest class to be placed in the museum buildings in Whitworth Park, and the remainder to be applied towards the building and equipment of the new Technical School, as part of the Institution.

All involved were euphoric and viewed the exhibition with great pride, Manchester had not only proved it was capable of holding a massive exhibition, but it had also brought together the arts and industry. Then out of the blue disgruntled murmurs could be heard all over the city. It would seem some Mancunians had decided the exhibition was not all it had been made out to be and that the city seemed to be neglecting the arts. Many thought this was ridiculous and asked "how on earth could the arts have been neglected after such an impressive exhibition and how could such an accusation be made when Manchester now had its own Academy, Art School and City Art Gallery?" This really did need looking into. When it came down to it the reason for all this unrest was more to do with the neglect of the city's artists rather than the city's art scene. Apparently a number of local artists had been invited to contribute one piece of work each to the present show where upon it was understood that one room or at least one wall would be set apart for their works. But this never came about. Their works were scattered throughout the exhibition without any attempt at classification. In fact, it was pointed out that works by Mr. Goodfellow - "Cheetham College Dormitory" and a small study of a female head by Miss Dacre (who worked so hard on the dome) were promoted to the ceiling.

---

3 4th January 1890.

Horrified at this treatment, some wanted to know why local artists and their paintings were being addressed in such a crass way?

One correspondent blamed the Academy of Arts: **The Manchester Academy numbers among its members: men who have to be reckoned with when the account of English art is made up. Surely, they deserved better treatment than this. Mr. R. Gay Somerset's solitary picture - a landscape is cruelly hung. Skied, in a cross light, it is impossible to see what the work is.** [4]

He was quite adamant that the Manchester Academy showed better work at its annual spring exhibition than any other provincial school could produce, and that London, Paris and the United States had already recognised the value of its efforts. "Why then had a stronger stand not been made by the President and Council of an Institution he had lately discovered called the Manchester Academy of Fine Arts?" he asked. **This body of men should have sought a better status for their fellow-members so they would not have had to undergo the disgrace of Manchester art being practically ignored at a Manchester Exhibition. The people who care anything about art in our own locality know the work of our own men. But people in the South of England, and an enormous number of persons from all parts of the continents of Europe and America who profess the higher culture have flocked and continued to flock to this exhibition, and they cannot fail to be struck with nakedness of the land, so far as local art is concerned.**

In his view this unreasonable treatment, with regard to Manchester's Artists, rested squarely on the shoulders of the Manchester Academy of Arts, and that local art was not one bit better off after thirty years of this Institution.

He thought a better status would be obtained if the president and council of this body were to make a firmer stand and look after their local artists. Not just stand there and let them be ill-treated at the hands of the recent Manchester Exhibition without daring to assert themselves. Also, he wanted to know why did they neglect to promote these artists and their work? He had been in conversation with one of them in his studio and was totally appalled at the way he had been treated.

---

4 Letter to editor of Manchester City News, July 1887.

To get to this studio he had taken a turn out of one of Manchester's fashionable thoroughfares down a dark and narrow street, where stepping into a dilapidated-looking building, he ascended a wearisome flight of dark and rickety stairs until he could get no higher. Here a door faced him upon which the legend "Mr. So and So," artist met his eye. After a short rap on this door it opened and he was confronted by a tall slim man of thirty years or more. He said a cheery "how do you do?" and "you are at liberty to look around."

The writer described the studio in the following way: **It was somewhat large and lofty, with a north light streaming through the roof. Pictures, canvasses, frames and easels are scattered about in artistic confusion. But the chief object that catches your eye is a large canvas upon which the artist is evidently at work, and as he lights his pipe and sits down with his palette you feel tempted to ask a few questions concerning it.**

The artist had been working on his picture for a number of weeks and complained how expensive it was to hire models and buy materials. When asked what he intended doing with the painting? He replied "that he intended sending it to London." "Why have you to send your work to London? Why not sell it in Manchester?" "Because most of Manchester's citizens cannot afford to buy large or important pictures. The few who can by-pass Manchester and only buy off fashionable London artists." "Have you no exhibition through which your work might be shown in Manchester?" "Well there is an exhibition, but again the more fashionable London artists have it to themselves, our local men - who don't get tricked out - get scattered and hung in every corner, or skied almost out of sight. The committee do not care about local artists just so long as they get a few sensational pictures to cover their walls to fetch in shillings."

As I fumbled my way down the steep and winding staircase I felt it was high time something was done quickly to relieve artists from these shameful circumstances.

Were these local artists being neglected? Some would argue a magnificent temple to the arts had been built especially for their exhibitions. But then should the local artists have it all to themselves? Perhaps the burning question was "how good was their work?" Was it as excellent as this correspondent and one (maybe biased artist) would have it? The Hanging Committee certainly did not think so. On the other hand it would seem a small number of people had a large number of artists within their grip, and could be seen as playing safe by exhibiting more important names. There was no doubt that a large number of Manchester's artists were struggling to make ends meet and were happy to place the blame on the Academy and a number of the city's industrial entrepreneurs. But there did seem to be much more bubbling away behind the scenes.

Another correspondent had a totally different slant on the reason why Manchester's artists were struggling so much to make ends meet. He thought it was unjust to accuse the authorities of neglect, and if some artists were struggling they only had themselves to blame: **For some years past artists even of considerable ability have found increasing difficulty in finding customers for their productions, and this has increased to such an extent that at present hundreds of men who a few years back could make with ease, say three or four hundred a year, now can scarcely make fifty.**

The prices have naturally fallen correlatively with the difficulty of finding a purchaser. The cause of this is simply the enormous production of pictures over and above the demand of them. These productions don't wear out like boots and shoes, and consequently dealers and painters alike are glutted with them. Pawnbrokers will in many cases refuse to advance money on pictures at all. [5]

His conclusion was that artists should agree to paint only a certain number of pictures instead of the unlimited quantity they at present produced and stop saturating the market.

There again, it was not just the Manchester Artists who were having a bad time. The artist Frank Spenlove-Spenlove wrote: **English Artists were passing through a very bad time and English Art was never at a lower ebb than at the present. He blamed the Royal Academy.**

So long as public appreciation of "Old Masters" is fostered and encouraged by the Royal Academy with its annual winter exhibitions how can the modern painter expect to make

5 Letter from W. H. Latham-Barnes to the editor of the Manchester City News, July 1887.

headway? [6]

He too thought the profession was overcrowded and many artists asked extravagant prices for their work in exhibitions.

Some Manchester artists, one in particular J. H. E. Partington, blamed Manchester's industrial producers for the lack of enthusiasm in the city's art scene. According to him these rich merchants were wreaking havoc throughout the city's landscape and supporting artists from further afield. He went so far as to say "they were not interested in the arts, just obsessed by making money."

If Manchester's art scene was being neglected could the blame really be put at the feet of its industrial producers? Surely many of these captains of industry (in their own way) had just fully supported one of Manchester's most prestigious exhibitions - helping to show Manchester as a caring city extremely proud of everything it produced - including its art.

Could it be that some of Manchester's artists were becoming too precious about their art? Criticising the city and its institutions, and complaining about its industrial landscapes, grey weather, and lack of patrons seemed to be their battle cry, though expatriate French artist, Adolphe Valette (1879-1942) lived and worked in Manchester and managed to overcome some of the latter difficulties.

J. E. Phythian, artist and art critic, disagreed with Partington declaring: **In Manchester, there was a wonderful picturesqueness – a certain subtle quality of light and shade constantly coming and going. Mosley Street he instanced was full of buildings, people, cabs and lurries, but if you half closed the eyes so as to get a general impression you experienced an infinite pleasure in noting the beautiful gradation and perspective as lines melted away, as it were, into the distance. All this is most consoling from the aesthetic point of view, and reminds us of that common place expression that it is not so much the world that's at fault as the people who are in it.**

---

6 Frank Spenlove-Spenlove, Pearson's Weekly, January 17th 1907, Why artists are having a bad time. This article states S-S had no fewer than three of his works purchased by the French Government, and was also known as the founder of the famous Yellow Door School of painting, to which students came from all over the world.

Was Partington right to criticise and blame Manchester's industrial entrepreneurs? Or was he being foolhardy since a large number of business men did patronise local artists, believing passionately in their art and trying to support them. They helped to keep the local art scene vibrant. Whether they were supporting Manchester, its art, or its artistic producers, who knows. Perhaps in their own way they were actually promoting all three, but without a doubt they were going out on a limb, and supporting a number of genres of art by an assortment of relatively unknown (at that time) producers, whose only common factor was Manchester.

Take Samuel Barlow (1825-93) for example. Barlow lived and worked as a partner in a bleach works at Stakehill, Near Middleton. His artistic and botanical interests were numerous. He was a founder member of the Manchester Arts Club, an active member of the Manchester Literary Club, and had special interests in Lancashire dialect.

He was an early patron of the Manchester School of Artists, and they were strongly represented in his collection. When his collection was sold the catalogue recorded twenty-seven oils and ten watercolours by Anderson Hague, seven watercolours by Joseph Knight, four oils and two watercolours by R. G. Somerset, twenty oils and eight watercolours by F. W. Jackson, and works by J. H. E. Partington, J. H. Davies and others. [7]

If Manchester was to stay an impressive centre of art there would have to be some give and take on both sides. Like it or not, the only way forward for the Manchester artist was to come to terms with the city and its industrial rhetoric and use it as a vehicle to promote their work. Listening to these professional artists' moans and groans it could be thought that any person with a leaning towards the turning cogs of Manchester could not possibly understand or be involved within its aesthetic scene. One business man (describing himself as an amateur artist) condemned this thought. [8]

---

7 All the information on Samuel Barlow has been taken from: John H. G. Archer, Art And Architecture In Victorian Manchester.

8 City News, February 1889, Business Men as Painters, An Art Society for Manchester.

In his opinion the professional artists were very selfish and furthermore the Manchester Academy of Fine Arts certainly did not meet every artistic person's wants, it confined itself to professional men only, and the working amateur could only join its ranks under heavy disadvantages.

A case in point being: for an annual subscription of two guineas one could have the privilege of attending the Academy's life class on four nights weekly and exhibiting at the Spring Exhibition. Being a business man he was unable to put in three or four nights per week and could only turn out once or twice a week and he knew others in the same position. He came to the conclusion the Academy was not interested in the non-professional business man: **The amateur is a social animal and the Academy does not offer him any inducement in that direction. The Academy does not meet the wants of the average lover of Art. It is a professional club, it does not attract anyone else and therefore does not meet the want of "An Art Society for Manchester."**

He also thought the other leading professional club, the Graphic Club, failed to meet the needs of an amateur business man. In fact, he thought neither of the clubs offered any advantages whatever to the art patron, or the lover of art who spent his money upon the productions of many local artists.

All these self-opinions darting back and forth via the local newspapers were very healthy and showed citizens cared. But, if the city's artistic reputation was to stay intact and prosper further, the powers that be would not only have to look after their local artists and start promoting their work more, they would also have to go out of their way to woo their local manufacturers. It was crucial that art and industry should be seen to be hand in glove.

Manchester's economy was changing once again, and as a city, Manchester was moving into exciting times. Mighty and Magnificent was how one newspaper described the city. It was bustling again. A new era of progress and expansion had begun and a new kind of prosperity was enveloping the city, and it was all thanks to the building of the Manchester Ship Canal.

Just stroll down to the docks of the Ship Canal, and you will see there the great vessels which have come to our very doors from the never most parts of the world bringing for our use the varied

produce of every country and clime, look upon the immense provision already made for present and future trade, and note the activity, the bustle, and life of a seaport which is already one of the great emporiums of the earth, in order to have borne forcibly in upon our minds that there is reason sufficient for the access of prosperity which we are beginning to feel and for the creation of that new era in which Manchester will become Mighty and Magnificent beyond the dreams of the most imaginative amongst us. [9]

The door was open, if those in authority were broad-minded and enlightened enough they could cream off some of this new prosperity. They could promote the arts and prove that Manchester was not just a thriving city - but was also extremely proud of both its artists and its manufacturers.

This same newspaper printed the following: **Instead of rushing off to London - visit the studios of our Manchester Artists. It is surely wiser and more to public advantage that a work of high merit even if it be from the studio of a comparatively unknown man should be displayed, rather than some inferior specimen from the hand of a "popular painter."**

It would have to be a two way situation. Professional artists through their Academy and the members of Manchester's various institutions would all have to pull their weight and gel with these new entrepreneurs. Then perhaps all would see that art did not always have to be serious and academic. It could be great fun and frivolous. It really was all right to giggle and squint awkwardly at a painting and not have the foggiest what it was about, and even think it would look much better the other way up. If the label was beyond belief it did not matter. It was perfectly acceptable to just look at a painting take in its variety of rich colours and wallow in its sumptuous broad brush marks, and if it made the viewer feel like running round the hushed gallery for joy – so much the better.

Art was an excuse for people to dress up and enjoy themselves. The Courier covered one arts event and showed its frivolity by allowing a peep into the female fashions of the day. **The Lady Mayoress wore a dainty pale Heliotrope crepe de chine blouse and black voile skirt.**

9 Manchester Weekly Times, Art In Manchester, 29th January 1897.

Mrs. Mandleburg was in brown voile, richly embroidered. Mrs. B. Mullen was in grey cashmere trimmed with panne velvet. Mrs Hatton's black silk dress was trimmed with Maltese lace. Mrs. Murray wore black crepe de chine with entre deux of Chantilly Lace. [10]

Manchester's bees were buzzing and so too was the Academy - gradually the arts and commerce became hand in glove, as advocated by George V when he visited Manchester in July 1913. After his visit he had sent his thanks to the Lord Mayor of Manchester for the reception recently afforded to him and made the following comments concerning Manchester's industry and its arts. **If Manchester has derived its wealth and prosperity from commerce, it has also shown that success in business is compatible with an active discharge of the duties of citizenship and a keen and practical interest in art, literature and science.**

Your city has specially distinguished itself by its intelligent and discriminationary patronage of the art of painting, and the efforts has made to establish and perfect its system of technical education are worthy of high praise. [11]

10 Courier, 24th January 1907, Friends of Art.
11 Courier, 31st July 1913.

CHAPTER 8

THE MANCHESTER SCHOOL OF PAINTERS AND THEIR MANCHESTER CRITICS

Some of the principal members of the Manchester School

Joshua Anderson Hague - 1850-1916
John Houghton Hague - 1842-1934
James Hey Davies - 1844-1930
Frederick W. Jackson - 1859-1918
William Meredith - 1851-1916
John Herbert Evelyn Partington - 1843-1899
Richard Gay Somerset - 1848-1928

During the late nineteenth century the above group of artists had a profound effect on Manchester's biased art scene. Biased in an overpowering way; the critics made it very clear they did not appreciate this group's eagerness to experiment.

Amazingly one Manchester newspaper went out on a limb and predicted their futures in the following way **It is most interesting to watch the progress and rapid strides daily made by a school of artists who have appeared comet-like before the Manchester public. We refer to Messrs: A & H Hague, Partington, Somerset, and Meredith. These men have given rise to no little controversy, not unmixed with jealousy.**[1]

"These men have given rise to no little controversy, not unmixed with jealousy" may seem a little melodramatic, but unfortunately as their biographies unfold it proves to be founded. It was also predicted by the same paper that: **The next two years will try their mettle, and if it keeps its ring those who have had appreciation enough to encourage their efforts will be amply rewarded for their nous and pluck.**

Their mettle was tried for a lot longer than two years, in fact, it took ten years of constant wrangling before their techniques were accepted.

---

1 The Critic, October 5th 1872.

What a beleaguered bunch of artists they were, constantly being criticised by the Manchester art critics whose comments at times knew no boundaries where rudeness was concerned.

Known as the Manchester School, this group of young artists first came together in the 1870's under the auspices of the Manchester born landscape painter and Mezzotint engraver, Joseph Knight. Enthusiastic and full of ideas they would gather at his studio in York Place behind the Union Chapel in Oxford Road on Friday and Saturday evenings.

Right from the beginning the newspaper critics condemned their working techniques. They described Joseph Knight as a gloomy character and decided this ultimately affected his painting. Some argued he had no talent, his technique was too wispy and he had a limited range of colour. One critic wrote: **Although he painted the Welsh mountains and valleys with the grand landscape gesture that is so rare in present-day art, he usually favoured a wispiness of technique that rather emptied them of interest after the pictorial idea and the grace of his evanescent colour had had their say.** [2]

Almost as an afterthought and very begrudgingly this critic announced that although Knight did have a limited range of colour, it was sometimes poignant and never dull.

Knight was an extremely successful painter and etcher, but the Manchester critics refused to admit this, they could or would not come to terms with the fact that his techniques were different. How were they different? He painted how he desired and refused to conform to traditional Art School rules.

This really appealed to all the members of the Manchester School. They not only admired his work but looked up to him as an artist, and suddenly their own work became exciting and different. He had opened a door for them - a door which would lead to exciting new theories and techniques.

But had they the confidence to practise and carry off these new techniques? What about the old school? This predicament of new techniques vying with old was nothing new. These artists were making

---

2 Obituary, The Manchester Evening News - 22nd December 1916.

waves within the hallowed walls of the Manchester Academy and the powers that be were definitely not impressed.

At first the group made small waves and minor changes to their techniques. These changes were hardly noticeable. They all desperately wanted to change their techniques but were not sure how to. Then the waves became much stronger. They visited an exhibition held by the picture dealer, F. W. Hamer, who organised several exhibitions in the early seventies in Manchester. This particular exhibition became known as the "Corot" Exhibition. When they saw his work they knew at once this was the way forward, and excitedly they began to incorporate some of Corot's techniques into their own works.

The tuts could be heard for miles and they became the talk of the Academy. What did these artists think they were doing blatantly copying this French artist's techniques? The critics made it clear they too were unimpressed with the Manchester School's style of painting and accused them of being totally unoriginal and positively boring copying the techniques of the French painter, Jean Baptiste Camille Corot (1796-1875). What the group had realised was Corot was not just an artist, he was an innovator. In the late 1840's he had been experimenting with a number of new techniques, including photography. He began to paint in soft grey-green tones and his landscapes became blurred and hazy with wispy feathery trees. These landscapes became immensely popular. [3]

The group were excited by Corot's techniques. They latched on to them and went through a green period of experimentation - painting in low tones with grey greens as their dominant note.

This looking at past techniques, taking them on board and then experimenting with them, was a very brave thing to do. During these experiments they tried applying their paint straight on to the canvas with a palette knife instead of a brush. One critic was outraged, declaring it was a very dangerous thing to play with edged tools, and

---

3 It has been suggested by Phoebe Pool, Impressionism, that Corot's experiments might have been influenced by a number of photographers known to him. He was particularly good friends with Grandguillaume and Cuvelier, who at that time were deeply involved in landscape photography.

that Anderson Hague's use of his palette knife caused some of his skies to lose something of their tenderness and subtleness in the greys. 4 When Hague experimented with his trees in a number of landscape paintings, making them seem almost flat, he accused him of using his palm and wondered if he had mislaid his paint brush.

All the critics seemed to relish in suppressing any move forward the artists made. The group were pushing their art forward all the time and every time they nudged it on the critics leapt in with their antagonistic comments.

When some of the Manchester School decided to experiment with a different landscape for their next exhibition and crossed the Channel to Pont-Aven, Brittany, someone signing himself as a "Bohemian," wrote the following disparaging comments: **It would seem that several artists have been studying in Brittany, if one may judge from the number of subjects taken thence. The similarity of treatment too, appears to point to a uniform style.**

What did he expect from a school of artists? The group never pretended to be anything other than a school - they used similar techniques and were influenced by a single master, Joshua Anderson Hague, the originator and father of the Manchester School of Painters.

The Bohemian also wrote: **The school may be called the grey and green school, since all the pictures are painted in variations of these colours. Their style is broad, the object evidently being to attain the largest apparent result for the least possible labour.**

We have by various artists: a variety of views at Pont-Aven, any of which might have been the work of one artist, for any discernible difference there is among them. In all these pictures there is an absence of sunlight and a monotony of sky, which strike an outsider as inconsistent with a true interpretation of nature.

In the summer of this year I chanced in Wales to meet with some knights of the brush, who in conversation, vigorously denounced this school and its sketchiness. 5

---

4 RMI Exhibition of Modern Art, Courier, October 16th 1877.

5 A Gossip About Pictures at the Royal Institution, City News, 2nd November 1872.

It does seem incredible how the writer of this article could just dismiss some of the members of the School painting in Pont-Aven, Brittany. To go and paint there must have been such an exciting experience.

This town with its magnificent surrounding landscape acted like a huge magnet pulling in writers, poets and artists from all countries, especially artists. The place was vibrant and full to the brim with an eminent and cosmopolitan crowd of painters. [6]

Richard Gay Somerset, Anderson Hague, John Houghton Hague, J. Hey Davies and W. Meredith stayed at the Hotel Voyageurs in Pont-Aven for four months April, May, June and July, 1872. They went especially to explore this unspoilt place. If the "Bohemian" writer had paused for thought he may have realised that they were in fact making history. As environmentalist painters their finished paintings reflected the times and the culture of this place. Freezing it in time - before Paul Gauguin's brilliant colours and words such as Synthetism and Cloissonisme crept in, took over, and made it famous.

The group's paintings reflected the quaintness of the region through its inhabitants and their every day life, and especially their traditional clothes. However it would of course be wrong to portray Pont-Aven as an unsophisticated place. It was a thriving commercial port exporting local materials to England.

6 All information on Pont-Aven has been taken from Catherine Puget and Julian Campbell, Peintres Britanniques en Bretagnes. Amongst the first to paint in Brittany were Charles Eastlake and Charles Stollard in 1818.

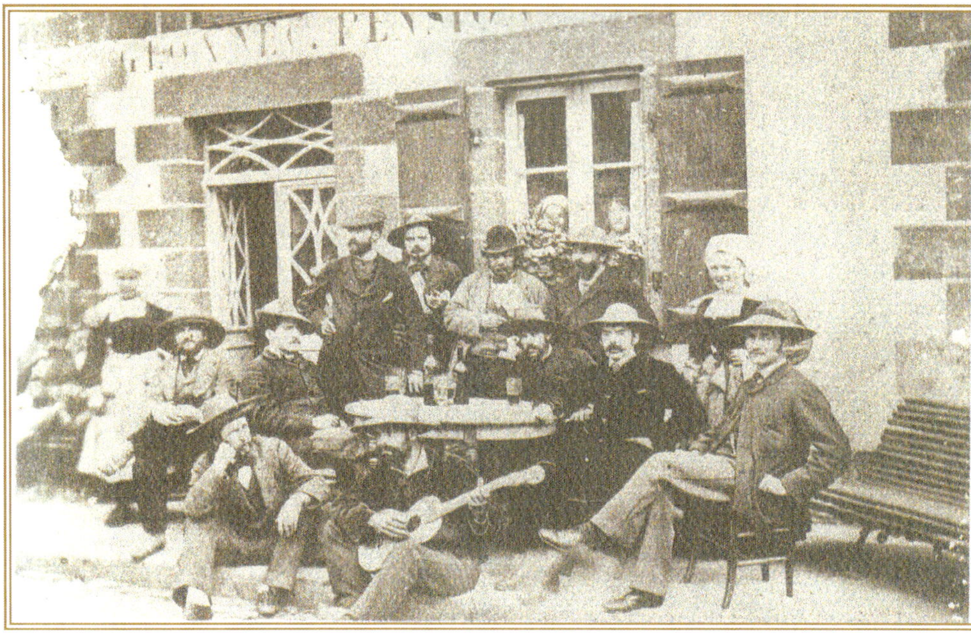

Figure 17. ***English and American artists sat outside the Hotel Gloanec. Richard Somerset on the extreme right.***
Musee de Pont-Aven

It was the atmosphere of the place British painters fell in love with, and soaked in when they excitedly rushed off their boats and trains. They were made so welcome. The locals were more than happy to model for them, and the artists' life styles were good for the town's economy. Pont-Aven's dominant ingredient was the way the light continually changed over the sea and surrounding landscape throughout the day. It never failed to capture every artist's imagination. It was exquisite, and perfect for natural painting. They responded to the light and watched how their French colleagues dealt with it, and slowly their own work became Impressionistic. They soaked in the atmosphere. In return they too were appreciated for their own particular style of painting and obvious Englishness.

At one time there were sixty to eighty artists seeking this agreeable, but hard working life at Pont-Aven. The artist, Caldecott said "On the approach into Pont-Aven the traveller remarks on the strange background noise coming from the woods all around." I would reply,

"It is the rapid movement of the brushes of the hard working painters which one can hear."

There were numerous nationalities painting in France, but it was the American artists Gustave Courbet wanted to know about. Whilst strolling through the Salon with his American artist friend, Walter Pach, Courbet asked him "Why do the Americans come to France to paint? Have they no landscape at home? Why do they go and make all those pictures of Brittany, its costumes and its people, whom they do not understand? In fact, why do you, a painter, come here?" His colleague replied "There are the museums; we have not those at home. One must not only have the landscape, but learn from the masters how to paint it." [7] France had a lot to offer and the Manchester Painters knew this.

Fired with inspiration the group began to experiment in a completely different way. They had been painting in the open air, and the changes in light gradually had some influence on the way they began to work. In particular, John Houghton Hague whose brilliancy of tone began to underpin his work. It was as though there was no hue too brilliant for him to use and harmonise into his colour scheme. His skies became aglow – he was under the spell of the French Impressionist Painters. His pictures were dazzling. Once again he and other members of the group were experimenting and once again the critics were unimpressed.

One critic decided to attack Houghton Hague's exciting new techniques in the following manner: **Comments on the artists of the Manchester - or, as we prefer to call it, the Naturalistic School.**

J. Houghton Hague's work "His Long Day Almost Done." Many visitors inclined to regard this picture as a study in Chrome Yellow, give it a look and pass on.

Mr. Partington has made profuse, though we believe, true, use of his yellow shades, but Mr. Hague has gone further, and suffused his sky with the same hue, so that the spectator wonders for a moment whether he or the painter suffers from yellow jaundice. [8]

---

7 Walter Pach, Queer Thing Painting.

8 Manchester Evening News, 22nd September 1875.

In the same year Houghton Hague was being accused of inflicting jaundice on his Manchester spectators the whole group were exhibiting at the prestigious Durand-Ruel Gallery in Bond Street, London.

Paul Durand-Ruel took over his father's small French business in 1865 and steadily built it up by purchasing and selling reputable works of art by artists such as Delacroix, Corot and Courbet. He moved to London when the Franco-Prussian War began and opened a gallery in New Bond Street.

The French Impressionist, Claude Monet also decided to leave France for the safety of London, and it was here he first met Durand-Ruel. The Impressionists and their techniques had a huge impact on the dealer who became almost obsessed with their productions, so much so, he spent years trying to get their paintings appreciated, taking knock after knock from French and English Critics. This Gallery was indeed an important step forward for the members of the Manchester School and what's more they received a good press:

Manchester Artists In London

Durand-Ruel Gallery in Bond Street, London has a special interest in Manchester, because it contains pictures of some of the artists belonging to what has come to be known as the Manchester School. It is in reality a collection of the works of English artists whose sympathies have an affinity with those of the modern French School, and in this collection the few pictures shown by the Northern painters take a by no means subordinate part.

This small and informal exhibition, we understand is held as an experimental step, and there is reason to believe that the success which it has met with is such as to lead us to expect to hear of an exhibition in London of the work of Manchester Artists on a much larger and more public scale. [9]

Here was praise indeed, what an ego boost for the Manchester School. This article must have helped to spur them on for their next round with the Manchester critics which came all too soon.

---

9 Evening News, 27th January 1875.

The Manchester critics were having a field day with their antagonistic views towards the techniques used by the French Impressionists, and at the same time they were taking an immense delight in criticising the Manchester School for copying this French Modern Movement. It was history repeating itself (old against the new). The group were trying to blend traditional techniques with some new and exciting ideas, and once again the critics were making a fuss. It was as though this undesirable French influence was seen as a sort of disease being blown over the Channel by the wind - hell bent on contaminating Manchester and its artists.

When William Meredith (once described as the pictorial alter ego of Mr Hague) exhibited his work at the Autumn Exhibition at the Manchester Royal Institution one critic had a field day pulling every inch of his painting to bits in the following way: **Standing close to this picture all the less agreeable features stand out - the crude transitions from light to shade, the flat pieces of paint, the clayey colour, the rude manner of execution - are painfully apparent.** [10]

In other words the traditional way of painting nature using composition and drawing were nowhere to be seen. Shadows were produced by using certain colour combinations rather than dark tones. This was all summed up as: "a rude manner of execution."

Arrogantly, the writer then takes it upon himself to explain where Meredith has gone wrong by not using traditional methods of art: **The fundamental rule respecting the degree of finish and amount of detail should be determined with exact reference to the distance from which the eye can easily take in the whole at a glance, no further, because that is the distance at which the spectator will naturally place himself. The rule is a very old one, and that it is a good one the discomfort caused by pictures like Mr. Meredith's proves.**

The writer of this article made a bigoted attack on the way William Meredith worked, arrogantly preconceived since he opened his article with: **No devices of clever men, no orations by art lecturers, no amount of examples by other clever men can make us see nature as**

10 Manchester City News, 13th March 1875.

this body of men see it. This body of men being the Impressionists with members of the Manchester School standing in their shadows.

There was a certain irony in the manner in which many of the Manchester critics conveniently parcelled this Modern Movement up and placed a French tag on it. Almost as though it was a seven day wonder and the Manchester School would soon come to their senses and see the error of their ways and return to being stalwart English landscape artists. But then was this movement entirely a French phenomena? A little unravelling needs to take place.

The Impressionists techniques were much influenced by the colour harmonies of the French chemist, Eugene Chevreul, and they were also intrigued with all the new scientific theories which were now being correlated alongside their already extensive knowledge of art. They were obsessed in trying to achieve ever greater naturalism by exact analysis of tone and colour and by trying to render the play of light on the surface of objects, in much the same way, the major painter of the Romantic Movement Eugene Delacroix (1798-1863) had underpinned his works with scientific colour theories. He and his techniques had a huge influence on the Impressionists.

When painting in England in 1824 Delacroix was extremely influenced by the English landscape painter, John Constable (1776-1837). Phoebe Pool writes: 11 Frederic Villot, who taught Delacroix the art of etching left an account of the effect "The Haywain" had on his pupil: **Although the "Massacre at Chios" was almost finished, Delacroix was so struck by the brilliance and texture of Constable's picture he gave his own an increased transparency by means of glazing and by the additional impasto (thick pigment) for effects of light. He covered the arm of the old woman with small patches of pink, orange, yellow and pale blue, and enlivened the sand in the foreground in a similar way.**

Here was one of France's most important painters (unashamedly) incorporating some of the techniques of the English landscape painter John Constable in his own work. If some one as splendid as Delacroix could copy English techniques and not be ashamed of it why then was it so wrong for the Manchester School to copy certain French techniques? If the critics had paused for a moment and thought it

---

11 Phoebe Pool, Impressionism.

through they may just have realised that some of the Impressionist's techniques were linked to those of one of the major English landscape painters of the 19th century, and whose painting the "Haywain" was shown at the Academy in 1821 and was awarded a Gold Medal at the Paris Salon. Perhaps the group were not so far off the beam with their experiments. Like many before them, they were taking traditional techniques and adding exciting new ones to them.

Should one person consider they alone have the right to say whether a piece of art is good or bad? The trial between the painter, James Abbott McNeill Whistler, and the art critic John Ruskin sails close to answering this question.

John Ruskin publicly humiliated Whistler over his painting techniques: **I have seen, and heard much of cockney impudence before now, but never expected to hear a coxcomb ask 200 guineas for flinging a pot of paint in the public's face.**

Outraged, Whistler sued Ruskin and won - gaining damages of a farthing. He may have saved his reputation, but his own costs ruined him.

This trial was an important landmark. Most importantly it showed that one man's critical opinion is not always right, and that a piece of art can be seen and interpreted in a variety of different ways.

Many impertinent questions were asked by Ruskin's representative at this trial [12] and at times they bordered on being absurd. The following being an example: **Let us examine the Nocturne in blue and silver said to represent Battersea Bridge. What was that structure in the middle? Was it a telescope or a fire escape? Or perhaps it was the tubular bridge sent from the Meni Bridge Straits to span the Thames. What were the figures on the top of the bridge? And, if they were horses and carts, how in the name of fortune were they to get off?**

12 Daily Telegraph 27th November 1878, Whistler v Ruskin, Exchequer Division November $26.^{th}$ Sittings at Nisi Prius, before Baron Huddleston and a special jury.

Was this really constructive criticism? This taunting seems almost frivolous considering a man's artistic career was actually in the balance. Then came the biggest insult of all - Whistler was told his paintings were not worthy to be called works of art.

It was admitted that Whistler had done exceedingly good things: **But as to these pictures they could only come to the conclusion that they were strange fantastical conceits, having some merit, but not worthy to be called works of art. There was a mania at the present day for what was called art and it was the fashion to admire everything that was incomprehensible, and to say how exquisite.**

Ruskin was not present owing to a nervous breakdown. It was his representative the Attorney General, Sir John Holker who said: **It was the opinion of Mr. Ruskin that care and conscientious labour in a picture were matters to be appreciated and that an artist ought not to present a picture to the public until he had, as far as he was able, brought it to a state of perfection.**

Obviously Whistler must have decided his painting had reached perfection or he would not have put himself through all this anguish. Ruskin's representative knew this and was deliberately harassing him. He went on to say: **If a man thought a picture was a daub he had a right to say so without subjecting himself to the risk of an action.**

In other words Ruskin considered Whistler's painting was a daub and it was his right to say so. But, was it also his right to publicly insult Whistler as an artist? No wonder Whistler was outraged. He was not only defending the way he worked, but he was also fighting for his reputation - that of a first rate artist. It would seem Ruskin considered himself indestructible and his accusations knew no boundaries.

It was then decided to ask a number of famous artists to give their own opinions upon Whistler's techniques.William Powell Frith said "I have seen Whistler's paintings and they are not serious works of art." Albert Moore said "In the qualities aimed at, Mr. Whistler has succeeded, and no other living man could have succeeded so well. I consider his pictures beautiful works of art." W. M. Rossetti was asked the following about Whistler's Nocturne in Black and Gold.

"Is it a gem?" "No."
"Is it an exquisite piece of art?" "No."
"Is it very beautiful?" "No."

"Is it eccentric?" "It is unlike the painting of most other painters."
"Is it a work of art?" "Yes, In my opinion it is."
"Is anything a work of art that produces a startling effect?"
"Yes I think so."
"Why is this a work of art?" "Because it is a picture painted with a considerable sense of the general appearance of such a scene, and with a considerable amount of the manipulated skill of an artist."
"I would rather not express an opinion as to the value of the picture, but if I am pressed I should say two hundred guineas was the full value of it, but it is worth that. It is a stiffish price."

Whistler did point out that "the price mirrored all his expertise."

Eventually Whistler won his case - proving his critic wrong. John Ruskin could not come to terms with Whistler's techniques. They were not familiar to him, he was not at home with them and they were far too experimental. Therefore, they had to be wrong and unacceptable as pieces of art. But, when a number of well known artists were also asked for their opinion it would seem obvious a picture cannot be judged by one person alone.

It did seem extraordinary that the Manchester critics were able to get away with the abuse they continually threw at the Manchester School. Fortunately their solidarity enabled them to rise above their individual critics, but it must have been extremely tiresome for them. At their next exhibition they were accused of producing disgusting subject matter and revolting canvasses by the City News: There are several members of the Academy who delight apparently, in painting poverty, gloom and desolation, squalid abodes, dirty and penury - smitten neighbourhoods.

One wonders what will be the fate of those revolting canvasses - whether they are destined to decorate the board room of some work house or the private apartment of Mr. Bumble, or whether they will carry their misery and desolation into the heart of some unoffending family? [13]

---

13 City News, 15th February 1879, and 22nd February 1879.

The Courier's critic decided: **Choice of subject is as important to the landscape painter as it is to the man who ascends to the higher realms of art, and it would be well for Mr Hague and those who follow him to ponder wisely over the road they are treading, and to pause before their best energies are expended, and before their hands lose their cunning.** 14

Before their hands lose their cunning. Whatever next? Something extremely unexpected. The conflict between the school and the critics suddenly ended. At the next Manchester Academy Exhibition's private view one critic decided that, after an hour or two's viewing, he could affirm that this year's exhibition would reflect increased credit upon the Manchester School of Painters, and that it had become apparent in the course of the last eight or nine years that Manchester was founding a school of painting, and that her artists had a style and quality of their own which were being recognised at a distance with appreciation and applause.

It was good news for the School, but what was unbelievably galling was he also ventured to say that "Such an exhibition as that which is to be opened to the public tomorrow could not have been predicted a decade ago." Oh but it was - by the writer for the Critic on October 5th 1872 who stuck his neck out and predicted the Manchester School of painters would be successful. He also predicted they would have to fight their corner against all the "controversy not unmixed with jealousy which was heading their way." When he wrote this article did he ever think it would be nearly ten years before there would be a major break through for the School?

Finally success had arrived. All at once the local newspapers were full of praise for the Manchester School of Painters: **The earnest work of this group of young painters cannot fail to have its effect far beyond local limits. There are influences continually at work which prevent any traditional form of art from maintaining a perpetual sway in progressive communities; and there has not been in England, since the formation of the pre-Raphaelite Brotherhood, so promising a movement for the advancement of landscape art, as that which has been led by Mr. Knight.**

---

14 Courier, 25th February 1880.

The Manchester School have now risen above the stage at which they had to endure either the laugh or the superciliousness of ignorance. It will be interesting to see what will be the ultimate future of our local aspirants for fame.

They will probably diverge to a further extent from the point at which they formed their combination. Their special tendencies will gain more prominence with time, but the truths which they have proclaimed in their work cannot fail to become a part of the permanent inheritance of British Art. [15]

As a group, the Manchester School of Painters had succeeded. They had stood by their techniques no matter how adverse their publicity became and put up with the constant jibes and jealousy from, what seemed over the years, a never ending source of art critics.

They pushed their boundaries further and further building their own individual styles and continually gaining in confidence. What a triumph, they could now confidently work as a group or feel free to experiment on their own. [16] Which was just as well because in 1884 one critic [17] writing about the Manchester Academy's Spring Exhibition decided that the Manchester School had dissolved away:

The exhibition represents an unusually strong local school of art, and by school we distinctly do not mean, nor would the present exhibition in any way suggest, the prevalence of a particular sentiment or style of work.

Ten years ago it was possible to refer to a "Manchester School" as an obvious fact. The identity of purpose, the sympathy in feeling among the artists, was then so palpably shown in their work that the use of the term was warranted.

---

15 Manchester City News, 5th March, 1881, The Pictures at the Manchester Academy - Landscapes of the Manchester School of Painters

16 Manchester Courier September 1900 - Compared R.G. Somerset and Anderson Hague's techniques, and came to the conclusion: their methods are widely different and the impressions produced by both are diametrically opposite.

17 The Manchester Academy of Fine Arts Spring Exhibition, Manchester Examiner and Times, 19th February, 1884.

It does not matter whether the horizon of that little band was widened, or whether the individuality of its members has become more intense; but of the "Manchester School," in the sense in which the term used to be employed, there is no longer obtrusive proof.

The Manchester School of Painters has not vanished, far from it. Their ghosts and paintings live on, just look on gallery walls, search in files, pull out dusty racks and they are there. Fortunately for succeeding generations they are indestructible. [18]

---

18 Richard G. Somerset, Musee de Pont-Aven.

CHAPTER 9

JOHN HERBERT EVELYN PARTINGTON 1843-1899

A PROMINENT MEMBER OF THE MANCHESTER SCHOOL OF PAINTERS

This multi-talented artist, played a major role within Manchester's Victorian Art Scene.

Unlike many of his colleagues he did not go about his daily life quietly. He considered it his duty to let his artistic opinions (rather a lot of them) be known to all and sundry.

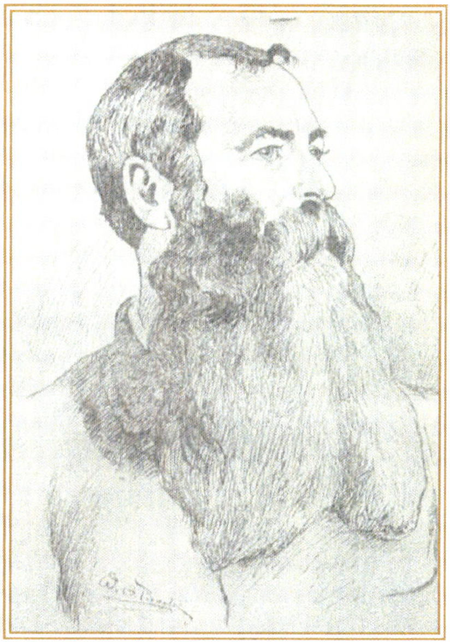

Figure 18. J. H. E. Partington,
Self portrait,
Momus 20th October 1881.
Manchester Central Library

Part 1: Manchester

Partington commenced painting and selling his pictures at the age of thirteen when his father bought him some oil paints and brushes. At the age of fifteen he was further artistically encouraged by a journeyman house painter, and received tuition from him for a time. Partington then discarded his art altogether and left England for America, but he was unable to settle there, he could not find an agreeable occupation and decided to return home. On his return he found employment as a mechanical draftsman for a Professor Scott Burn who was so delighted with Partington's work he engaged him to make some drawings for a projected work on freehand drawing. Suddenly, all his former ambitions came flooding back and he was determined to become an artist.

He entered the Manchester School of Art under the Head Master Mr. Muckley who helped Partington to obtain a position at Messrs. Shaw of St. Chad's at Saddleworth as a designer of cartoons and painter of figures in stained glass. Partington learned a lot about the technical processes and the principles of art from Mr. J. R. Shaw who encouraged Partington to become a student at the Manchester Academy. He was right, within a month Partington was singled out by the artist Mr. Joseph Knight for proposal to become an Associate of that body. At the age of twenty-eight, and twelve months after his election as an Associate, he received the honour of full membership. [1]

His work found a ready market and a number of sketches made in Holland and Brittany sealed his reputation and brought substantial rewards. Joseph Knight invited him, together with Anderson Hague, Houghton Hague, Davies, Somerset, Bancroft and others, to his house on Saturday afternoons. After much talk and swapping of ideas they would sketch for a couple of hours and practise the theories they had put forward. Knight left Manchester, but this group of young artists stayed together, and became known as the Manchester School of painters. Even though Momus [2] did make the following comment: **He is, moreover, qualified to rank as a true colourist outside the group of his fellow artists, and his method, as may be inferred is more independently his own than that of most of the rest of the Manchester School.**

Partington first exhibited at the Royal Academy in 1872 - fulfilling his aim to be presented in the first of English galleries before he was thirty. He became a member of the Manchester Literary Club, producing various articles and drawings for its volumes and also helped found the Stockport Literary Club.

---

1 Brasenose Club Manchester, Catalogue of Exhibition Of The Works of J. H. E. Partington, 1879. Introduction by J. L. Aspland.
2 Momus, 20th October 1881, J. H. E. Partington, p.58.

Here we have an extremely energetic man with many talents, writing and painting were his strongest, but he also lectured and taught with great flair and enthusiasm.

Where teaching was concerned: he was very disillusioned with the South Kensington methods of art training (laborious and precision drawing from the antique) and was determined to make sure the whole of Manchester's art scene knew so. In one speech he stated: **I have to say something tonight in condemnation of the South Kensington system of art education. Partly founded upon actual experience of its working at our Manchester School of Art.**

I cannot state my case fairly without pretty frequent reference to that school. But I wish it to be distinctly understood that it is the system, and not the school for any speciality of its own, which I am criticising. I feel the South Kensington system of art education from the beginning is terribly detrimental to the art of the country. [3]

To justify his assault on the South Kensington system he explained how he took a young student under his wing and when he decided he had taught him all he could, and that his work was becoming too similar to his own, he had him enrolled at the Manchester School of Art.

Apparently the first task set for this young man was "as in the old time," outline drawing from flat copies, chiefly geometrical. The student could not understand any of it. He then quoted Partington, "There is no outline in nature, that I must never look for such a thing, as I shouldn't find it." He was extremely upset that the school was trying to force him to see things in that way - and definitely no other.

The student passed three months at this work. Partington said "He wished he had never sent him there." Finally, taking matters into his own hands and knowing that Antwerp Academy had a common sense system he decided to send the student over to Antwerp.

Comparing Antwerp to Manchester he made the point that: if a city like Antwerp with a population of 200,000 inhabitants, takes it to be its duty to give an art education of the highest order to a lad of any nationality entirely free of expense, Manchester with its population of

---

3 Manchester Guardian, English Art Education, 1887

500,000 should at least see to it that such an education is possible here for its own sons.

Then raising his voice for extra effect he said "An art education of the highest order should be possible in this city and it is a great pity a young person cannot have a proper training here at the School of Art instead of abroad."

Having assailed the city for its lack of art education he went back to its School of Art declaring he had been told by one of the ablest and advanced art teachers in Manchester, who had been educated in the first of the French studios, "I would far rather take in hand a pupil who has never received a lesson at all than a pupil from your Manchester School of Art. I have such great difficulty in unteaching them."

A reader of the Manchester Guardian pursued with interest Partington's attack on the Art School's methods of teaching and wondered if the artists of Manchester and district (professional and amateur) were sufficiently numerous to start a studio to be conducted in accordance with Mr. Partington's ideas?

Since The Manchester Academy whose life classes he had attended certainly did not supply the want.

The writer of this letter probably had no idea the effect it would have on Partington, who decided to take the matter into his own hands and establish an art school in Stockport. This would be run on the same lines as the Academie Julian, Paris where masters and students worked together from a live model.

The City News reported its opening as follows: **A new Art School established by H. E. Partington, opened on Tuesday evening at the Hatherton House Academy, Royal George Street, Stockport. Mr. Partington is head-master and Mr. Alexander Bain and Mr. R. C. Partington are his assistant-masters.**

There are three classes for elementary drawing, model and figure drawing and oil and water colour painting from life. During the Spring, Summer and Autumn months a class will meet for landscape sketching and painting direct from nature. The opening proceedings promised well for the future of the school. [4]

---

4 City News, September 8th 1888, Art At Stockport: Opening of Mr. Partingtons School.

Partington was triumphant - in a spacious studio filled with the students of the elementary and advanced classes he briefly lectured them on elementary drawing. Now all his artistic principles could be brought to the fore. He was also adamant that during the winter evenings his studio should be used to meet the working classes and prove to them that art and beauty could penetrate through clouds of smoke, or as he put it, even into the dingy dwellings of a neighbourhood such as Ancoats, where hundreds of men, women and children were herded together under vile conditions.

He wanted to help them make their homes more beautiful within the limits of a working man's means, and advise them on what sort of papers they should have on their walls, and what kind of chairs and tables they should buy and what pictures they should decorate their houses with. In his own words "If we can do this we shall have done a stroke of work in the right direction."

Opening a new Art School in Stockport would seem to be a simple enough thing. Unfortunately, Partington's timing was not appreciated by a number of people. He had coincided with the opening of the new Technical School. A letter was sent to the local newspaper and it was straight to the point. 5 It stated the Committee of the Technical School were making arrangements to supply the needs of the town in every phase of the art question and all Stockport people would be well advised to avoid any unnecessary introductions outside of that building. In other words "Boycott" Partington's School of Art.

Partington wrote a blistering reply to this letter. He accused the Art Department of the Technical College of associating themselves with South Kensington, not to foster art, but to gain Government money.

He ended his letter: **Permit me in conclusion to say that our course of conduct is clearly marked out for us. It is simply to mind our own business, which is the teaching of the fine arts of drawing and painting in their application to the education of artists, amateur and professional. We shall leave any art in relationship to our manufacturing industries to those establishments - South Kensington, Technical Schools and Mechanics' Institutions - to which they legitimately belong.**

---

5 Manchester City News, 31st August 1888,

The Art School advanced so rapidly in public estimation that new and larger rooms had to be taken at the Borough Chambers, St. Petersgate Bridge. The school was extremely successful, but unfortunately for Partington and his son no rich patron stepped in to help them. This meant the school was not financially viable and had to close. It would be some time later in California his dreams of a successful art school would come true.

Partington did have very set ways on learning how to draw and paint, so how did he learn to paint? In one of his lectures [6] he explains where and how he learned the art of water colour painting. He was adamant that "a lad" learned to paint by seeing a master paint and not by being told what to do, and this was definitely how he had learnt his trade. After leaving the School of Art he had gone down to Conwy to join a dozen young artists who were working alongside the artist, J. D. Watson, who, in his opinion, was one of the most accomplished figure draughtsmen in England and a master of water colour art with no living superior.

Amongst them were Anderson Hague, Richard Gay Somerset, E. M. Bancroft, Henry Measham, and William Meredith. They too were trying hard to free themselves from the miserable futilities of the South Kensington system.

With knapsacks over our shoulders, easels in our hands, and the entirely indispensable pipes alight we used to start after breakfast in search of the picturesque, Watson ever on the alert for a subject.

Something would suddenly arrest his attention. He would often stand absorbed for a moment or two, and then turn round to us. "Well, boys, do you think this will do?" He would rapidly analyse the subject to us, painting out its main masses - but not in a school masterly way. Then we began work and we did work as I had never worked before.

---

6 Manchester Guardian, 25th August 1888, The Right and Wrong Methods of Teaching.

All the while we were at liberty to watch Watson. He would explain his reason for doing a particular thing. This was of inestimable value to raw youngsters in art, such as ourselves. After an hour he would shake himself up and come and look at what we were doing. It is difficult for me to describe his humorous fashion of criticising. This was something like it: "Well, now, look here, my boy there are different ways of doing things. You have yours - I have mine. I shouldn't try myself, you know, to get the solidity of that stone in transparent colour; for I couldn't do it. I should paint it in body colour. Let me show you. Don't you fancy me cheeky? I'm getting an old man; look at these revered grey hairs." He would lift up his hat and run his fingers through the magnificent aureole of his silver curls. "Here give me your box and squeeze some of that Chinese White out for me."

One's poor, petty niggling School of Art stuff was swept out with a few strokes that took one's breath away. Then loads of body colour were piled on to the ruin. In a few moments more there arose in its place, as if by magic, a lovely creation - and Watson would get up, just remarking, "mind you, Partington, I don't say that is better than yours, only it's the way that I should do it."

Partington finished this lecture by having another dig at the South Kensington School of Art by saying "alas the men who can paint and teach others to paint are not the men who hold certificates as drawing masters from South Kensington."

It is one thing to see a picture when it is finished and to allow yourself the pleasure of letting your imagination run riot over it. If this picture is being exhibited it may have an explanatory label divulging where and when it was painted. However, it is an altogether different experience to have the picture's producer actually narrate the story behind his creation - suddenly it takes on a history of its own and becomes real. This is exactly what Partington decided to do.

On 7th February, 1881 Partington read a paper to the Manchester Literary Club allowing a fascinating insight into the moralities and culture of the time and in particular their impact on what was being painted and how. 7

In his "Story Of A Picture" he confirms: How it came about, where it was painted, the sort of day on which the idea occurred to him, certain influences, and an outline of the general grounds on which the form, the light and shade and the colour were based. The story began with Partington being invited to paint in Tenby, Pembrokeshire by a friend: **Just the place for you Partington. You can get any kind of subject you like here. Figures of all sorts, boats any quantity, landscapes. You should see the coast of Carmarthen Bay from Pendign to Saunders Foot.**

Weather - cool mornings followed by day after day of sunshine and sunshiny harvest noons and evenings of broad red sun sinking down into a tranquil sea.

And see here. There's no society down here we can be as free and as solitary under the shade of melancholy boughs in those deep woods as Jacques in the forest of Arden. We'll paint occasionally and smoke continually. So clap on sail for Milford Haven, and the devil take the hindmost.

This was such a contrast to Manchester, the temptation was too much for him and he set forth. **Early next morning I steamed up the whole length of the Haven to Pembroke Dock, thence drove to Pembroke, and on by train through Tenby and Saundersfoot to Kilgetty. I was then driven bag and baggage, by an up and down winding road. By now it was dark, lights flickered from far off cottages and glow worms had lit their little lamps and hung them on trailing branches. All that could be heard was the regular plod of our horse's hoofs and the roll of carriage wheels. Then Colby Lodge, which was to be my home for the next ten weeks.**

Setting the scene for his audience Partington describes in detail the sky on the morning of the 2nd September 1880 as follows: **It was like a smile on the face of a beautiful woman. Soft gleaming clouds spread thinly over the field of ether from zenith to horizon -**

---

7 J. H. E. Partington, A Story Of A Picture, Papers of Manchester Literary Club, vol 7, p.p. 19-36.

tender, amorous, dreamy, utterably beautiful. About the sky, over the horizon line was spread out a thin mist, the colour of a tea rose, slowly unrolling itself on the morning wind. It was shot through and through with the softly dappled radiance of tender sunlight.

He now had everybody's attention and continued to describe his walk down to the Black Hall Rocks: **I** fell in love with these rocks the first day I saw them. I loved to watch the play of sunlight and cloud shadow, and fancied there was a cold smile on them like that on the face of the sphinx, as they looked down on the childish tremulousness of the sea below.

These rocks were covered with a close network of mussels and barnacles, and decorated with brilliant green beards of dripping seaweed. The sand, varying endlessly with the washing of the changing tides. The pools - are there many things in Nature more beautiful than such a pool? Sand, pebbles, shells, seaweed - all things steeped in the soft translucence become fairer, their colours deeper and richer, their charms in every way enriched by the exquisite veil of subtle transparency thrown round them.

His lulled audience could feel the warmth of the sand and hear the lapping of the sea and the cry of the herring gulls as they were slowly being sucked into this eloquent speaker's painting. Imagine how they must have sat up with a start when he suddenly introduced a beautiful young women into this idyllic scene and began to speak extremely intimately about her beauty and goddess like figure.

There I saw one, such a woman, eyes so soft and lips so red;
On her neck the small face buoyant,
Like a bell-flower on its bed,
O'er the breasts superb abundance where a man might base his head.

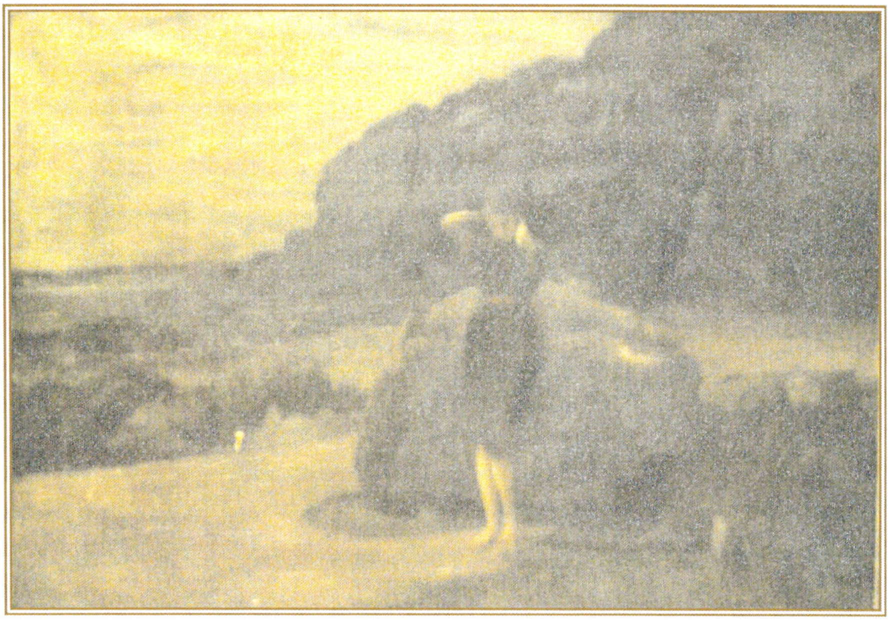

Figure 19. J. H. E. Partington, P*ainting of a Girl on Black Hall Rocks*
Stockport Art Gallery

Her head slightly turned upon the rounded neck, arms raised to fasten in a closer coil the wavy hair that was her crown, the full breasts lifted by the action of the arms, the drapery loosely supported by the swell of the hips – she stood in complete and nobly innocent womanhood, looking out dreamily on the waiting sea, the most perfectly beautiful thing that God has made. In an attitude not unlike this stood that Spartan woman whose loveliness inspired the sculptor of the Venus of Milo to fix for ever the type of the highest womanhood.

Here was my subject; here was the cementing link to bind the parts together which I have attempted to describe. The presence of the woman softened the sky into a delicious dream, the incoming tide seemed to hasten forward to get a nearer look at her beauty; the savage rocks turned their faces towards her with a modest gaze: the little pool beside which she stood opened its bosom to receive the reflection of her lovely figure - all of them were made

glad by her; their queen had come amongst them. I had found my key stone – my subject was complete.

He then calmly announced that he really wanted to paint the most beautiful thing God had ever made "naked," but knew if he did he would not be able to exhibit the painting for moral reasons, since a large selection of the general public would not tolerate a nude painting on display. **My main concern was - suppose I had painted that woman as God made her and I saw her, and had succeeded in getting the picture exhibited, what would have been its reception by a correct and decorous public?**

Turning to his bemused audience he asked: **Do you remember how ten or a dozen years ago the Heywood Prize was given to a French picture of a nude woman lying on a rug. (M. Lecardre's painting of "Le Reveil.") A lovely picture it was too, and in my opinion well worthy of the honour, but it was too much for the unco'guid?**

There was a number of murmurs and groans, and it was obvious the majority did remember this painting. It had caused quite a sensation and a large portion of the public were disgusted with the decision of the Council of the Royal Institution to hang this painting at all.

What had really incensed Partington was the fact that some Manchester artists signed a round robin condemning it on the grounds of its immoral tendency, and he was grieved by the fact that one of Manchester's more well-known artists, Fred Shields [8] was one of the prominent signatures.

In a disconsolate manner he said: **I am sorry to have to admit that this prevalence of philistinism had something to do with my determination to drape the figure. I confess to having sacrificed those white breasts curved and coloured by the hands of God, because the British public prefers to see blue serge to flesh and the folds of drapery to the rapturous lines of the figure of a naked woman.**

Partington conveniently omitted the fact that many letters were sent on the painting "Le Reveil" and a good many of them were written by middle class members of the Manchester public, similar to his audience. People with their own set of values, underpinned by social

8 See Chapter 11.

position and influence, especially where art and its producers were concerned. Whether they could be called philistines is debatable.

Anyway, he soon resolved his dilemma. He decided, as an artist, he owed it to himself to paint this picture, and did exactly that on his return to Manchester. **Let me say, though, that this defection from the ideal has been only temporary. On my return to Manchester I ordered a canvas 7ft by 3ft., and that canvas will ultimately contain life size and entirely naked the figure of that beautiful creature, as nearly as I can realize it.**

I am not responsible for getting it hung on the walls of an exhibition. I am responsible to myself at any rate for getting it painted.

The galling point was, not once did he think how this young woman might have felt if she had the slightest inkling she was going to be displayed as Partington's "Pose Plastique of the Venus di Milo" on a 7ft by 3ft canvas. Did he realise she was not a willing model? Did he even care? The moral connotations wrapped around the female Victorian model, especially the nude model, were dire. Society immediately presumed her to be a prostitute and words such as depraved and contagious were often bandied around. It was only towards the end of the century the female model was actually seen as a social victim. What was Partington thinking of? He knew the score, should he as an artist have taken it upon himself to decide he was different, some kind of genius so wrapped up in his art he had the right to violate a person's privacy?

Apparently he thought so, and was quite at ease admitting it to his audience, perhaps he had decided they were not philistines, but simply like himself a follower of the avant garde at any price. Fortunately for his audience he had also found a younger paragon of beauty to paint on the sands. He waxed lyrically about her youth and compared her to his goddess and then, at long last, the moment many of his audience had been patiently waiting for came.

This innovative artist began to explain in great detail how he had painted his picture. He used words such as values, weights of light and shade, and chiaroscuro. He described his techniques and how certain textures were got by heavy impasto and how other effects of atmosphere were got by transparent films of colour. He had won his audience over, they were completely enthralled.

Partington was ahead of his time in a number of ways, not least by telling this unique "Story Of A Painting." He captured his audience and allowed them an insight into his innermost feelings. This could be seen as brave or foolhardy, either way it allowed an amazing insight into how, as an artist, he thought and worked.

Over a period of time Partington painted a number of beach scenes. In a "Manx Note Book vol; 1885 the following appeared: **Mr. J. H. E. Partington, of Manchester, now residing in Ramsey, has painted a variety of Manx subjects. "A Ramsey Wrecker" depicts a handsome barefooted lass, with a bundle of wreckage in her arms, on Ramsey Shore, during a gale. This beautiful picture was painted in 1883, and first exhibited at Stockport, where it was purchased by Mr. Edwin Lawrence. Mr. Partington then kindly lent it to the Douglas School of Art for exhibition purposes, and finally sent it to the Royal Academy, where it was hung at this year's exhibition. The size of the canvas is 5 feet by 4 feet.**

He also produced a very dramatic painting named "The Rescue." **The Rescue," showing the Manchester Lifeboat *The Two Sisters* rescuing a schooner in Ramsey Bay, is now on exhibition at the Manchester Corporation Art Gallery. It is the most important picture in size and motive which Mr. Partington has painted. The figures of the crew of the lifeboat are full size.**

Partington was passionate about Manchester's art scene, or as he would have it - its lack of it. He presented a paper entitled "Lancashire Artist's Doubts And Guesses" to the Bolton Art Club. In this paper he blamed Manchester's so called lack of artistic enthusiasm on its residents and: industrial manufacturers. It was as follows: **I sometimes doubt whether in Lancashire in these modern days the game of art is worth the candle.**

Society gets what it deserves. If an age can content itself artistically with portraits, bastard classicism, galvanised Gothicism, prosaic landscape, tragedies in evening dress, pictorial punning, Yankee wood cuts, Mrs. S. A. Allen's posters, pretty Christmas cards, advertising almanacs printed in 23 colours and striking portraits of prize fighters in the Police Gazette and pay no attention to true art - the art of the past, the fair and the graceful, it was on its way to being depraved.

It was not just people's social behaviour towards the arts he was discontented with. He was exasperated with Manchester's manufacturers and their industrial pollution, their greediness and their non-supportive role towards the arts.

What does it matter if we destroy all that is dear to us, just so long as the factories can carry on spewing out their contents, whilst their owners become better off and more and more selfish. When they erect a mill chimney, a certain part of the sky is shut out. I do not know a single factory chimney in Manchester, Salford, Oldham, Ashton, Stalybridge or Stockport for example, in which the element of architectural beauty is strikingly prominent, the same remark applies to most of the mills themselves. I am afraid that in the towns named, the Smoke Nuisance Act is mostly a dead letter. Nobody seems to obey it, and nobody seems to care much whether they do or not. In the same way nobody seems concerned with manufacturers turning refuse into our rivers making them hideously black and causing horrendous fevers.

The truth is we Lancashire people have had an aim and a purpose which in our view were a thousand times more important than the Cultivation of the Fine Arts. We are the richest manufacturing community in the world of our size, and we have all along intended to be richer. We have built up one of the biggest industries in the world, and we have been determined that it shall be bigger still.

With indomitable British energy we have shouldered competitor after competitor to the wall. Ships freighted with our cotton goods cover the seas, and we may be said to clothe all the children of men who live within the tropical belt of the world's surface. We keep an unceasingly vigilant eye upon even the uttermost parts of the earth; and no slightest chance of opening out a new market is ever neglected by the merchants of Manchester and Liverpool.

One manufacturer, Mr. Morgan Brierley, incensed with Partington's somewhat pious attitude, decided to take him to task. He had seen a letter written by Partington in the City News stating that where art was concerned he condemned anything to do with industry and supported anything to do with the classics. [9]

9 Manchester City News, Art in Lancashire, 18th February 1888.

Brierley was angry, how dare this artist criticise Manchester and its industrial manufacturers? He sent a letter to the City News stating Partington should stop harping back to the classics and take a good look at what was happening around him. He declared: As a work of art I have seen nothing more beautiful or magnificent in either Rome or Florence than a pair of 100 horse-power condensing engines, such as may be seen in many Lancashire Cotton Mills. They are as graceful in outline as the finest tracery on the choir-screen of York Minster.

The battle was on, and Partington replied: I don't know the screen referred to, but there are one or two objects of art in Rome and Florence which seem more beautiful than any steam engines I ever saw.

He then challenged Brierley to draw in outline two of the loveliest and most graceful 100 horse-power condensing engines and he would draw in outline two statues, the one in Rome, say the Apollo Belvedere, the other in Florence, the Venus di Medici. These could then be reproduced in the City News. In so doing they could each show in some slight degree what was meant when they wrote about art, beauty and gracefulness. He wrote: Recognizing that Art in Lancashire is not in a healthy condition, that painting here is either a mere dilettante pursuit or simply a means of keeping the pot boiling, Mr. Brierley comes to the help of the poor bewildered fraternity of Lancashire painters and recommends us to make a round of visits to the busy workshops and mills of Lancashire and Yorkshire. There real works of mechanic art, charming as the mural paintings in the Vatican, in the Dome of St. Peter's, or in the Cathedrals of Pisa and St. Mark's at Venice, will often fall in line with their surprised and delighted powers of vision.

Here again I am unconvinced. I have seen the Exhibition boilers, Duncan and Ruston's steam navvy, several spinning Jennies and Billy slubbers gas and doffing frames (I worked in fact at a gas frame before I was ten years of age), and am indeed, like most Lancashire folks fairly well acquainted with the external appearance of these real works of mechanical art.

I have also seen the mural paintings in the Vatican, the Dome of St. Peter's and the Cathedral of St. Mark. For beauty I prefer the paintings, but despite the specialism pointed out by Mr. Brierley I am earnestly desirous of enlarged vision.

Perhaps the drawing of the Condensing Engine will give us discontented painters some new ideas, and incline us to work more in accord with the dominant forces of our native county.

Now in full sail Partington decides to comment on the Lancashire mill girls comparing them to the statue of Venus di Medici, and wisely agrees they too are beautiful, but he is quite unable to accept their apparel. In the busy workshops and mills of Lancashire and Yorkshire he says we shall find living subjects beautiful as the Venus di Medici. By all the Graces and Goddesses I swear Yes, that is so. There are no girls on earth so beautiful as our Lancashire witches. But, how about the costume? I think the costume of the Venus di Medici absolutely perfect despite the horror stricken remonstrances of Mr. J. C. Horsley RA and the whole tribe of outraged British Grandmothers.

If, however, you could breathe into the statue the breath of life, cover up her hair, neck and breasts with a shawl in Lancashire fashion, slip her into a striped-flannel petticoat, and partly hide this by a bishop, then let her dainty feet be shod in a pair of clogs - it is safe to prophesy that after six months work in an Ancoats Cotton Mill, poor Venus would be no match in beauty for the sturdy lasses of the County Palatine.

Partington wrote a number of papers with regard to Manchester and its arts, described by him as "bold and argumentative pieces." He did take a great delight in keeping everybody concerned with the city and its arts on their toes. When he decided to leave England for health reasons, some were mortified and others sighed with relief.

Part 11 California

The City News reported the following: For health reasons Mr. J. E. Partington the artist with his wife and seven children, sailed for New York on Saturday last on board the steam ship Nevada.

On arrival in the states they will proceed to Philadelphia, where Partington has a portrait commission to execute. His family will

leave him there and proceed to San Francisco, their future home where Partington will join them when he has completed his commission. [10]

They made Oakland, California their home living in a tent at Lake Temescal until suitable quarters could be found. The family moved often making formal schooling for Partington's children difficult; he solved the problem by training them himself. After teaching them to read and write, he taught them drawing, painting, poetry and music.

Two of his children, Richard and Gertrude became well-known Californian artists. **Gertrude and Richard Partington daughter and son of the admirable portrait painter J. H. E. Partington, whose heads of Ambrose Bierce and other famous men won something more than local renown for him in his day, are graduates of the Newspaper School, beginning as illustrators of the San Francisco Examiner and working their way up to higher things.** [11]

Ambrose Bierce's portrait did earn Partington a good deal of kudos. Bierce was an enigmatic man with a rather spectacular ending. Legend would have it he was killed in the Mexican Revolution in 1913.

At the outbreak of the Civil War he joined the Union Army which he later wrote about. After the war he moved to San Francisco where he became a newspaper columnist and editor. His caustic criticism earned him the nickname "Bitter Bierce." He became well known for his "Devil's Dictionary" (1906) a volume of ironic definitions.

---

10 City News, October 4th 1890.

11 Millard Baily, History of the San Francisco Bay Region.

Partington portrays Ambrose Bierce casually standing with one hand in his pocket and the other relaxed besides a skull.

When used as a symbol in art the skull is known as a memento mori. It is a reminder that man is mortal and will die.

Partington may have met Bierce through his daughter Blanche or it could have been the other way round. Blanche and Ambrose did have an affair for a number of years when she was twenty six and he was fifty.

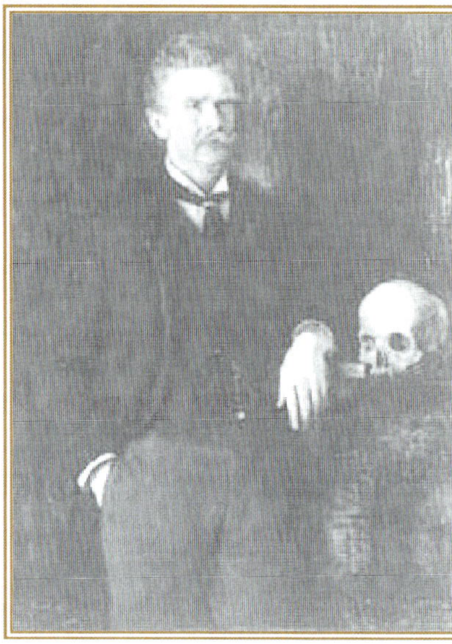

Figure 20. J.H.E. Partington,
Ambrose Bierce
Library of Congress Washington DC

Gertrude Partington (1883-1959) followed in her father's artistic footsteps. She illustrated society and court room sketches for the San Francisco Examiner, and then went to Paris for further study at Academie Delecluse with G.X. Prinet.

On returning to San Francisco she established a studio where she produced etchings, portraits and oils.

She was a cofounder of the Californian Society of Etchers in 1913, and a Director of Society of San Francisco Women Artists. She was also a well respected teacher. His son Richard Langtry Partington (1868-1929) helped him established the Partington School of Illustrating in San Francisco at 414 Pine Street.

When a fire in 1906 destroyed the school, he returned to Oakland and became curator of the Piedmont Art Gallery. He died in Philadelphia on June 3rd 1929.

On balance, Partington was more appreciated in San Francisco than his native England. He was well respected in Oakland where he played a lively role in the cultural life of the San Francisco Bay area. The

Observer 12 confirms this: Partington spent some time studying art at the Pacific Exposition and followed his bent for painting portraits. About this time his work attracted the attention of a prominent Philadelphian who engaged Partington to go to the Quaker city to paint family portraits and such was the success of the Californian's genius that he at once attained the place in the world of art that had been with-held from him in his home state.

He painted some of the most notable people in Philadelphia, among them being Governor Sproule. He also exhibited in a number of prestigious exhibitions. 13

A cutting from the Oakland Observer, taken from the Society Column states: Tomorrow the masterpiece of the late J. H. E. Partington will be formally installed in its permanent home in Oakland Art Gallery. This celebrated picture is entitled, "The Old Bell Ringer," and was presented to the Gallery by Richard L. Partington. 14

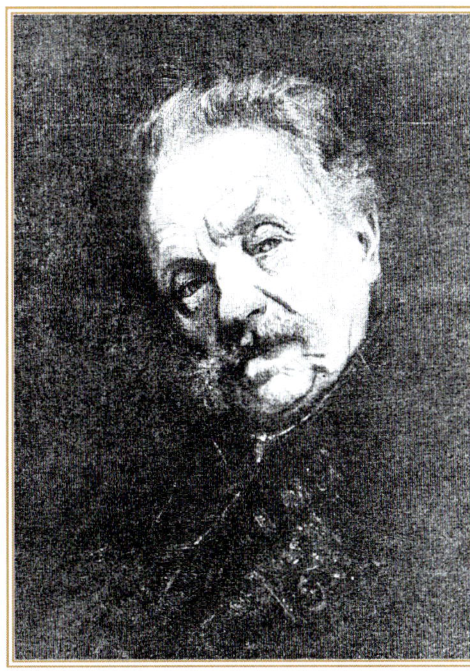

Figure 21. J. H. E. Partington, ***The Old Bell Ringer***

This portrait was given to the gallery by his son at the request of Dr. Porter who said "the picture would remain as a lasting reminder of the

12 Oakland Observer, 6th November 1921, Masterpiece to be Hung.
13 Mark Hopkins Inst., 1897 (portrait of Tilden Dakin), Panama-Pacific- Int. Exposition, 1915 (The Old Bellman). Awards: gold medal, California Midwinter Int'l Expo, 1894. Works held: de Young Museum (Cliff House), Society of Calif. Pioneers.
14 Observer, 11th June 1921.

Partington family, the members of which had attained fame in art and music that had spread all over the world."

Dr. Porter could have had no idea that eighty years on this painting would play a major role in identifying another of Partington's portraits in England. The clue was in the title.

Stockport Art Gallery also own an oil painting named "The Old Bell Ringer."It has no signature, date or information on it. On close inspection this picture seemed uncannily similar to other paintings executed by Partington, and especially the one hanging in the Oakland Art Gallery.

Could this anonymous portrait, which had been hidden away in the Gallery's store room for years, possibly be a painting by Partington?

Anne Swift, 15 provides the link between the two paintings and their similar titles.

The sitter for "The Old Bell Ringer" was George Cooper (1824-1895) Stockport's Last Town Crier. He was her great-great uncle and quite a character.

One member of his family described him as "a bit of an agitator, a soldier of fortune."

At the age of twenty-nine Cooper organised and won a seven months strike which centred around the poor pay and conditions which had

Figure 22. J. H. E. Partington,
The Old Bell Ringer
Stockport Art Gallery

15 Anne Swift, George Cooper - Stockport's Last Town Crier. All information on Cooper has been taken from this book.

been imposed upon Stockport's poverty stricken workers by the wealthy cotton mill owners. It was Cooper's responsibility to make sure the strikers had food and he was not sure how he was going to achieve this. The country came to his rescue. In his own words, "Money flowed in to us from all parts."

When the strike was over in 1853 Cooper and his wife decided to leave England for a while and visit Toronto, Canada. Unfortunately, his wife died whilst they were living in Canada in 1855. Cooper decided he would leave Canada, travel around the United States for a while, and then return to England.

He ended up in Philadelphia in 1858. It was whilst he was in Philadelphia his old feelings for even-handedness seemed to come flooding back and in 1861 he enlisted to fight for the newly elected President of the United States, Abraham Lincoln, who was determined to maintain the solidarity of the Union and also pledged to oppose the extension of slavery in any states. He had an appalling time and was badly injured in the head. "For thirty months I never slept in a bed or building. The hardships I underwent at that time left their mark upon me. I never felt the same man afterwards." On being discharged he left for England immediately and returned to his home town Stockport where he helped his brother Alick in his bill posting and town crying business.

It was at this point in his life he met Partington. **It is a true though old saying that "God never closes one door for us without opening another." Just as my physical powers were failing, I obtained work as an artist's model. My employer was Mr. J. E. Partington who took care that I wanted for nothing.**

This phase of my life was a very interesting one. The Art School and its environment during Mr. Partington's time formed a little world of itself that was quite unique. I can tell you I loved to think about those happy days and the pleasant associations connected with them. I delight in recalling to mind each face of the bright band of students who gathered around Mr. Partington and his gifted son. I felt as though I were an inseparable constituent of the organisation. Every young lady or gentleman who joined the school was as soon as ever he or she knew anything about the use of colour put to painting the features of the old George Cooper. Mr. Partington used to say –

"When rusty is the clapper of his bell,
And corroded is the clapper of his tongue
Whilst canvas holds the face it knows so well,
George Cooper's name will always remain young."

Anne Swift writes: There is an oil painting of George in the Stockport Museum. Partington's prophecy proved true.

Cooper said: **My portrait in one fancy costume or another hangs on the walls of many a home in Cheshire. Mr. T. Alderley of Bramhall Lane has "Touchstone and Audrey" in which I represent the jester whilst Miss Gertrude Partington is the model for Audrey.**

Others who painted me were Miss Nellie Leah, 16 **Miss Emily Rostron, Miss Edith Young, Mr. S. Ludlow, Mr. Arthur Margison and Mr. Wheatley Jones. They all possess portraits of me which they executed themselves.**

Cooper was devastated when Partington decided he and his family would have to move to America. **I was one of the invited guests at the garden party and presentation to him at Sykes' old house that Saturday afternoon in August 1890. I could not help breaking down at the kindly reference that Mr. Partington in his public good-bye make to his old model.**

Partington taught at his school in San Francisco for eight years until he was taken ill and died at his home in East Oakland. He was buried 30th January 1899 at Mountain View Cemetery. 17

16 This portrait hangs in The Stockport Story – Stockport's local History Museum.
17 J. H. E. Partington died at 5 a.m., on January 28th 1899 at the age of 54 years and Six months. It was signed by Dr. Andrew Fine (whose portrait Partington had painted.) Information obtained from Partington's Death Certificate, Oakland Library, California.

The following appeared in the Oakland Enquirer:

LIFE WORK ENDED
Death of J. H. E. Partington
The Artist

He was a man of very quiet habits, living a retired life, engrossed in his family and his art. He was a very kind hearted man and a perfect gentleman.

CHAPTER 10

ALFRED DARBYSHIRE
1839-1908
ARCHITECT,
THEATRICAL DESIGNER
AND LANDSCAPE
PAINTER

Darbyshire was born at 8, Peru Street (later renamed Melbourne Terrace,) Salford on 20th June 1839.

The day of his birth coincided with the opening of the Victoria Bridge linking Salford to Manchester. [1]

The family moved to Peel Street, Salford but not for long. His father was made the manager of a dye works at Egerton near Bolton, and it was here as a young boy Darbyshire met a number of the great men of the day, including Richard Cobden and John Bright who were friends of Edmund Ashworth of Egerton Hall, the owner of the dye works.

At the age of ten the family moved again to Irlams-o'-th'-Height and Alfred attended Mr. Charles Cumbers' school in Peter Street Manchester. He then attended a Quaker boarding school at Ackworth near Pontefract in Yorkshire where he was extremely unhappy. Consequently he was moved to Lindow Grove Academy at Alderley in Cheshire. Where he says "Life at Lindow Grove was delightful." He became articled to an architect, Mr. P. Alley and went to work in an office at the corner of Chapel Walks and Cross Street, Manchester.

Whilst he was still qualifying as an architect he was desperately anxious to act, but the Quaker sect of which he was a member did not approve of the theatre. In 1861 he was chosen to play the part of Jacques in "As You Like It," but on religious grounds he was forbidden to appear. Three years later he ignored opposition and played Jacques at Bury in honour of the three hundredth anniversary of Shakespeare's birth. His debut was a great success and he was there and then offered a professional contract, which he refused having set his sights on becoming an architect.

However, he did not abandon the theatre, nor cease to act. In 1865 at Bury he played Polonius to the Hamlet of Henry Irving. It was after a rather disastrous "Othello" at the Theatre Royal, Hereford, Darbyshire decided that perhaps he was far happier building a theatre

---

1Information from: T. A. Lockett, Three Lives "It Happened Round Manchester," and Alfred Darbyshire, The Art of the Victorian Stage.

than performing in one. His last appearance was in 1879 when he again played Jacques in "As You Like It."

This was a special show for the benefit of the widow and family of his great friend Charles Calvert who had died earlier that year.[2] Another member of the cast, playing the part of Le Beau, was the artist L. Alma Tadema. As a result of this particular performance and his other theatrical activities, Alfred was expelled from the Quakers.

In 1862 he completed his indenture as an apprentice architect and left Mr Alley to set up his own chambers in St. James Square, from here he would go on to design and execute many buildings not just in Manchester but in a number of prominent cities.

In 1869 Charles Calvert, employed Alfred to redecorate his theatre. Darbyshire said "It was during the progress of this work that I became conscious of the shortcomings of English theatre planning and its lack of safety to the public in case of panic. I was convinced that in the event of fire panic, the consequences would be fatal and disastrous."

Unfortunately he was proven right, but it was not until the awful disaster at the Exeter Theatre in 1887 when over two hundred people were killed, that it was realised just how inadequate theatre planning and construction was in England. Darbyshire said "At Exeter, the poor creatures sitting in the gallery never left their seats, for when the cloud of poison burst from the stage it instantly ascended, enveloped them, and left them sitting there, rows of ghastly corpses."

Sir Henry Irving, one of the leading actor-managers of the day, and a good friend of Darbyshire, was also appalled at what had taken place at Exeter. He approached Darbyshire in his architectural capacity to help him make all future theatres safe."It was time for a complete revolution in theatre planning." He said. This was how the famous Irving-Darbyshire Safety Theatre was born. The essence of the plan was a fire-proof safety curtain separating the stage from the auditorium; the theatre was to be separate from any other building and with easy access to the streets, and plenty of emergency exits; finally

---

2 Charles Calvert was actor-manager of the Prince's Theatre, Manchester. When he died no fewer than 50,000 people turned out between Manchester and Brooklands Cemetery where he was laid to rest.

every space upon which the human foot was planted in the auditorium and escape staircases would be absolutely fireproof and unburnable.

Darbyshire was absolutely adamant that his first consideration was for the people, not the building, which meant ample and direct means of exit must be obligatory. No theatre should in the future be allowed to be erected unless it stood upon an isolated site, i.e., it must be surrounded either by open spaces, streets or roads.

This vital condition became law with the Corporation of the City of Manchester, and the Palace Theatre of Varieties was built upon these lines. On three sides of the site streets existed, and by decreasing the width of the building a narrow street or roadway was created, and direct exit was achieved. In his book, [3] Darbyshire makes this task sound simple.

However, before he could even put his plans into action there was a great deal of opposition to the building of the Palace of Varieties. [4] Many people feared that a music-hall would become a den of vice, especially as it was proposed that alcohol should be sold in the refreshment bars. The Church of England Temperance Society, the Methodists and many individuals opposed the granting of a licence. It was decided this would have to be taken into consideration and sorted out later.

Meanwhile building began, but it was not long before there was further trouble. The licensee of the nearby Railway Inn brought a legal action against the contractors to restrain them from using any more explosive to clear the site for the foundations. Compensation was also demanded for damage done to the inn. Darbyshire forbade the workmen on the site to enter the Railway Inn on pain of instant dismissal.

Then the rear wall of the building when about sixteen feet high collapsed because of the pressure of the water from the nearby Rochdale Canal. Eventually the theatre was finished and a music and dancing licence was granted, but it was not licensed to sell intoxicating liquors. The Palace of Varieties opened its doors to 3,000 people on the night of 16th May 1891.

---

3 Alfred Darbyshire, The Art of the Victorian Stage.

4 T. A. Lockett, Three Lives It Happened Round Manchester.

Darbyshire was a man of many talents most of which centred around the theatre. He built them, acted in them and now he was becoming famous for his Histrionic Art i.e., extravagant stage productions.

> *"Although the Elizabethan era will ever be held in respect and reverence as having given birth to the world's greatest dramatist, the Victorian era will also be respected and honoured in historic annals for having given truthful and beautiful stage expression to the Shakespearian creations."*
>
> A. Darbyshire.

In his book "An Architect's Experience," Darbyshire considered the term Histrionic Art meant the combination of local expression and bodily action, with such adjuncts and surroundings as was possible for the stage to supply.

To achieve this result had been the aim and high ambition of those responsible for the art of the Victorian stage: **"In my opinion all that art, intellect and stagecraft can produce, should be forthcoming to provide a glorious setting suitable for the brightest jewels which have ever sparkled from the human brain."**

In the autumn of 1902 Sir Henry Irving was in Manchester at the Theatre Royal. He accompanied Darbyshire to a morning performance at the Prince's Theatre of "As You Like It," the last revival by Roger Courtneidge. When the curtain finally fell they quietly rose and he offered no comment on the theatrical background. Darbyshire looked at him, and asked "Well! Is the effort a good one, will it do?" He looked at me with a quiet, happy smile, and said, "Well, my boy, I have seen exactly what Shakespeare saw as he wrote the immortal comedy."

At a luncheon given by the Lord Mayor of Manchester Irving spoke in the highest terms of praise of the revival by Mr. Courtneidge. Thanks to Irving thousands of playgoers from all parts of the country crowded the little historic Prince's Theatre to see "As You Like It" as Shakespeare saw it when he wrote the words as coming from the mouths of those who lived and moved amid the sylvan shades and under the "melancholy boughs" of the Forest of Arden.

Calvert was of the opinion that Shakespeare wrote to be acted, and not to be read. So when the Manchester Prince's Theatre was under Calvert's regime he and Darbyshire became close colleagues and best friends. Darbyshire was quick to praise Calvert's revivals stating "they made sure that the works of Shakespeare were carried on in a provincial city in a superior manner, with increased knowledge and unlimited finance."

In 1872 a spectacular set was designed by Darbyshire for the triumphal entry of the King into London in "Henry V." Calvert saw an opportunity to illustrate the life and manners of medieval England, and the pomp and circumstance of medieval warfare. It was the epoch of plate armour, flowing robes, picturesque architecture, and of that pictorial splendour which could appropriately be cast around Shakespeare's favourite hero.

Darbyshire was delighted to be able to work alongside his friend in this celebrated revival. He wrote: **When this work was being contemplated I happened to be a resident at Marple Hall, in Cheshire, formerly the home of Bradshaw, the regicide, and it was in this house, surrounded by armour, tapestry, old pictures, and quaint furniture that I planned out and designed the architectural scenes; and it was here also that I conceived the idea of realising the correct blazon of the arms and banners, as they were actually used on the heroic field of Agincourt.**

Calvert would spend hours with him in the gloomy old mansion, and would pace about its rooms and corridors in delightful restlessness and excitement, as Darbyshire described and explained his portion of the work.

Calvert wanted a faithful historical picture of the period of the early part of the fifteenth century. The architecture and the scenery had to be as nearly as possible reproductions of the streets of London, the seaport of Southampton, the walled town of Harfleur, the battle field of Agincourt, the palaces of Westminster and Rouen, and the cathedral of Troyes.

The costumes were made from a series of splendid drawings by the artist J. D. Watson, whose, according to Darbyshire, "enthusiasm knew no bounds." He not only made his careful drawings from best authorities, but actually cut out the patterns to ensure correctness and exactitude; and personally superintended the work of the costumier.

Apparently "The Entry into London" was the most difficult scene to represent. Darbyshire followed the accounts of the old chroniclers of the period. This was a colossal task, not only was the architecture of old London to be reproduced but also the decorations and incidents which constituted "The Pageant." Many practical difficulties had to be overcome, for example Darbyshire wrote, "the "wings" and "flats" were of such a height and size that they had to be hinged in several flaps for convenience of movement and for transmission to other countries."

And then there were the "supers." According to Darbyshire "the super was an individual, as a rule without intellectuality, in fact if he had any he would not be a super." The entry into London in "Henry V" contained between two and three hundred persons (supers) and it was only by incessant drilling that the crowd of soldiers and the mass of London citizens could be got to do the right thing at the right moment. It was a nightmare, but on the night it went like clockwork.

To Darbyshire it was the realisation of an ideal: it represented all that art and stagecraft could do to illustrate a great historical poem. Heraldry of the time, and the banners, shields, and other devices actually used at Agincourt were, after much labour and research, faithfully reproduced and for the first time the Agincourt roll-of-arms was blazoned. It cannot be doubted that this production of "Henry V" in Manchester was an event of importance in stage history.

The production was carried through the United States [5] and into Australia until - as Darbyshire put it: "It finally disappeared from the stage with my old scenery worn out and the proudly-waving banners of Agincourt tattered and torn till their devices were beyond recognition." He continued his Histrionic Art, and in 1887 when the Royal Jubilee Exhibition was held in Manchester, Darbyshire designed a most elaborate setting depicting Old Manchester and Salford.

As a landscape painter he sketched and painted in Italy, France, Belgium and Germany, and knew many of the leading artists of the time, and met and corresponded regularly with Dante Gabriel Rossetti, Ford Madox Brown and Walter Crane.

One of Darbyshire's favourite painting places was Whitby, North Yorkshire. Here he painted its harbour and bridge in 1892.

5 In 1875, Calvert took the production to Booth's Theatre, New York. "The Boston Herald" wrote: More than 100,000 persons have already visited Booth's Theatre to enjoy the magnificent revival of "Henry V."

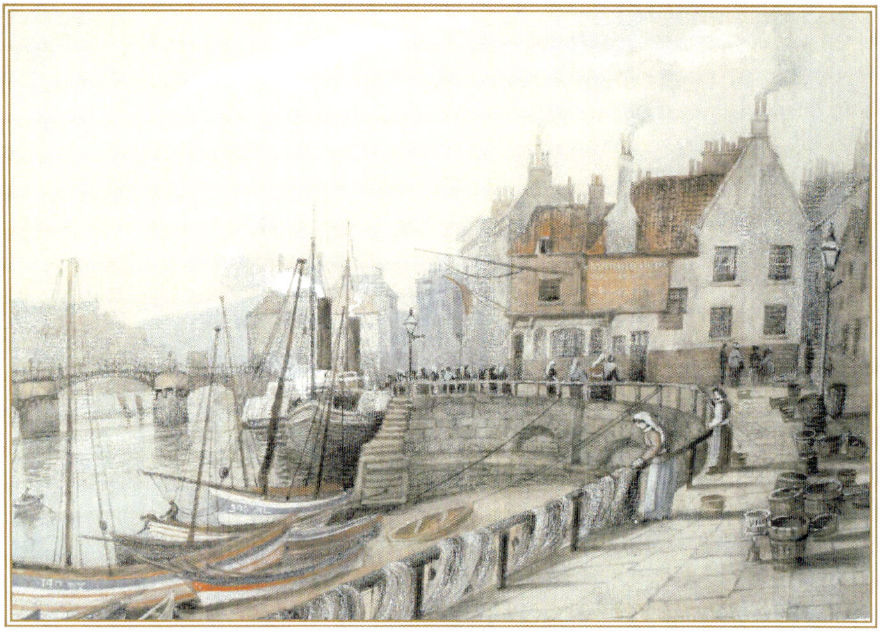

Figure 23. Alfred Darbyshire, *Harbour and Bridge Whitby*
Stockport Art Gallery

This busy watercolour, packed full of history, would make an excellent jigsaw puzzle. The eye really does not know which bit of the scene to rest on first. Perhaps it should be the bridge. Darbyshire has depicted a section of Whitby's cast iron swivel bridge spanning the banks of the River Esk. [6]

He has included a number of people walking along the top of the bridge thinking their own thoughts and going about their every day lives. Underneath this cast iron structure sailing boats pass silently by.

6 Designed by Francis Pickernell and completed in 1835.

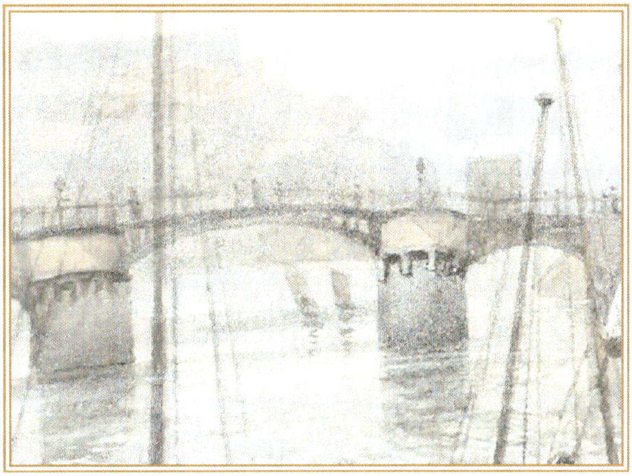

Figure 24. ***Section Of Whitby's Swivel Bridge***

The large green steam boat is also an important piece of Whitby's history. It is anchored to the harbour wall whooshing steam out of its funnels waiting for all its excited passengers to embark. 7

The steep harbour steps lead down to the beach below, where a number of brightly coloured sailing boats with long slender masks are waiting for a wind so they can unfurl their sails and be off. Unused rowing boats litter the beach. One man, now on the move, pulls the anchor up on his rowing boat closely watched by his colleague.

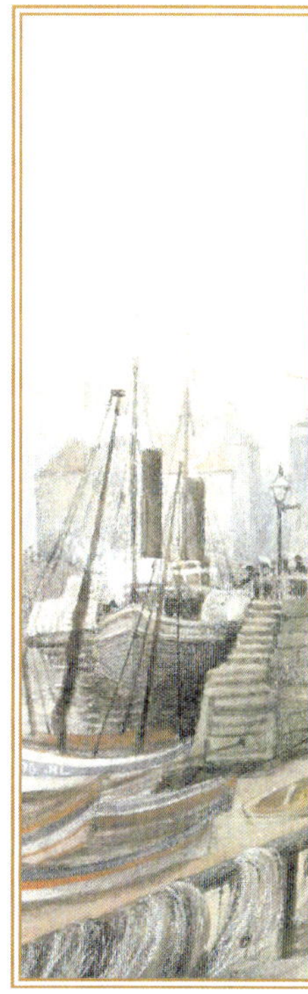

Figure 25.
The Whitby and Robin Hood's Bay Steam Packet Company's Vessel

7 The Whitby and Robin Hood's Bay Steam Packet Company ran a scheduled passenger service to Hartlepool and occasional excursions to Scarborough and Sunderland.

At various times of the day there would be a hive of industry on the quay, but it is quiet at the moment. Local women in their traditional Whitby dress are scattered around the quay mending their nets and drying them on the harbour railings. All the empty baskets now stashed along the side of the quay would have been heaving with fish a few hours previously. Behind them smoke pours out of the Marine Hotel's chimneys and a bunch of people stand near by in a circle talking. What a feat to capture all this in one painting.

Darbyshire was an extremely accomplished artist. He could turn his hand from a colourful busy picture such as "Harbour and Bridge Whitby" to an architectural watercolour depicting Durham's splendid cathedral.

The Cathedral was built in the late eleventh and early twelfth centuries to house the relics of St. Cuthbert.

In his water colour Darbyshire depicts Durham Cathedral's west towers from the cloisters. These cloisters are clustered around a small square green called the Cloister Garth. The buildings surrounding the garth were once monastic priory buildings of the cathedral and they took in the Chapter House, the Monks Dormitory, the Rectory and the Great Kitchen. Around this square are four covered cloister walkways where the monks spent considerable periods of time during the heydays of Durham priory. [8]

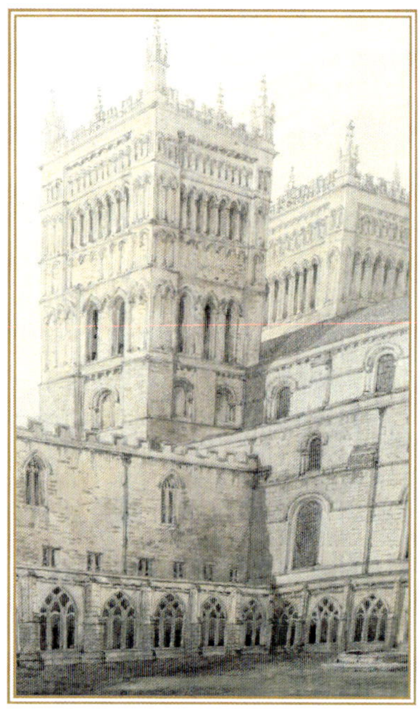

Figure 26. Alfred Darbyshire
Durham Cathedral
Stockport Art Gallery

8 Thenortheast.fsnet.co.uk/DurhamCathedral.htm

Darbyshire lectured to many societies, wrote for the Manchester Guardian, The Courier and the British Architect, and was also an author of a number of books on architecture, heraldry, and art including "A Book of Old Manchester and Salford" containing about seventy illustrations of ancient buildings. 9

He was appointed Secretary and then President of the Manchester Society of Architects, and from 1902-5 he was Vice-President of the Royal Institution of British Architects. He was also a member of the Manchester Academy of Fine Arts (1867), Manchester Arts Club (1879), Manchester Literary Club (1880-84), Brasenose Club (1870) and council member for the Lancashire and Cheshire Antiquarian Society.

When writing he very seldom mentioned his family. He was married in 1870 and had four children, one son and three daughters. He died on the 5th July 1908 at the age of sixty-nine.

Sarah, his wife lived to be ninety-five and two of their daughters were eighty-five.

> *"Who will ever forget his gentle voice, his gracious and courtly ways?... Alfred Darbyshire was one of Manchester's cherished possessions, a man of fine brain, and with a heart of gold."* 10

He certainly had a profound effect on Manchester as a city. He designed houses, churches, libraries, clubs, schools, factories and theatres. He will be especially remembered for his architectural and artistic contributions towards Manchester's theatrical scene. He made it bigger, better, more safe and a joy to see and experience.

9 Published in connection with his reconstruction of "Old Manchester and Salford," at the 1887 Manchester Jubilee Exhibition.

10 City News 1908 taken from Three Lives "It Happened Round Manchester."

CHAPTER 11

FREDERIC J. SHIELDS
1833-1911

The following artist played a huge role within Manchester's Victorian Art Scene.

"So Mr. Shields will remain unrecognised except by those who seek him out."

Charles Rowley. 1

In 1907 when Shields had achieved his well earned reputation as a professional artist, Manchester decided to honour him with an exclusive exhibition.

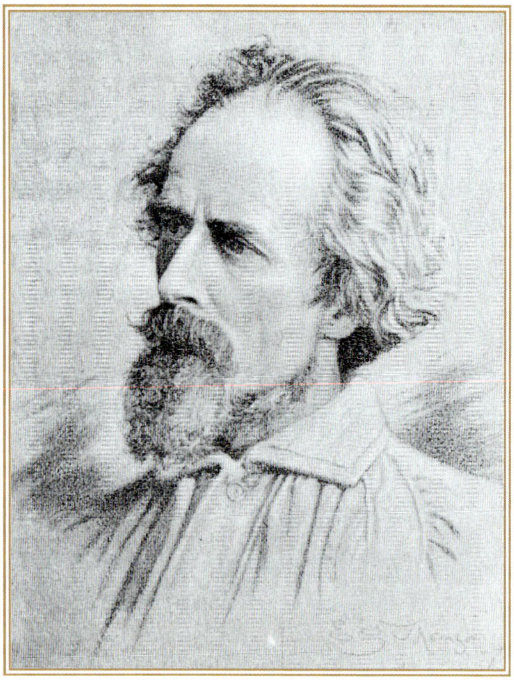

Figure 27. E. G. Thomson, *Frederic J. Shields*
Manchester Central Library

The City Art Gallery's foyer was tranquil. A number of attendants were on duty and the public slowly wandered through on their way to their relevant rooms.

Behind the scenes it was a different tale. The Art Gallery Committee of the Corporation had decided to hold an exhibition of Frederic Shields's 2 collected works during the coming months of March and April, and this meant for some there was a lot of organising to be done.

The main objective of this exhibition was to make sure the gallery had enough pictures to fill three rooms.

1 Charles Rowley 1840-1933 was a councillor, philanthropist, art dealer, author and founder of the Ancoats Brotherhood.
2 Also known as Frederick J. Shields.

An advert was placed in a number of newspapers asking if any private owners would be willing to lend their paintings for this exhibition. These adverts were a great success, numerous owners replied, and the exhibition duly went ahead with over one hundred and sixty three works on display, executed in a number of different media - oil, watercolour, tempera, chalk and pencil and several reproductions in autotype. It was summed up by the Manchester Evening News as follows: **One of the first impressions derived, in our own case from a tour of the three rooms full of well hung drawings and paintings at the City Art Gallery, is one of admiration for Mr. Shields's command of design.**

Everywhere you are struck by spaces ingeniously and yet naturally filled; every work is a pattern well laid out, without cramping or padding, or the dragging in of irrelevant accessories to help out the composition, by way of set-off to something that is there because it was essential to the meaning.

All his Biblical subjects are treated with a certain quality of seriousness that we do not quite remember in any other artist.

Mr. Shields is at his best by far in large decorative designs and that his employment of the past twelve years, on the interior of the Chapel of the Ascension, Bayswater Road, London, is one of the happiest of modern instances of a considerable talent put to the very fruitful and most stimulating use. [3]

At the formal opening of this exhibition the Lord Mayor praised Shields and said "his work was much admired." He then launched into the tale of the Manchester Town Hall murals and Shields's immense generosity towards his good friend and fellow artist Ford Madox Brown. He wisely left out the fact that these two artists very nearly missed out on this commission, and that not only had the Decorative Committee approached Shields and Madox Brown to paint a number of murals in the Town Hall, they had also approached some foreign competitors, Guffens & Swertz of Belgium. In fact a sub-committee, with the architect, Mr. Alfred Waterhouse and the Town Clerk, Sir Joseph Heron had actually been over to Belgium to see some of the decorative works produced by this firm. Guffens & Swertz had

---

3 Manchester Evening News, 27th March 1907, Frederic Shields Exhibition.

sent an estimate to do the work for the sum of forty pounds a yard, and to do it within a short time.

On hearing this, via Madox Brown, Shields immediately wrote a letter of complaint to the Committee accusing them of insulting all English artists. Maybe his letter had an effect upon the Committee (it was an extremely strong one) because they did eventually give the commission to Shields and Brown who agreed to take on the commission at the Guffens & Swertz price of £40 a yard. Coincidently, Brown had spent some time studying in Belgium.

It was agreed by all to have the history of Manchester painted on the walls and the two artists would have one side of the room each. But this never came about. Shields did not undertake this work. Things came to a head when Madox Brown had written to Shields thinking he had been working for months on the Wycliffe cartoon in his studio. Shields had been busy on a number of other things, and had nowhere near finished this cartoon. He decided that it was now time he admitted to Madox Brown that he would rather he took over the whole commission.

For financial reasons alone, Madox Brown was indeed overjoyed to receive this commission. Madox Brown immortalised his stern bearded friend by making him sit for Wycliffe in the fresco of the Reformer's Trial. As the Mayor had said " Shields had been immensely generous to his good friend Madox Brown."

After the Mayor's speech it was decided to send the following telegram to Shields: **The Lord Mayor and Art Gallery Committee offer you hearty congratulations on a beautiful and impressive exhibition. Express admiration of life and work, and wish you health and strength to complete the Chapel of Ascension.** 4

Here he was, much later on in his life, receiving a great deal of accolade from the citizens of Manchester, but by birth Shields was not a Manchester man. 5 He was born on the coast of Durham and his father was a Perth man, by trade a bookbinder's finisher. Shields spent his childhood in London in the squalid surroundings of Clare Market in London, described as a dismal network of alleys and mean streets,

---

4 Courier, 27th March 1907, Shields Exhibition - Formal Opening.
5 Biography taken from: City News March 4th 1911, Frederick James Shields: A Great Manchester Artist. And the Guardian, February 28th 1911, Frederic Shields.

which were cleared away later to make room for the Royal Courts of Justice. It was here he first began to practise his art. He had found some old antique prints hidden away in a garret in the house, and he would spend every minute he could drawing from them.

At fourteen he had to leave school because his father, who was now foreman at M'Corquodale's printing works, Newton-le-Willows, was very ill and he was desperately needed to help earn money for his mother and the rest of the family. A year later he joined his father at Newton-le-Willows. At the age of sixteen Shields found employment with a Manchester lithographer named Cowen at 5/- a week. His early days in Manchester were not happy - he often went with out a meal and his beloved father died.

After a number of different jobs at places that kept failing Shields said "I began to think myself fatal as the plague to all who entertained me." He resolved to be his own master and took a small house in Clopton Street, Hulme. He now executed commissions for lithographic firms, and also began to paint in water colours. Later he resided in Cornbrook, and from 1872 until he finally left the district, at Ordsall Hall.

As a youth he was intensely religious and was delighted to receive his first religious commission from Mr. Harry Rawson of the Manchester Examiner to illustrate Bunyan's "The Pilgrim's Progress." The twenty designs for the book, engraved on wood gained praise from Ruskin and the friendship of Rossetti and Ford Madox Brown.

"I know no one in England," wrote Ruskin in his impulsive way, "who could have made that drawing but yourself. Even should you never be able to colour, you may be more useful and (if that is any temptation) more celebrated than any painter of the day."

Charles Kingsley sent Shields a letter suggesting he might become the English Gustave Dore. A notion not popular with one critic: **In matters of art the Canon was always at best something of a Philistine. He never could bring himself to appreciate the Pre-Raphaelites. His comparison of Shields to Dore was about as inept as such a parallel could be, for no two men of genius were more unlike in their aims and methods. Still his administration was**

honest, and its expression kindly and no doubt encouraged the struggling youth. [6]

Ironically, Shields decided that wood engraving did not do justice to his drawing and he lost interest in black-and-white work.

He found temporary employment with a landscape painter, C. H. Mitchell, for whom he introduced figures into his pictures. On a working trip to Devon he had passed through a village named Porlock and noticed, from an artist's point of view, it was rich in rustic personalities and subjects. When he finished working with Mitchell he returned to the village and stayed there for a considerable time painting and getting to know its inhabitants, who readily accepted him and were happy to model for him. It was these rustic portraits that helped to make his reputation and if he was short of commissions or in need of money he would return to Porlock and paint for a while.

In May 1864 Shields met the artist Dante Gabriel Rossetti for the first time. "Face to face, I felt such a sense of littleness as I have never experienced in contact with any man but himself. This, through the long years of intimacy that followed never diminished but increased." Shields showed Rossetti some of his designs, and admitted to feeling incompetent towards them at times. "Tut, tut, you design better than any of us, but cultivate your imagination," said Rossetti. Shields felt elated, but not for long. He was next introduced to Madox Brown who said very little about his work.

Rossetti really did admire Shields's working techniques. Rossetti's brother, William writes: **Another matter of technical practice is brought out in an interesting way in a paper which my brother's intimate friend Mr. Frederick J. Shields, the distinguished painter, contributed to The Century-Guild Hobby-Horse (No. 18).**

---

6 City News, March 4th 1911, Frederick James Shields, A Great Manchester Artist.

My brother always valued much the works of this artist, and held him in the highest esteem as a devout-natured man of the strictest principle and the warmest feeling; the bond between the two friends being singularly close in the last four or five years of my brother's life, when Shields became his frequent and unflagging visitor, sparing no effort to keep him in heart and hope.

Mr. Shields, it seems, had towards 1864 come upon a certain French "compressed charcoal," which he approved, and showed to Rossetti. The latter at once adopted this material alone for all his larger studies, which were altogether very numerous, and as high in quality as anything he produced, and many of them done in varying tints.

When the Franco-German war broke out in 1870 - this truly atrocious and insufferable war," as Rossetti called it in writing to Shields - that chalk became unprocurable, and it has never again been in the market. Fortunately Rossetti had previously laid-in a large stock of it, which he continued using, and even at his death it was not nearly exhausted. [7]

In one of Rossetti's letters to Shields [8] he writes about chalk drawings, and wonders what paper Shields uses."The blue grey is of course the one tending most to deaden redness; but it is apt to resist covering for a long time and leave the drawing cold. I have been using a slightly greenish tint instead, which has great advantages, but requires caution as to redness.

---

7 William Michael Rossetti, 1895, Family-Letters with a Memoir, vol 1.

8 All photographs, personal information on the artist, and excerpts from Shields's diary and letters have been taken from: Ernestine Mills, The Life And Letters Of Frederic Shields 1833-1911.

I have had great success by making a mixture of black and red powdered chalk, dip a stump in it, rub it almost off the stump again and then rub the stump all over the paper you are going to work on before you begin.

The tint thus rubbed should be no stronger than a sky, but is neutral and pleasant with the greenish tint underneath, and gives a good ground to work into, as the white tells on it and you can bread out lights." Rossetti spent many hours with Shields in his studio teaching him the art of colour. Shields was a very fine draughtsman but not a good colourist.

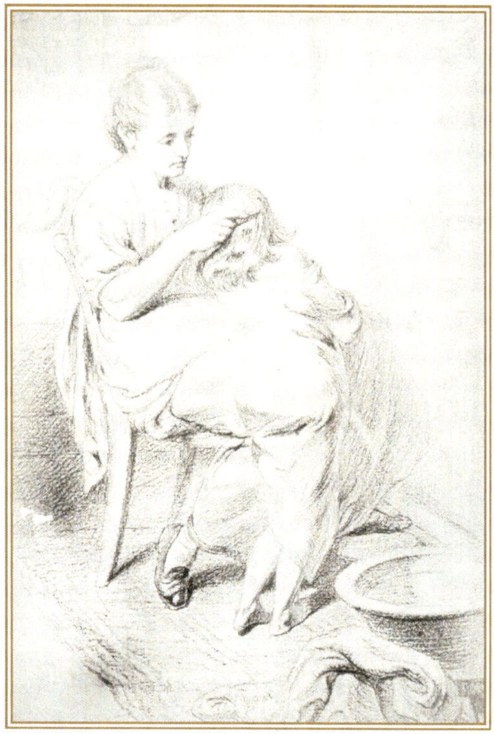

Figure 28. F. J. Shields, *Saturday Night*
(a drawing in red chalk)
Manchester Central Library

Inevitably Shields, Rossetti and Madox Brown became the very best of friends. They would sit up half the night exchanging ideas, write copious letters to each other, spend Christmases together and would frequently come to each others aid if they were short of financial funding. Later on in their friendship when Rossetti had bouts of illness Shields sat with him for hours on end. They were the closest of friends with entirely different natures. Rossetti was an agnostic, vigorous and impetuous. Shields's nature was totally opposite, but he enjoyed their friendship so much and feasted on Rossetti's genius. At the same time he had a real terror as to the ultimate fate of Rossetti's immortal soul.

When Rossetti finally died Shields was the one to run and fetch the doctor: Gabriel, who was sitting, fell back, threw his arms out, screamed out loud two or three times close together, and then lay, breathing but insensible. Nurse raised the alarm. Mr. Watts hurried back, and, one on each side, they held Gabriel down; but there was not the slightest struggle or return of consciousness. All assembled round the bed. Mr. Shields flew for Dr. Harris, and in the shortest time returned with him.

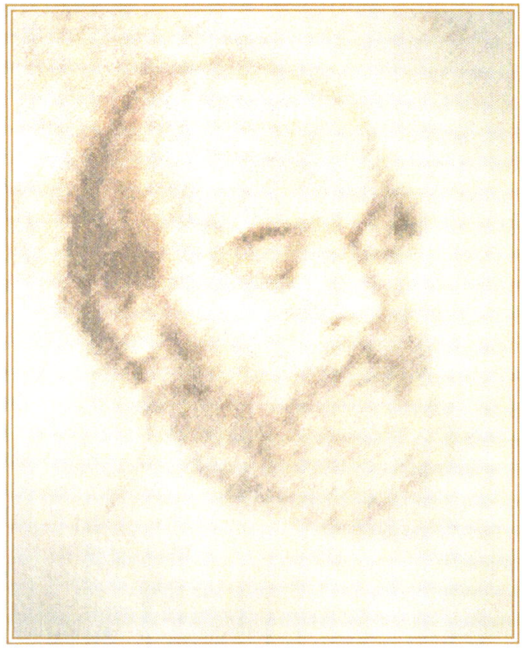

Figure 29. F. J. Shields, *The Dead Rossetti*

The following is an extract from Rossetti's brother's diary: A man from Brucciani's, London was sent for to take a cast of Gabriel's face and hand (these casts were taken with no less skill than that which the Brucciani firm always command; but it is a fact that the head proved extremely disappointing to all of us, and seems barely to suggest what my brother was like). Gabriel looked quite peaceful, with a tendency towards a smile. Mr. Shields made a drawing of him (this was done at my request, and it was a truly self-sacrificing act of Shields, the most high-strung and susceptible of men, and my brother's devoted friend, to whom such a task was a wrench indeed: I possess the drawing, and the artist afterwards made a copy of it, and presented it to Christina).

Shields recorded in his diary "Made two copies (in misery) of the drawing of Rossetti's face for Christina and Watts." Shields had a cast of a hand, a small fine hand which could easily have been mistaken for that of a woman had it not had pencilled upon it the words: "D. G. Rossetti's cunning right hand, that clasped mine in friendship once."

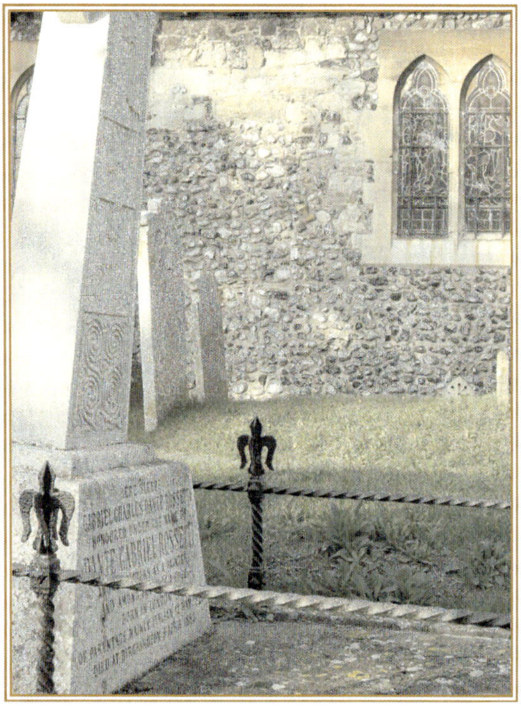

Figure 30. ***Rossetti's Grave at All Saints Church, Birchington***

In July, Shields received a letter from Christina Rossetti written on behalf of her mother, expressing her mother's wish to commission a memorial window over looking her son's grave at the church in Birchington.It seemed Mrs. Rossetti had decided that she would like to secure the window (nearest to the grave) as exclusively her own gift and would devote £100 for this purpose. Christina then asked Shields "if this would be a sufficient amount for him to take the window as a commission?"

She continued, "Mr. Alcock, the vicar, is inclined to a subject in some way appropriate to Holy Baptism since the window belongs to that part of the church which forms the Baptistry. He also requests that the lower section of the window which consists of two lights should be made slightly ornamental in some simple way independent of the figure subjects, as these panes of glass are made movable for the purpose."

Shields was rapturous at the thoughts of this commission and prepared two designs, one of his own, the subject being: "The Healing of the Blind Man," and the other was adapted from Rossetti's design of "Mary Magdalene."

Can you imagine Shields's horror and despair when on submitting his two designs to the Birchington vicar for approval he replied "I do not think this picture of Mary Magdalene is likely to inspire devotional thoughts and feelings, and fear that in some cases it might rather do the reverse?" With his temperament and fierce religious pride he must have been mortified. He replied to the vicar "My friend Rossetti himself would have shrunk with shuddering at any supposition that the design could have an impure effect."

He then religiously lambastes the vicar, but the vicar does not flinch. As a very last resort Shields asked him "if he realised how ill-mannered he was being towards Mrs Rossetti and her kind commission towards his church?" Alas this was to no avail, the vicar would not be moved, so eventually Shields gave in and another design of Rossetti's, "Passover in the Holy Family," was mutually agreed upon.

When the window was finally in place Christina and her mother went to view it. Christina wrote to Shields praising the beautiful window. "We saw it on such a lovely day and it excels my mother's highest expectations. Thank You."

On entering All Saints Church through the South porch way the window is on the left hand side.

It has two lights, the first being Rossetti's own design adapted by Shields from "The Passover in the Holy Family: Gathering Bitter Herbs." [9]

The second window is designed by Shields and portrays "Christ leading the Blind Man Out of Bethsaida."

The inscription under the window reads:

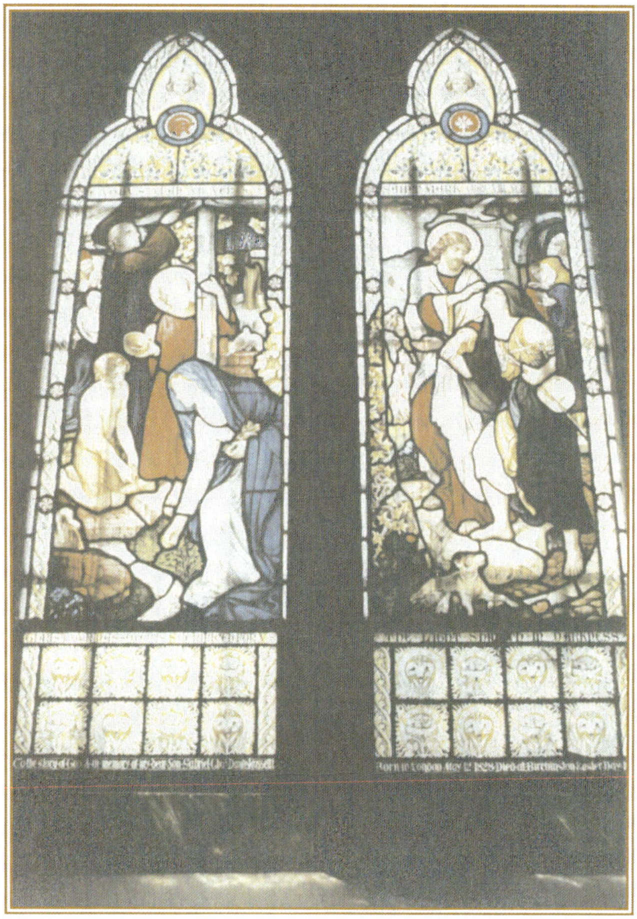

Figure 31. ***The Rossetti Memorial Window***
P. E. Blanche.

"To the glory of God and in memory of my Son Gabriel Charles Dante Rossetti Born in London May 12th 1828. Died at Birchington Easter Day 1882."

9 A Watercolour dated 1855-56 in the Tate Gallery, London.

In 1865 Shields was elected as an Associate of the Old Watercolour Society resigning in 1900. During his membership he exhibited over one hundred watercolour drawings. He never exhibited at the Royal Academy.

In 1865 he went to London with a view to staying for a long time. He took lodgings at Chelsea, near Rossetti's house. Shields was at an extremely low ebb in London and ceased working for a time. Any kind of noise would jar his nerves and cause deep depression. He said "I have counted as many as seven organs in a morning at Chelsea, with German bands, and it is this kind of noise infliction that makes me so low – nothing else." It was around this time Ford Madox Brown advised him to take hydrate of chloral, 1 dram in 1oz of water several times a day to make him sleep. Unfortunately, he became addicted to it for quite some time. He described the drug "as giving deathlike stupefaction without restorative power."

He decided to visit Boulogne to ease his nerves. This was the first time he had left England. He was not there very long before he started painting again. He returned to his adopted city steadily producing little watercolour and chalk drawings, a few figure pieces and portraits in oil and some designs. He was a prominent member of the Manchester Academy and gained the Heywood Prize at the Royal Institution in 1871.

In 1874, at the age of forty, he married Cissy a striking sixteen year old with long auburn hair. She modelled for him before they were married and afterwards. Cissy was entirely uneducated and was more than glad to leave her monotonous family surroundings behind. But did she really understand how different her life would be with Shields? Yes, he was a professional artist and as a model she enjoyed receiving attention from him and his colleagues. But would this be enough? Did she realise how different her life with this completely selfish and intensely religious man would be? An entrance in his diary, August 15th 1874, reads as follows:

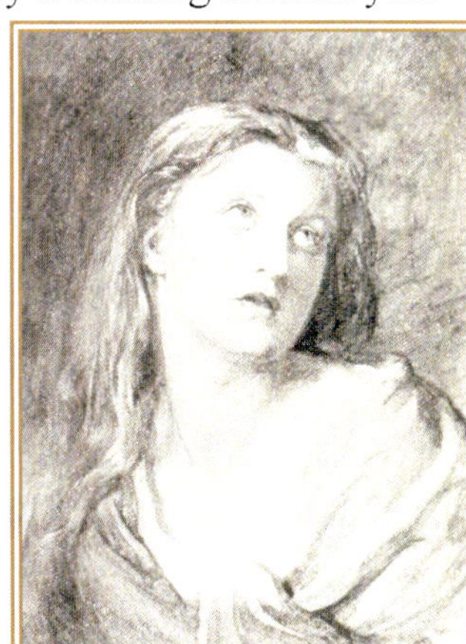

Figure 32. F. J. Shields, ***The Artist's Wife***

Married at Irwell Street Chapel. Revd. Mr. Codling. Off to Blackpool alone with Mac. Did me wonderful good. Thank God."

Shields often left Cissy to her own devices and as a result she became good friends with a former student of Shields, Miss Emily Gertrude Thomson. Shields wrote to Emily on 1st November 1875 from Blackpool:

We have longed for and in vain expected your promised advent. But I rejoice that you are working so hard, indeed I am envious.

All our house salute you. My wife specially, who would write to you in gratitude for the pleasure which your letter afforded her; but that its brilliant excellency of descriptive power and perfect calligraphy have abashed her soul into silence and her pen into rust. But she desires me to say that if you will get her the aforesaid number of yards of the "bobby fringe" she will be your obliged and faithful servant, if not correspondent, all the rest of her life.

Shields insulted Cissy and her lack of education many times over.

In the past he had visited a well-known girls' school at Winnington, Northwich, for whose pupils Ruskin wrote "Ethics of the Dust." Ruskin appreciating the way Shields worked introduced him to Winnington Hall's principal Miss Bell.[10] They became life long friends.

Into this Eden I was introduced, a shy, bashful fellow, alone in the presence of many ladies, for I suppose there were usually seventy girls of varied ages being educated there, with their unique advantages.

Winnington Hall was full of beautiful rooms with chimney pieces of Italian work. It boasted a very fine library jam-packed with art works. Dotted around the Hall's interior were exquisitely carved fine casts, Turner and Raphael engravings, and many of Ruskin's drawings of Venetian architecture. The Hall stood in widespread grounds bordered by the River Weaver with its magical musical weir.

Unfortunately, Miss Bell and Ruskin fell out and Ruskin tried very hard to persuade Shields not to continue his friendship with her but it

10 Lady Burne-Jones says in her book, Memorials of E. Burne-Jones: "Miss Bell was an extremely clever woman, of a powerful and masterful turn of mind."

was to no avail. Due to financial difficulties Miss Bell moved her school to a house near Brighton called Winnington Pines.

After a spell of ill-health and giving up their current home Shields decided to tour Italy with his good friend Charles Rowley. This was when he decided to send his wife Cissy to Miss Bell's, very alien, select finishing-school for young ladies, Winnington Pines. He was adamant this would enlighten her. He recorded this in his diary as follows: **May 16th left London for Brighton – saw Cissy to school. Parted with darling at 8. To Newhaven, Boat cold, no sleep, very sick, morn at last.**

He wrote copious letters to her when he was away, and became inconsolable if she did not write back immediately. His letters were diabolical, and it was little wonder she took some time to reply. Each letter had a definite pattern. He would start with how miserable he was, and how lucky she was, then he would make cutting remarks about her handwriting, spelling and general character. There was also an overwhelming devoutness entwined within his abhorrent pettiness.

He wrote in one of his letters whilst staying in Florence: "Behave as my wife, so that in all things I may hear such an account as shall make me proud of you, in attention, in seriousness, in courtesy and obliging behaviour." The following appeared towards the end of this letter: "Not till we crucify ourselves can we have any real life," and in the very same paragraph, "I wish you could learn to spell little simple words better than you do, for you spell worse than you write. I could make a dreadful list of your wrongly spelt words if I chose from your letters, only I have not the heart to pull them to pieces seeing how full of love they are, my darling. My very kindest regards to Miss Bell and Miss Bradford, and the lady with whom you have a bedroom – I forget her name."

Did Cissy love him? She was amazing, for all her youthful inexperience she put up with his selfish pettiness, and managed to accommodated his pious obsessions. She must have felt something for him to have persevered the way she did. Her perseverance paid off, and over a certain time their marriage altered and Shields began to treat her as a mature woman, he mellowed and became far more tender towards her, but even so, some years later, they did split up.

Shields not only toured Italy but Switzerland too, returning to Brighton on July 17th where he stayed with the Madox Browns while he searched for a new house. Poor Cissy, constantly ill, and completely out of her depth, was still living at the school under the influence of Miss Bell and would continue to do so for some time to come, in fact it was early in 1877 they moved into their new home.

It was around this time Rossetti wrote to Shields with the prospect of designing stained glass for a firm with which he was connected (Messrs. Morris, Marshall, Faulkner & Co.) Amongst some of its artists were Madox Brown, E. B. Jones and himself. "Unfortunately we do not always have the time to spend on these designs. We do have an excellent full time colourist, William Morris, and all that is needed in the design is the drawing – the colour rests with him. Are you interested?" Shields was not interested and wrote back saying "he really did have too many commitments." Ironically, he became more and more involved in the design of stained glass over the next years.

Through his friend Alfred Waterhouse, Shields received a commission to design a set of stained glass windows for the private Chapel of Sir William Houldsworth's house at Coodham, Kilmarnock. [11] The subject was to be "The Triumph of Faith," and he worked upon it from 1876 to 1880. With this commission he established a reputation as a decorative artist of the highest degree and had no lack of commissions.

Alfred Waterhouse introduced Shields to the Duke of Westminster who commissioned him to design his stained glass and mosaics in the Chapel at Eaton Hall, which Waterhouse was then building. The subject of this remarkable decorative scheme was the hymn of St. Ambrose, the "Te Deum Laudamus." It occupied Shields for about ten years, from 1880 to 1890.

11 The original cartoons illustrating "The Triumph of Faith," now belong to Manchester Corporation.

He wrote about the commission as follows: It revolutionised all my views of design, imposing bounds upon me that purified and ennobled my style, while the practice in drawing upon a large scale gave me great increase of knowledge and power and the necessity of grappling with the fine disposition of drapery gradually taught me how much the dignity, grace and action of a figure depended upon this feature, and made me seek after excellence in this respect eagerly. 12

In 1884 Shields actually visited William Morris at Merton Abbey. He wanted Morris's advice on the designs to be made for the south wall of the chapel which would be carried out in mosaic. Shields did not like mosaics saying "they were flat and feeble in their effect." Much to Waterhouse's horror, he got around this by introducing a black background. As well as the mosaic designs he was also designing some windows for Cheltenham College, undertaken at the request of a friend. The subject was Spenser's "Faerie Queene." But all did not go well. Miss Beale, the head mistress of Cheltenham seriously disagreed with his treatment of one of the figures – that of a small Cupid. She was adamant that, as the figure was undraped, it could only be allowed to appear festooned with roses. Shields was furious, "my lovely little figure does not need any alteration." He immediately resigned and his former pupil and good friend Miss E. G. Thomson took over the commission. 13

Shields designed the windows in the chancel of the Parish Church of St. Ann, St. Ann's Square, Manchester. When St. Ann's Church was consecrated in 1712 all the windows were in plain glass. During the church's restoration in 1887- 89 the windows in the semicircular apse were filled with stained glass of a high quality for the Victorian era. Six other windows in the nave had their glazing replaced with stained glass at various times to commemorate royal and ecclesiastical occasions.

12 On Shields's death all the designs were presented to the Young Men's Christian Association, London Headquarters in Tottenham Court Road.
13 Ernestine Mills, The Life and Letter of Frederic Shields 1833-1911.

Shields was very fond of St. Ann's Church, and for a nominal fee he drew out a complete scheme for the church's stained glass based upon the theme of The Shepherd. 14

The three east windows behind the altar and the centre of the north and south aisles carry forward this theme and are the work of Heaton, Butler and Bayne. 15

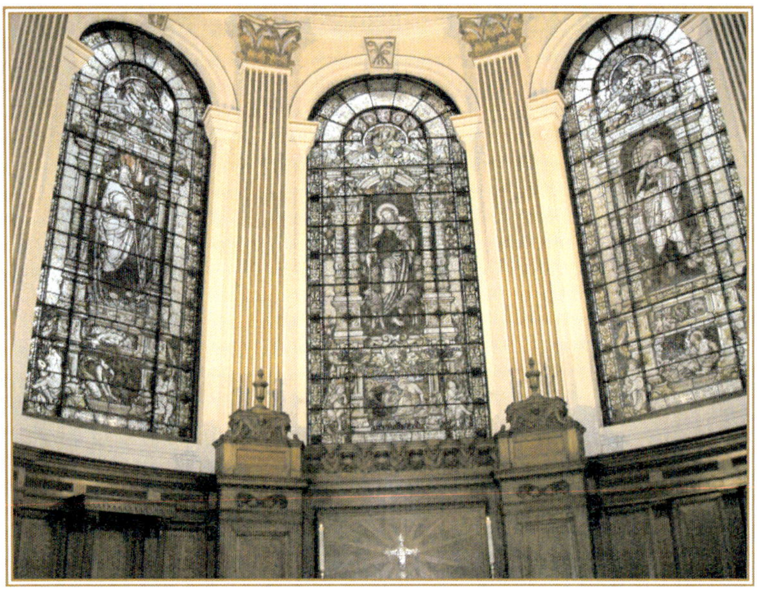

Figure 33. ***The Three East Windows Above The Altar***

14 Taken from a Booklet compiled by Su Holland and Researched by Paul Campion, The Parish Church of St. Ann, St. Ann's Square, Manchester: About our windows.
15 The firm was known as Heaton, Butler and Bayne from 1862, when Robert Turnill Bayne (1837-1915) a Pre-Raphaelite artist became partner and chief designer. Bayne's striking and linear designs were carried out in an exceptionally wide range of coloured glass, developed by Heaton as a result of his researches into medieval techniques. Their work can be seen at Westminster Abbey. The Grove Dictionary of Art, 2000, (Oxford University).

North Aisle Windows
The Jubilee Window:

This window was installed in commemoration of the Diamond Jubilee of Queen Victoria. Shields's design incorporates a shepherd slaying a lion between highly ornate pillars, with the crown and Royal Coat of arms above.

The dates on either side are 1837, when Victoria came to the throne, and 1897, the date of the Jubilee anniversary. The shepherd is almost certainly David.

In 1996 the IRA launched a vicious bomb attack on the City of Manchester. St. Ann's church took its share of the damage.
Many of its windows had to be replaced - including the Jubilee. After the explosion the window was restored in memory of Maria Isabella Blythe 1898-1985.
She was married in 1945 in St. Ann's Church with which she had a long and affectionate association.

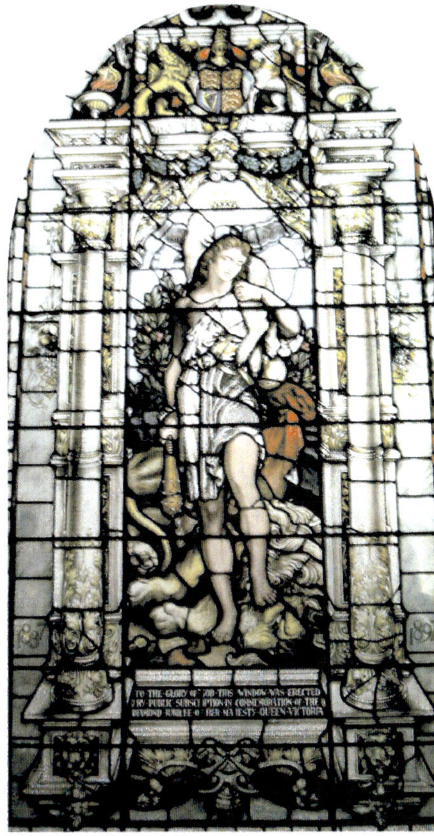

Figure 34. ***The Jubilee Window North Isle Windows***

South Aisle Windows
The Coronation Window:

In this window Adam appears in the Garden of Eden. It has numerous symbols including the serpent and apple in the bottom right corner. Adam stands with his hand on his brow looking towards heaven.

He is superimposed on a background of finely detailed flowers and leaves. He is no longer naked and wears a sheep skin around his waist. He is perfectly framed by two decorative architectural panels, which blend flawlessly with Shields's Garden of Eden theme.

The inscription reads:

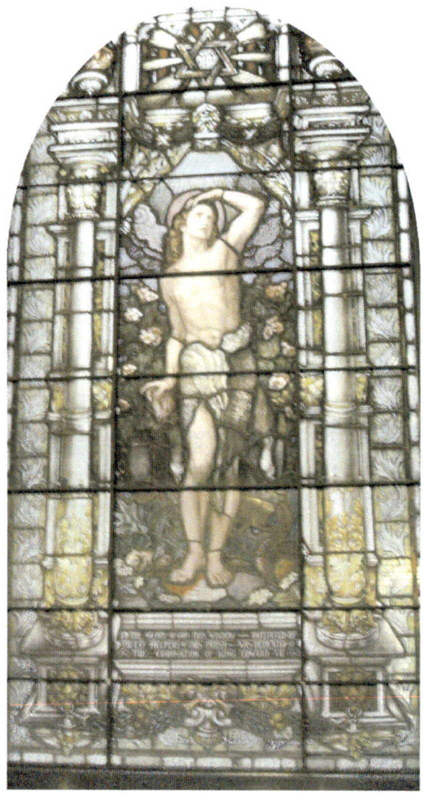

Figure 35. ***The Coronation Window South Aisle Windows***

To the Glory of God initiated by lay helpers of this parish, dedicated at the Coronation of King Edward V11 (1902).

The Coronation and Jubilee windows are splendid examples of the Pre-Raphaelite movement and prove Shields was indeed a distinguished Pre-Raphaelite painter/designer.

The Jubilee Window

David in the Jubilee window depicts a romantic interpretation of Pre-Raphaelitism.

The window is sumptuous and abounds with textures. David's tunic is a mass of rippling folds against his pure skin. The lamb with its woolly form contrasts skilfully against these silky folds.

David's foot rests upon the lion he has just slain, a splendid lion, a king among beasts, with huge pads and a flowing mane.

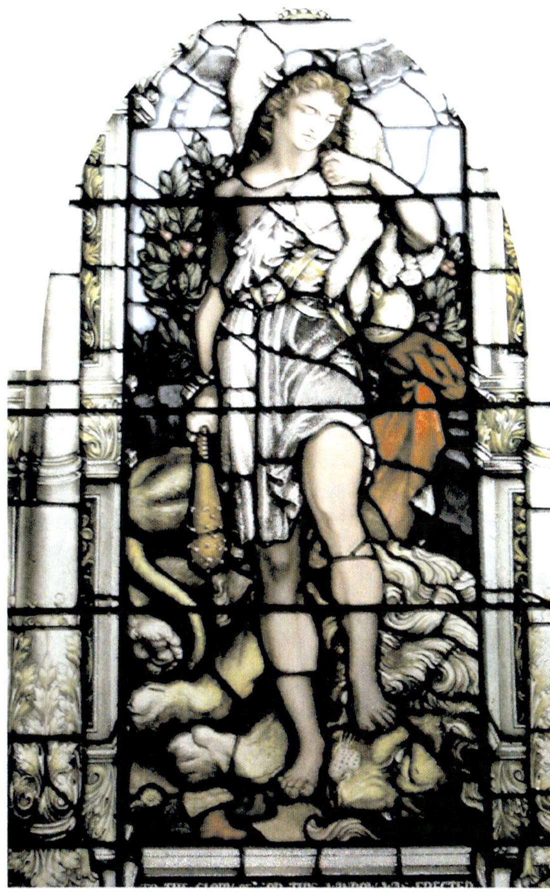

Figure 36. ***Section taken from the Jubilee Window***

Shields has used conventional Renaissance perspective to achieve all this sumptuousness. His background is simple and natural with finely detailed leaves and berries against a bright blue sky.

His piece de resistance is David's face. It is truly striking and full of serenity. He has the well known Pre-Raphaelite trade mark - cascading curls. David has just killed a lion but his face is at peace. His tunic is pristine. It is as though some mystical paint has been used to conceal any signs of the gruesome battle which must have taken place.

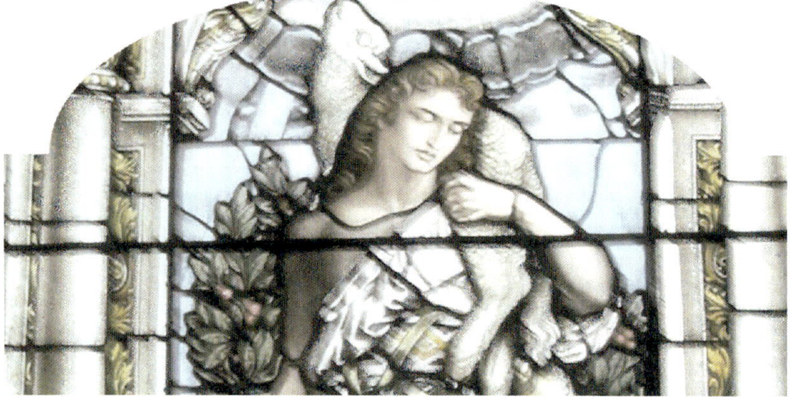

Figure 37. ***Jubilee Window - Close up of David's face***

Shields combined his deeply religious thoughts and artistic talent within St. Ann's Church for future generations to enjoy.

However, the greatest work of his life yet remained to be done - in the Chapel of the Ascension. 16 In June 1877 Dante Rossetti introduced Shields to Lord and Lady Mount-Temple and they became firm friends. Early in May 1882 when Lady Mount-Temple brought Mrs. Russell-Gurney to Shields's studio, little did he know then that she would become his nearest friend.

The widow of a Recorder of London, she was a woman with strong religious sentiment who recognised in Shields a kindred spirit. She first asked him to paint some frescoes in a country church. Then she conceived the idea, in Shields's words, "to plant in some great highway of London a place of rest for wayfarers and for prayer and meditation, wherein body, mind, and spirit, oppressed with the hurrying roar of the city's life might find repose and a refreshing feast ever liberally spread upon its walls for whosoever willed to enter." This sanctuary would be built to the memory of her husband.

16 The following account has been taken from the Guardian, Tuesday, February 28th 1911, Frederic Shields.

After much difficulty she obtained leave in 1890 to build her oratory in the old cemetery of St. George's, Hanover Square, facing the Bayswater Road a little to the west of the Marble Arch.

The Chapel of the Ascension was designed as a basilica, with a porch, without aisles, and with windows near the roof. The church at Pietra Santa, Carrara, was indicated by Mrs Gurney as the kind of building that she wanted, and Shields and the young architect Herbert Horne visited Northern Italy to study some of the principal churches and decorations. He wrote: "My Dear Mrs. Russell-Gurney, it is not possible for me to say what I feel about this journey, nor the rich rewards that meet us after the long railway journeys." The finished plans were submitted in February 1890 and there were endless complications from the moment the site was suggested. Only a skilled ecclesiastical lawyer succeeded in reconciling the various interests that barred the way. On April 9th 1890 Shields began his work.

To cover the great bare walls with religious pictures was the task to which Shields devoted the rest of his life, from 1890 onwards. Mrs. Gurney died in 1896, and for some time there was some doubt as to whether the work would be continued. Happily, the difficulties were overcome, and Shields, though hampered by ill-health, made steady progress, until at last the work was finished.

The pictures were not in fresco but in oil, and therefore, had not to be executed on the spot.

They were painted in his studio, first at St. John's Wood and latterly at Merton, and were then affixed

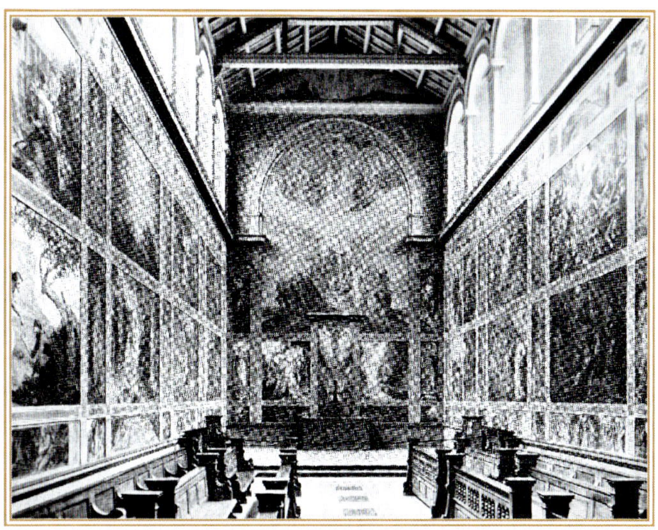

Figure 38. F. J. Shields, *Inside the Chapel of Ascension, Bayswater Road, London*

by means of a white lead compost to slate blocks let into the wall, on a plan adopted by Puvis de Chavanness. He also states in his handbook to the Chapel that his object was "to avoid anything like framed pictures."

The City News printed an article with reference to Shields, the Chapel and some Manchester visitors: 17 **Some of your readers may be interested in the following instance of Mr. Shields's unfailing kindness and loyalty to Manchester.**

In Whit week, 1906, three Manchester girls, of whom I was one, went to London for a holiday. In our program of sight-seeing we had included a visit to the Chapel of the Ascension. (Our interest had been aroused by an account which appeared about that time in the Manchester City News).

When we arrived at the Chapel we were keenly disappointed to find it closed. We lingered about the entrance for some time hoping to see someone pass in or out. It was our only possible day for the visit, and we had looked forward to it so eagerly that our disappointment was very great.

We examined the outside and wandered into the burial-ground behind, trying to make the best of what seemed a hopeless disappointment. Then we found a side door, which we thought might belong to the caretaker's house. After much hesitation one of us knocked gently at the door hoping the caretaker might prove friendly and allow us a special visit.

The door was opened by an elderly man in an artist's overall, whom we knew at once to be Mr. Shields. We were so surprised that for a moment none of us could speak. Then one of us began a confused apology, mentioning that we were from Manchester and we quite thought we were knocking at the caretaker's door.

---

17 City News, Saturday March 4th 1911, The Artist and His Manchester Visitors.

Our apology must have been very incoherent, but Mr. Shields heard the word "Manchester" and at once began to question us. His interest soon put us at our ease.

I can remember that he said, "You've come all the way from Manchester? Then certainly you must be allowed to see the Chapel." Going to the door he opened it and instructed the attendant to let us stay as long as we liked. Then he seemed to change his mind, and to our great delight followed us into the Chapel himself. I think we all count the next half hour as one of the golden ones of our life.

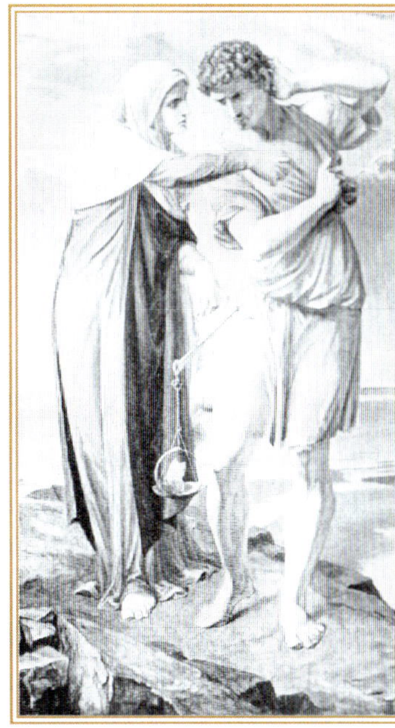

Figure 39. ***Man Harkens To The Appeal of Conscience***

When at last he left us it was as if a dazzling radiance had been removed. His interest in us was evidently unfeigned, and was no doubt due to our coming from Manchester.

This information on the Chapel of Ascension with its various photographs of Shields's tireless work is extremely precious to art historians, because the Chapel was bombed during the Second World War and had to be demolished in 1952. Tragically depictions such as these and The Despised Manna Frieze were obliterated.[18]

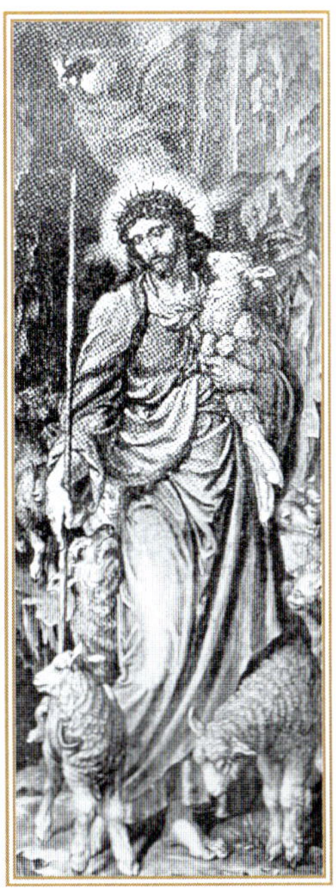

Figure 40. ***The Good Shepherd***

[18] Taken from Ernestine Mills, The Life And Letters Of Frederic Shields

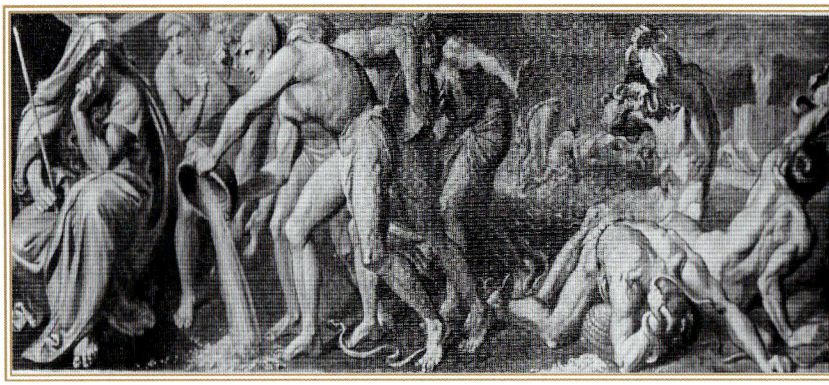

Figure 41. ***The Despised Manna Frieze***

When Shields's task was finished he finally retired to Merton in Surrey, but he never lost his Manchester contacts. Whilst working on the chapel he had mourned the death of many of his artist friends, especially Madox Brown and Holman Hunt. Emily Gertrude Thomson his old friend and favourite pupil for whose work and personality he had the highest regard frequently visited him.

CHAPTER 12

MANCHESTER'S LEADING MALE ARTISTS

By the end of Victoria's reign Manchester had an exciting and thriving art scene. One with roots that reached out all over the world.

None of this could have taken place if it were not for its artists. They set the ball rolling and kept it going. Men and women working hard behind the scenes. Tucked away in their different studios, living on a cocktail of angst and joy, always believing in themselves, but never quite sure whether the Manchester art critics would make or break them.

The following are some of the prominent male artists who helped to make Manchester's art scene become a reality.

Mark Henry Anthony - 1817-1886

In March 1904 the following statement was made:

> *"Here, at last, is one master who will claim some posthumous glory whenever we begin a careful estimate of what England has produced."*
>
> Shepherds Gallery, Athenaeum.

Mark Anthony was born in Rusholme Lane, Manchester and baptized on the 4th August 1817 at Chorlton-on-Medlock. At first he trained for the medical profession and at the age of sixteen was placed with a doctor in Glamorgan who, being a painter of some skill, recognised Anthony's artistic talents and gave him great encouragement. Anthony was very fortunate on inheriting some property he was able to give up his medical training and pursue his love of art.

He decided to study in Paris and the Hague and was a pupil of Delaroche and Vernet at Beaux-Arts and Atelier de Nuit. In 1837 he met Corot and Dupe at Fontainbleau and was greatly influenced by them. On his return to England he exhibited in both Manchester and Liverpool. In 1854 he was awarded the annual prize of £50 for the "best" picture in the Exhibition of the Liverpool Academy.

He travelled in Ireland and Spain painting their landscapes. His works usually had a restrained element of poetry or sentiment.

He first exhibited at the British Institution and became a member of the Society of British Artists in 1845. He exhibited at the Royal Academy in 1847, 1849, 1852, and thereafter had either one or two pictures annually at Somerset House until 1866. He constantly hoped to become a member of the R.A. but never did and stopped displaying there after 1879.

Anthony was on intimate terms with the Pre-Raphaelite painters and their friends, particularly Ford Madox Brown. They seemed to appreciate his French way of painting. An entry in Brown's diary dated January 1884 was as follows: **He has a habit (of late particularly) making his skies so heavy that they quite spoil all the fine qualities otherwise evinced in his works. The picture of Stratford Church, however is magnificent in every respect, save the sky, which if he can paint it will be one of his finest works.**

From another of Brown's letters in the Autumn of 1885 to Lowes Dickinson, it appears Anthony had managed to paint his sky. He wrote: "He has been very successful indeed."

William Frank Bradley - 1801-1857

When Mr. Alex Brogden sold some of his paintings in London he noticed there was one by an artist named William Bradley of Manchester. Bradley's painting had sold for £65 and Brogden was curious to know more about this artist. He decided to write to the Manchester City News to find out if any of the newspaper's readers had any information on Bradley. He particularly wanted to know if any of his art was appreciated during his life time, did he realize a fortune, and were there any other particulars of a man whom Manchester ought to be proud of?

It was suggested by another correspondent, the artist Thomas Letherbrow, that either Mr. Crozier or Mr. Percy, two of Bradley's students might write a piece on him. Crozier saw the article and stated he would like to write very briefly his ideas of Bradley's powers as an artist, together with a recollection of his last visit to him when on his death bed.

He deliberately wanted to write about his last visit to see Bradley before he died because he wanted to rectify what he considered malicious remarks made against this artist by a correspondent named Joseph Johnson, an auctioneer in Newall's Buildings, Manchester where Bradley also had rooms. In a previous article Johnson had stated that Bradley's ending was very wretched and that apparently he was under the impression that he was not paid and appreciated according to his ability and this had induced intemperate habits. He claimed that for days running into weeks Bradley had employed a lad constantly to bring him brandy from the "Thatched House" until one morning he was discovered lying dead on a stretcher in his work-room.

Johnson had sold the contents of his studio and declared that the furniture was simply valueless. There were many original sketches which he sold from 2s.6d. to 20s., and he sold Bradley's palette for 35s. He finished his article: "so ended, ignobly and pitifully, the career of one of Manchester's most gifted artists."

This sorry account of Bradley's last days incensed Crozier and he was determined to set the record straight. The first part of his letter consisted of a number of biographical details and read as follows: William Bradley was born in Bloom Street, Manchester, January 16th 1801. His father eventually became a partner in Thackray and Co., and died when William was about three years of age. Our future artist first became a Manchester warehouse boy at 3s. a week (White, Armitage, and Co, New Brown Street). At the age of sixteen he began the practice of art, and styled himself "a miniature and animal painter."

In 1819 he lived at 43 Major Street, where his prices ranged from one shilling to six guineas for portraits of horses and dogs, according to their size. He had a limited number of lessons from Mather Brown. [1] When he reached twenty-one he went to stay with a friend, Mr. Levenson in London, and gained an introduction to Sir Thomas Lawrence, who kindly expressed his opinion from time to time on any work Bradley took to show to him.

---

1 Mather Brown (1761-1831) was an American artist who was in Manchester between 1817 and 1824.

He occupied a house in Fitzroy Square for nine years, namely from 1829-1838 at a rental of £3000 a year. He then came back to Manchester and in the house of the late Charles Calvert [2] he shared a studio with another artist, B. R. Faulkner. Crozier said "he was now considered a great man and his society much sought in this his native town."

In 1833 he married Eliza, eldest daughter of Charles Calvert, some sixteen years his junior. They had two sons, William and Basil who both became artists, and two daughters, Julia and Blanche. The last twelve years of Bradley's life were spent in Manchester. He died of typhoid fever in the room adjoining his studio, July 4th 1857.

Crozier had visited Bradley on the Wednesday before he died, and had taken a large book in which were engravings from Venetian masters and seating himself on the side of the bed they had discussed them. A little later Bradley had said "Crozier, I am going to die." He spoke of the portrait he had in hand of the late Mr Absalom Watkin saying "It is, I know, weak. I am weak; my brushes don't seem fitted to my hands. I try to get to my work, but as I get out of bed on the floor I go down, and on my hands and knees have to get back to bed."

Bradley then alluded to the Art Treasures Exhibition. "Do you happen to recall a portrait by Landseer of Sir A. W. Calcott, which allegedly Landseer painted in two and a half hours? It had a fabulous brown background, in fact, it was one of the most perfect shades of brown I ever saw. I just could not believe it, I go to this prestigious exhibition and see a work which has been dashed off in so short a time, and it is one of the finest things I ever beheld." Crozier left, remembering in substance all he had said, and feeling the truth of the saying that "the ruling passion is strong to death." Two more nights and Bradley had passed away, and after resting in the grave for twenty-one years the question is asked, "Who was William Bradley?"

---

2 Charles Calvert (1785-1852) was a Manchester landscape painter.

According to the artist William Percy a former student of William Bradley "he was an excellent portrait painter." He describes Bradley in his Manchester studio in the following manner: **He was painting the large portrait of the late Sir Thomas Potter, now in the Town Hall. He had also one on hand of Dr. Dalton, which I do not think was ever finished. The chalk drawing was very fine, and I remember I made a reduced copy of it for my master. There were a good many portraits in his studio, recently done, as I supposed. There was one of Peter Clare, another of Mr. Agnew, one of old Mr. Zanetti,. I think that of Sir Benjamin Heywood in the Mechanics' Institution had only just been finished.**

When Bradley moved to London he almost immediately sent for Percy, who went at once. He found Bradley busy with a number of portraits of eminent Conservative statesmen and others. He was painting them for some publishers. Amongst them were the portraits of Lord Francis Egerton (afterwards Earl of Ellesmere) Mr. Gladstone, Lord Sandon, J. Emmerson Tennant and Lord Derby, whose portrait made a considerable sensation in the Royal Academy. The list was long and very impressive. But, Bradley's engagement with the publishers was rather a disastrous one, and he was left with a good many of the paintings on his hands. He had to give up his house in London and a year or two later he returned to Manchester. [3]

Another correspondent, R. E. Bibby was adamant that Bradley's tastes lay not in dry portrait painting but in sketching the female figure and he also confirmed that Bradley's portfolio, generally accessible to callers, showed scores of fancy subjects. "He had an especial fondness for young and chubby children, particularly if a spice of mischief lurked in their countenance. These sketches could be regarded as gems in conception and art."

Johnson wrote apologising. He was sorry if his information had caused even the slightest displeasure, but still persisted he had told the truth about Bradley. Bibby then suggested that perhaps Johnson should have considered for a moment some of Bradley's living relatives and their feelings.

---

3 Manchester City News, June 16th 1878, Notes and Queries.

One of Bradley's relatives, Elizabeth Bradley Croft, showed her feelings: **I sat often as a child for my uncle. He was an eccentric, secluded character, but his despondency was no doubt caused by domestic troubles and intemperance. As he did not correspond with his near relatives they were not generally aware of his death.**

The letters continued for quite a while longer. All this information just from one small enquiry. Did Mr. Alex Brogden ever imagine he could have caused such a furore within Manchester's art circles?

Walter Butterworth - 1862-1935

A Leading Authority and Patron of the Arts

Walter Butterworth was highly revered within Manchester's artistic circles. In 1975, his son wrote a manuscript [4] based upon his father's work linked to the arts. This is a delightfully written, valuable piece of art history, allowing its reader an intimate look into Walter Butterworth's life, a life brimming over with art.

Angus Butterworth informs us his father was an accomplished linguist, speaking eleven languages, and that his favourite hobby was visiting art galleries and museums on the continent and in North America where he came to know well many of the leading art directors and curators.

As a patron of the arts he filled his home with his favourite pieces, described by his son in the following way: **The disposition of pictures and other objects d' art in my father's house was on a definite plan. Off the small outer hall was a cloakroom lit by two stained glass windows of Pre-Raphaelite design reminiscent of Burne Jones. There were a few oil paintings in the main inner hall and two Della Robbin plaques. On the staircase in accordance with tradition were most of the family portraits, while in the bedroom were watercolours and pastel drawings giving the effect of air and light. The long dining room had oil paintings, bronzes and silverware, together with the Rodin group now in the Tate. The square drawing room, a delightful**

---

4 Manuscript of "Belfield Papers," No 2, 1975, Walter Butterworth A Patron of Art.

room with windows facing South and East, which always seemed full of sunlight, had watercolours and some elegant Venetian and other glassware.
The breakfast room had pencil drawings and watercolours.

Butterworth's life style revolved around the arts. He founded the Society of Friends of Art, and was chairman of the Arundel Art Society and the Athenaeum Graphic Club. He was on the Council of the National Art Collections Fund, and for several years chairman of the Manchester City Art Gallery virtually acting as curator. For a long period he was also chairman of the Trustees of the Whitworth Art Gallery. Among the other offices he held were those of Vice-President of the Manchester Academy of Fine Arts and chairman of the Manchester Regional College of Art.

Angus writes: While chairman of the Whitworth Gallery he successfully established, with the support of the trustees, a policy which showed great wisdom and foresight. When first opened the collection was a miscellaneous one of watercolour and oil paintings without any distinctive character, so that there was risk of it becoming merely a repetition of the kind of thing commonly found elsewhere.

From the time my father became chairman, the Whitworth confined itself without exception to the buying of drawings and prints, to avoid overlapping. The scheme included drawings in every sense of the term – watercolour, sepia, pen and ink, pencil and pastel. In consequence the Whitworth collection became the finest and most representative of its kind in the country outside London.

When he retired from the City Council in November 1912 the Manchester Guardian wrote: In a few years he has made Manchester's public Galleries famous throughout England.

In 1913 Butterworth visited Poland, Russia and Finland. He was eager to see the first Russian Medieval Art Exhibition in Moscow, especially the icons which were the pride of the museums at Moscow, St. Petersburg and Novgorod.

On receiving his father's inheritance Angus thought it seemed fitting to present two fine examples to the national collection at the British Museum:

British Museum, Bloomsbury, London WC1:
Russian Icon, 16th century, 18.75" x 6.75" of "Our Lady's Tenderness."
Russian Icon 17th century 12" x 10.75" probably painted in Moscow, with scenes from "The Life of Christ."

The inheritance of his father's collection posed a difficult problem for Angus, "I had not the room to house it, and so I decided to give the majority of the works to national and other galleries in my father's memory. This I did between 1960 and 1975, many of the gifts were given through the National Art Collection Fund, to commemorate my father's long connection with it." The following are some interesting items from the collection and its beneficiaries.

Imperial War Museum, Lambeth London, E.C.1:
Crayon Portrait 16" x 12" by C. M. Horsfall of: Walter Butterworth as "Mayor Of Ruhlefen." The portrait was painted in January 1917 in the **Ruhleben Concentration Camp, near Berlin,** for over 4,000 British civilian prisoners-of-war. Walter Butterworth gave an inspiring lead here, and was elected "Mayor" by his fellow-prisoners.

The London Museum, Kensington Palace, London, W.8:
Lithographs by J. A. McNeill Whistler of: "Blacksmith at Work" and "Exterior of Fish Shop." James Abbott Mc Neill Whistler (1834-1903) was famed for his paintings of the Thames. He lived and died in Cheyne Walks, Chelsea, within a short distance of Kensington Palace, where these examples of his work, notable for the finished elegance, are now preserved. Walter Butterworth met him on several occasions and owned other works by him.

Tate Gallery, Milbank, London SW1:
The original plaster model by Auguste Rodin (1840-1917) of his famous group called – "Soeur Et Frere." The master modelled this work with his own hands about 1890.
Walter Butterworth, to whom the sculptor gave it in 1911, describes in his essay "A Visit To Rodin," published in 1912, as "very pure and tender." It was given to the Tate Gallery by L.M. Angus Butterworth in 1960, and was then reported as being "a worthy addition to the collection of Rodin's works which the sculptor presented to the British Nation in 1914."

Walter Butterworth visited Rodin at his Parisian studio in 1911 to commission "The Age of Bronze" for the City Art Gallery. This was the first full-scale figure Rodin exhibited. His model was a Belgian soldier, Auguste Neyt. Rodin worked on this piece for eighteen months observing the form from all angles, using a step-ladder to see from above. When it was exhibited, the figure looked so natural that Rodin was accused of casting it directly from the figure. 5

Butterworth described his visit to Rodin in the following manner:

Rodin was a great host and placed a whole day at our disposal to show us his work in all stages, to conduct us over his house and to drive us himself to Meudon Station. A last glimpse of him as the train pulled out made me realise although Rodin was seventy-one years of age he was extremely youthful - having just bounced down the station steps and thrust us into the carriage - he was now waving frantically at the moving train with great enthusiasm.

Rodin is about 5ft 3ins, thick set, even massive, with a great head set firmly on broad shoulders. Eyes clear, quick observant and a long and ample beard. Restless hands always seeking to do something when he talks. In these days of pre-eminence and prosperity he has houses and work rooms to spare. His studio in the Rue de l'Universite is a fine old historic house, separated from the Rue Va Senner by a courtyard with a series of large lofty work shops and at the same time distinguished exhibition rooms. Over twenty years Rodin has lived at Meuton, building an extension to the house and a remarkable museum – chiefly of Greek sculpture and vases. His great studio, a lofty structure of glass was first built to exhibit his work at one of the Paris international exhibitions.

We first called upon the sculptor at the Rue Va Senner, where he was busy with assistants who now, I understand, do practically all the work in marble – Rodin restricting himself to modelling in clay.

He was greatly interested in our descriptions of Manchester and the populous industrial parts of Lancashire having had no idea of the teeming multitude in the thickly-set towns.

5 Taken from A Century Of Collecting 1882-1982, Manchester City Art Galleries. P132.

As we passed from bronze to clay, from clay to marble, he freely commented upon his own works sometimes with simplicity so natural and unaffected as to seem the expression of a child's-mind. His hand caressed the lines of contours, his face lifted with a smile of pleasure, he passed before a small marble group embodying the immortal instinct of love and said, touching the shining curves and undulations very delicately "see how the little fingers and toes embrace, echoing the idea of love." This naïve enjoyment of his own creations made us warm to him. There was no pretence or pose, we felt we were in touch with the inner man.

We visited his house and the vast studio also served as a museum containing not only sculpture but many details of architecture of different periods. It contained so many of his works, chiefly in the form of clay models, as to form almost a compendium of his life's work. There stood the great portrait (in plaster) which has been the object of his ambitious aspirations.

The Penseur now placed in the square before the Pantheon – in all there were over 100 statues.

Amongst these many gifts taken from Butterworth's incredibly diverse collection is a watercolour by F. W. Jackson. It was presented to the Walker Art Gallery, Liverpool.

Walker Art Gallery, Liverpool, 3:
Watercolour 10.25" x 6.75" by F. W. Jackson, "An Old Lancashire Woman."
A masterly study of a grey haired keen eyed old woman, in an unrelieved dark dress, with gnarled hands holding knitting needles. The head and hands are thrown into relief by the otherwise dark colouring. F. W. Jackson (1859-1918), a Lancashire artist was chiefly known for his landscapes.

This final item demonstrates how he also patronised local artists such as F. W. Jackson. He and Jackson were good friends and Butterworth accompanied him on several painting trips. When they returned from a Russian painting holiday Butterworth said "The country had a profound effect on this artist making his work virile and glowing."

He also lectured on the arts and offered advice to any beginners wanting to start their own art collection. In his own way, he played an extremely important role within Manchester's Art Scene.

George Gordon Byron Cooper - 1849-1933

> *"I have always thought that Manchester is an awful hole, and that if there is any place in the world which needs art in it is this city; although all my previous public exhibitions have been held in London all my interests have been centred in the North."*
>
> George Gordon Byron Cooper 6

Cooper thought the city of Manchester itself was ugly, not because the architects were bad, he thought they were a fine lot, but simply because they were not given a chance. "The town planning is all wrong," he said. "Take Italy as an example; the people love art and artists and they erect towns and villages as picturesquely as possible and that is precisely why so many artists are so fond of Italy."

"But give me England anytime. There is more variety and more beauty in the English countryside and seashore than in any country." Cooper took a great delight in painting the English countryside and its seashores, especially those of Cornwall.

On the 18th February 1928 Cooper wrote from The Birches, Bowdon, Cheshire, to Mr. Haward the Curator of The City Art Gallery thanking him for his recent letter and for the kindly interest he always took in his work.

He also thanked the members of the Art Gallery Committee for purchasing one of his watercolours "A Cornish Landscape" for their permanent collection. 7

---

6 Signed his work Byron Cooper (not Byrom as christened), see Painters in the Northern Counties of England and Wales.

7 Information taken from a file at Manchester Art Gallery.

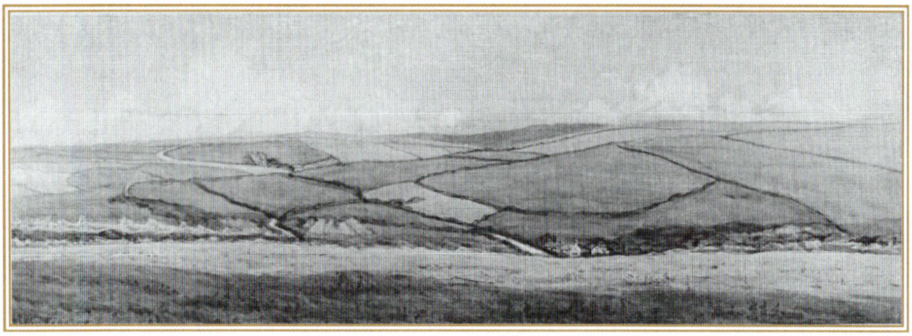

Figure 42. G. G. Byron Cooper, ***A Cornish Landscape***
Manchester Art Gallery

At Haward's request he supplied them with the following information. "A Cornish Landscape" was finished just in time for the present MAFA Exhibition. Like all my watercolour work, it is painted in pure colour without body colour or medium. The colours used were all permanent. It is not merely a sketch or memorandum but a thoroughly studied work, intended to interpret and express the thoughts and emotions experienced by the painter.

It may be of interest to here mention that I took upon prose landscape art not only as a decorative art but also as a language, its factors of expression being of course, colour, form, tone, design, composition, aerial and lineage perspective etc., and by these means thoughts and emotions can be more convincingly interpreted and expressed than by means of words.

I have not the power to describe my picture in words, but perhaps the words of the poet George Eliot will give some idea of it. She says "The time of sweet serenity, when colour glows, and the soul of visible things shows silent happiness."

Cooper had an extremely impressive successful artistic career. His pictures in oil and watercolour were chosen to represent British Art at seven great International Exhibitions at Paris, St. Louis, U.S.A., Irish, Spanish, New Zealand, the Coronation, and Franco-British. At the Paris International in 1889 his watercolour "Grange Fell" was hung in the place of honour in No 4 Gallery - The Watercolour Gallery. "I have had more works hung in the Royal Academy I believe than any Lancashire man with the exception of

R.A.'s, and on two occasions my watercolours have occupied the place of honour. My first oil picture was exhibited there in 1881." Eighteen Corporations held special "One Man" shows for him and his works were shown and purchased by the Corporations of Rochdale, Blackburn and Manchester.

The Cornish landscape provided a constant source of inspiration for Cooper during the early 1880's. One of his paintings "Godrevy Light, Cornwall," was purchased by The City Art Gallery in 1905. According to the accession card, the artist was nearly drowned in a storm at sea and only survived through the aid of a lighthouse. This event inspired the subject of the picture and the quotation which appeared on the original tablet: **"Across the moonlight water flashes the light of Man's humanity to man,"** which is a variation on the words of Burns' **"Man's inhumanity to man makes countless thousands mourn."**

Born in Manchester he became a pupil of the Rev. James McDougall at Chadderton Hall and attended the Manchester Academy of Fine Arts life classes. He then studied under two French tutors, Jules Breton and Carolus Duran. The RMI awarded him a silver medal for the best picture of early morning and he became a Council Member of the Manchester Academy of Fine Arts, 1896-99 and a member of the Athenaeum Graphic Club 1881. In his youth he was an amateur champion of athletics. [8]

His studio was at 61 South Corridor, Royal Exchange, Manchester where he held exhibitions twice a year. He was obsessed by Tennyson and eventually held an exhibition, comprising of 100 oils and watercolours centred around his hero.

The city news enlikened Cooper's painting techniques to Hardy's writing:

"Like Hardy he has watched for
the charm in the changes of day
As the cloud-colours came and went." [9]

Although he became well known for his Cornish paintings, his really exceptional and unique pieces were his so-called "mood

8 Manchester Art Gallery.
9 Manchester City News, 17th May1930.

paintings." Summed up by one art critic in the following way:
Cooper's painting is above everything else, concerned with moods. In its power of evoking a particular emotion Cooper's style is, of course, impressionist rather than photographic. He feels colour values acutely and has apparently a grand passion for blue. At any rate, the extraordinary range of his seas and skies gives the impression that he cares less for green days in forests than for blue days at sea.

Some of his pictures are studies in half tones, they catch the faint afterglow of sunset or the steely menace of lowering clouds with the same elusive mastery of technique which enables him to suggest the blue haze of wild hyacinths without painting a single flower. 10

When asked why none of his pictures contained a human figure - he said "They take up too much attention, and are not worth their place on the canvas. They are a blot on the landscape. In my earlier days I had to do a bit of portrait painting, but I soon tired of depicting old aldermen and stout mayors with gold chains. Women are more interesting to paint, but there are not many beautiful enough and of the right type for an artist."

Cooper knew his forte, and he became a celebrated painter of landscapes. He was very professional. He had many one-man-exhibitions. At the prestigious Manchester Salon Club he included several of his major pictures which had been hung at the Royal Academy and other international art exhibitions.

This exhibition was a huge success and represented the largest number of pictures ever shown in a one-man-exhibition at the Club, with over 169 pictures ranging in price from 8 guineas to 500 guineas. He remained loyal to his roots and was a highly respected member within Manchester's art circles.

Robert Crozier - 1815-1891

Thomas Letherbrow wrote a valuable biography on Crozier, depicting his artistic career as well as his working methods. 11 In 1845 Crozier studied under the artist William Bradley, and to quote

---

10 Manchester City News, 30th November 1929.

11 Thomas Letherbrow, 1891, Robert Crozier: Career as an Artist, Chap 3.

Letherbrow: It was at his hands Crozier experienced a new birth. His work underwent a complete metamorphosis. The old hard aurelia (of manner) vanished and gave place to wings.

Bradley founded his instructions in form (so far as the head and face were concerned) on that great antique, the head of Mars, which the pupil would carry on his shoulder, when he went to receive a lesson, all the way from Great Jackson Street to Strangeways. His studies from this head drawn with white chalk, were, as has been intimated, remarkable for delicacy and fine drawing. The secrets of refinement, beauty, nobility, grandeur of form, were revealed to him, the witchery and mystery of shadow and gradation; the preciousness of parsimonious light. Every feature of the head, the face, the hands, was subject to exhaustive analysis, and the standard, of primal type of form, made known.

Crozier had a lot to thank the artist William Bradley for. He had been taken under his wing and had his techniques nurtured.

Born in Blackburn in 1815 Crozier was the son of George Crozier one of the leaders of a remarkable band of working male botanists. The family left Blackburn in October 1825 for Bolton, and then in the following April they moved to Warrington where at the age of 12 he was apprenticed to William Maskery, coach painter of Winwick Street.

Through Letherbrow we find Maskery was not an easy man to work for. He was a tremendous Tory and thorough-going Church and King man. He was for three successive years warden of the parish church, a strong pillar and buttress of the establishment, a scorner of dissent (especially of the followers of Priestley) and an upholder of rigid orthodoxy. He insisted at confirmation time all his apprentices should be properly grounded in the vital principles of religion and confirmed by the bishop of the diocese.

At the same time he was a man who gave the reins to ungovernable rage, and who elevated blasphemy to the rank of a fine art. Apparently he passed through the shop like a whirlwind and knowing that a rich branch of the Crozier family were Unitarians, he would take the opportunity of cursing the orthodox boy for a condemned Unitarian scion of a female dog. Although Crozier's life was difficult at times he did gain a good deal of practical theoretical knowledge which enabled him to see how a painting could be cleaned and restored without injury. He also became skilled in the mechanical arts connected with painting and drawing.

In 1836 he moved to Manchester and settled there. He studied under a local artist, Henry Travis and two years later became a pupil at the Manchester School of Design under John Zephaniah Bell. In 1845 he studied under William Bradley and began to build up a flourishing practice principally of portraits and subject pictures of children.

At Bradley's suggestion, Crozier in 1851 opened a studio in a top room over the shop of Mrs. Mellor the bookseller in St. Ann's Street. He exhibited regularly at the R.M.I., and in London intermittently at the Royal Academy (1854-82). He was on the organising committee of the Peel Park Exhibition of the Work of Local Artists in 1857 and exhibited nineteen of his own works. The success of this exhibition led to the establishment of the Manchester Academy of Fine Arts in 1859, and Crozier's name was fourth on the list of ten artists by whom it was established. Two years later he became Literary Secretary, in 1868 Honorary Treasurer, and finally President in 1878-1890, holding this post for thirteen years up to one month before he died. He had numerous Manchester commissions including the painted Shakespearian medallions at the Theatre Royal in 1883.

Dear Old Crozier: What an oasis in the arid desert of Manchester was his studio to me in the thirsty days of my youth, when I oft panted for the waters of knowledge. Untaught, save by my own instincts; living in a city almost destitute of fine public examples of art (Etty's noble "Sirens" and the casts of the Elgin Marbles alone excepted) it was no slight blessing and privilege that such an artist as Crozier took interest enough in my feeble doings to admit me to his friendship, and make me the sharer of his cultivated tastes.

Such praise came from the pen of his very good friend Frederic Shields, [12] who was extremely grateful to Crozier for sharing so many of his techniques with him. For example Crozier had taught him to look for the bright spots of light on objects; and by using his own drawings (which began by touching in the points of light with white chalk) as examples, he showed him how much could be expressed by these alone, without any dark other than the tinted paper.

"Once" said Shields "when a drawing I had sent to old Rowbotham from Somerset, got injured in the carriage, Crozier volunteered to repair it, and I know it must have been well done, so well that I, probably, could not have discerned the injuries had I sought to do so. He had the most intense delight in getting a good picture under his hands for restoration. The conviction he had that he could penetrate its constitution, diagnose its disorder, and apply the healing remedies, made him gloat over the employment. Added to which was the pleasure he had in saving it from ignorant pretenders and quacks, who prey upon sick pictures to their utter ruin." Shields had often found his friend in reverent consultation over some cracked or darkened masterpiece with the late William Smith, of Grundy and Smith, each animated with the like aim, that of true restoration.

Crozier once showed Shields a fine, unfinished portrait of a man by Sir Joshua Reynolds the face lacking the eyes. Apparently it was Sir Joshua's admirable practice to carry the features almost to completion, securing likeness, as a sculptor did, without the eyes. Shields found this a most valuable method of procedure. He said "when at last the eyes were put in the whole face suddenly flashed into life."

Shields recorded that "he never knew a man so fitted to teach where he found a receptive mind to which he could impart his knowledge. But that he had a bitter caustic wit ever ready for the unworthy."

---

12 Thomas Letherbrow, Robert Crozier - An Artist's Tribute by Frederic Shields, Chap 1V.

J. Hey Davies - 1844-1930

Davies was born in Manchester on 11th February, 1844. He attended the Manchester School of Art under J. Muckley (1868-70). Protesting against the teaching methods practised by the school he, J. A. Hague, W. Meredith, J. H. E. Partington and R. G. Somerset left the school and enrolled as students at the Manchester Academy where they were greatly influenced by the artist J. Knight.

He attended the R.A. Schools and won the Turner Gold Medal for a painting "Under the Opening Eyelids of the Morn." Davies first exhibited at the Royal Manchester Institution in 1872 and was an Associate of the Manchester Academy of Fine Arts in 1873, a year later he became a full member. He visited Pont-Aven in 1872 with Meredith, Partington and the two Hagues exhibiting French scenes on his return. He then spent some time painting in North Wales, around the Conwy area, and in 1874 studied art in France and Sweden.

The City Art Gallery added two of Davies's paintings to their collection through a rather round about way. Its curator had visited Irlam Hall to view a statue named the Wrestlers by Molin, owned by the late George Thomas. His executors were hopeful that the Gallery might be interested in adding this statue to their collection.

On entering the hall Haward noticed one of Davies's paintings, "Late Autumn: Irlam Hall, Near Manchester" hanging over a door way.

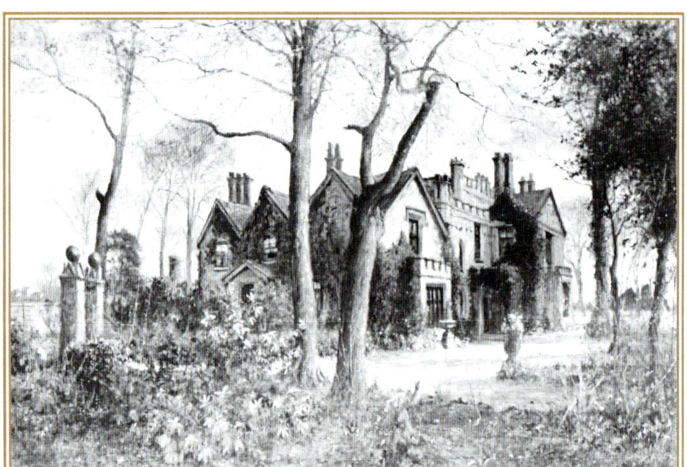

Figure 43. J. H. Davies, *Late Autumn- Irlam Hall*
Manchester Art Gallery

Declining the statue, he promptly purchased this picture along with another of Davies's paintings entitled "Stiggins Lock."

Davies was a member of the Royal Cambrian Society, a committee member of the Limners Club and a committee member of the Manchester Art Club in 1887. His address when he died was Fenwick Street, Hulme, Manchester.

John Houghton Hague - 1842-1934

Hague was born at Newton Heath on October 29th 1842 and died at his home Glencairn, Queens Road, Oldham in April 1934 at the age of ninety-one. The family moved from Newton to Oldham some time in the 60's. In 1934 he was numbered among the oldest residents of the district. His father, Samuel Hague, founded the cotton spinning business at Hawthorn and Newlands Mills later known as Messrs. Samuel Hague and Co., (1920) Ltd.. Houghton retained an interest in this business. 13

He was educated at a boarding school near Altrincham and also at the Manchester School of Art. He studied art in France during 1872, then accompanied by four other artists, he stayed for four months at Pont-Aven near Concarneau. On returning to Oldham he became master at the Oldham School of Art and was associated with, Charles Potter, R. O. Bottomley and Tom Heywood. Amongst his pupils were Fred Jackson, William Stott and George Wimpenny. The school was demolished in 1878.

A past Gallery Oldham catalogue 14 states: **His paintings form an immaculate record of people and places of Chadderton.** 15 **He first exhibited at the Royal Academy in 1875 with a picture named "The Chadderton Taxidermist," also known as "Owd Jesse, the Chadderton Miser," "The Ornithologist" and "The Naturalist." It is one of a great number depicting old Chadderton. Owd Jess was known as the Chadderton Hermit because of his eccentric nature. Born in 1799 he used to dress**

---

13 Oldham Chronicle, April 14th 1934, Mr J. Houghton Hague: Death at Age of Ninety-Two.

14 The Oldham Collection, Later Oldham Artists, Nov 1990 – October 1991.

15 The Gallery Oldham has in its archives a collection of dialect poems, songs and works transcribed by Hague.

up in early period costume much to the amusement of the visitors to his "Hermitage Museum." The Museum shown in "The Chadderton Taxidermist" was full of exotic stuffed birds and animals. Tetlow charged a copper to visit the house, which still stands at Heald's Green, Chadderton Fold. The collection was sold in 1892, and Tetlow died in December 1894.

Hague's works are precious pieces of social history. In one of his paintings named the "Oldham Street Sweepers" (1873) he beautifully captures Oldham's cobbled Market Place being swept clean by a gang of street sweepers.

For the powers that be it was a full time occupation trying to keep Oldham's streets and its popular cobbled Market Place clean.

Donald Thomas writes: [16] **Henry Mayhew made a careful analysis of "Food Consumed by and Excretions of a Horse in Twenty-Four Hours." He weighed the animal's food and excreta "in their fresh state," and tabulated the figures to the last ounce. He calculated that each horse deposited over forty pounds of dung a day in London's streets, a ton in less than two months. Multiplied by the tens of thousands of working horses in a city crossed by 150,000 vehicles a day, this posed a formidable problem of health and civic cleanliness.** [17]

Of course the figures for Oldham would be far smaller, but even so, it was still a huge problem trying to keep the town free from all kinds of debris.

---

16 Donald Thomas The Victorian Underworld.

17 Henry Mayhew , London Labour and the London Poor.

Here Hague's painting portrays six men sweeping the cobbles clean in Oldham's Market Place.

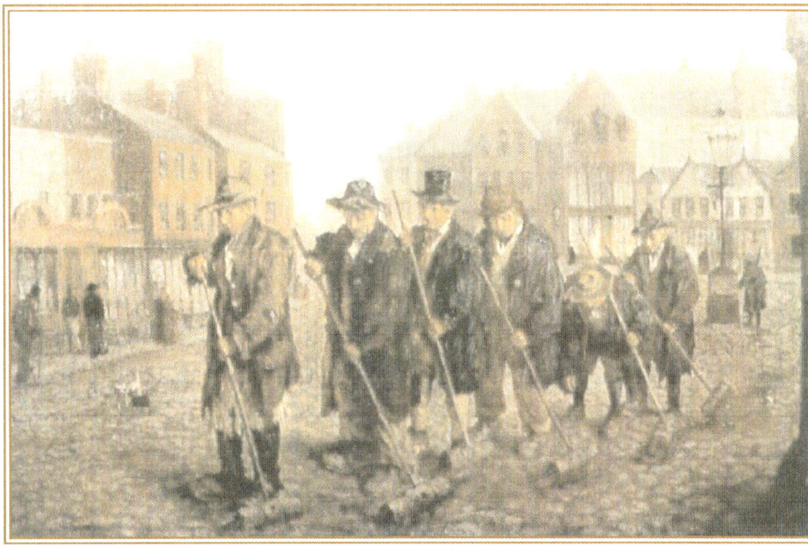

Figure 44. John Houghton Hague, *Oldham Street Sweepers*
Gallery Oldham

Their garb is shown in different degrees of shabbiness and helps to expose their lowly way of life. The third man from the front stands out a little with his black top hat and seems to echo the man walking on the pavement to his right. Had he too once walked along the pavement with no worries and money in his pocket? The fifth man stoops to pick something up the others have missed. They walk along sweeping the cobbles in right handed unison almost like a conveyor belt, whilst two scrappy looking dogs play along side them. The architecture and the glass fronted shops all add to this picture's heritage. It is a real gem.

Stephen Whittle [18] states: **The market square was the centre of activity in the town, staying open until 11p.m. on Friday and Saturday nights after the mills closed. The drinking fountain visible on the right of the painting was provided in 1859 by the**

18 Stephen Whittle, Museum & Gallery Manager, Gallery Oldham.

Oldham Industrial or King Street Co-operative Society. There were 400 old age paupers in the town in 1870 and 250 to 300 vagrants staying at the Workhouse each night, most of whom were put to work the following day stone-breaking, scrubbing floors etc.. More than likely some of these would be employed as street sweepers.

For many years Hague was an active member of the Antiquarian Society, and was also keenly interested in the work of the Oldham Microscopical Society. He had an unbroken membership of the Oldham Lyceum extending over 62 years, having joined in 1872. He was also a keen member of the Oldham Football Club and attended their matches for over forty years. He was enthusiastic about old lore and extremely interested in natural history.

In company with his friend, R. O. Bottomley, he did much work in and around Chadderton Fold, which in the seventies was a delightful old-world village, with a stream and rustic bridge and quaint cottages. He was to be seen there frequently between 1870 and 1880, and got much of the groundwork for his picture illustrating the works of Edwin Waugh, Ben Brierley and Samuel Laycock. He also painted in Belgium and Sweden and was a member of the Belgium Academy of Fine Arts. [19]

He was a great story teller. One of his favourites was a train ride: **I remember once travelling by railway with my father from Manchester to Patricroft. We had to stand up in open wagons and when we came to a public house near the railway line the train stopped. Waiters came out of the public house with trays loaded with ale and whisky and they went along the train selling drinks and collecting the empty glasses and tankards before the train started off again.** [20]

---

19 Oldham Art Gallery, Oldham Art and Artists represented in the Public Gallery.

20 Oldham Standard, August 25th 1933, In Other Days- Oldham Man Of 91 Looks Back.

Records [21] show in 1870 Hague had spent some time painting in Conwy with his artist friend Elias Bancroft. He fell in love with the North Wales landscape and over the years made many painting trips to this area. After 1885 he would make them with his wife Ada and then eventually with Ada and their daughter Nellie who was born March 19th 1888. Houghton wrote in his Holiday Book: 1885 Honeymoon, stayed in London at the Arundel Hotel, the Strand, from April 15th to 22nd and then crossed over to Rouen for a week and finally Antwerp for a further week.

With reference to his painting in Conwy in 1884 the Manchester Examiner and Times critic wrote: Mr. Houghton Hague has contributed better work than he has shown for a long time. He has abandoned the smoke of Lancashire for the sunshine and freshness of the Conway Valley and the result is seen in a new accession of light and colour and brilliancy to his canvas." [22]

In this same year he painted in Northern Ireland, and sailed from Liverpool around Scotland to Edinburgh. His Holiday Book is a valuable piece of history and goes to prove just how much time and effort Houghton put into his painting trips. He was always fond of his roots and before his death he was the last remaining original member of the Manchester Academy of Fine Arts.

Joshua Anderson Hague - 1850-1916

"He never seems to be up in the middle of the day." [23]

This is the sort of press Hague received and would keep on receiving for many years. Yet he played such an important role within Manchester's Art Scene. He was once described as the father of the Manchester School of "tone" painting.

---

21 Holiday Book of John Houghton Hague, Gallery Oldham, 1987 c/o Mr & Mrs Susman.
22 Manchester Examiner & Times, 19th February 1884.
23 City News, 1873.

Born in Rusholme his first school was Birch and later Withington. At sixteen he went to the School of Art in Cavendish Street and was much appreciated by its head, Mr. Muckley. He became an excellent draughtsman and won a number of prizes. One prize was a silver medal awarded for a still life study of a gold casket.

Hague's first professional works were studies of street Arabs. Here he had a captive audience. Street Arabs were young boys who during the day had time on their hands and played about the back alleys of the city. Night time was altogether different, they would set to work selling their News or Mail.

His painting techniques changed over night after he visited a local "Corot" Exhibition. This French artist had a terrific influence on him and Hague decided this was definitely the way forward and how he would paint in the future.

Leaving the busy city with its crowded alleys he and his artist friend, R. G. Somerset went into the fields and lanes to paint. Here the air was hypnotic and sweet and time seemed to stand still. Intoxicated by this atmosphere they decided to go and paint in Pont-Aven, Brittany.

Here they found the ambience they had been longing for. They found themselves in the closest sympathy with the French artists and their techniques and when work was over for the day the evening talks put fresh thoughts and ideas into their enthusiastic and receptive minds.

On leaving Brittany Hague went to live at Crossens near Southport, and here the cottages and lanes, with low undulating grey distance, gave him material for many excellent pictures, and where the influence of his French break came to the full.

The art critic Maxwell Enoch wrote: **He now painted with a delightful and delicate greyness, and gradually becoming stronger in colour and more dexterous in handling, commencing to paint in a manner that was absolutely his own, or "himself" as painters say - there is no landscape painter at present working in England who shows so much individuality in his work. The most simple subjects he is able to invest with a beauty and tone that is delightful.** [24]

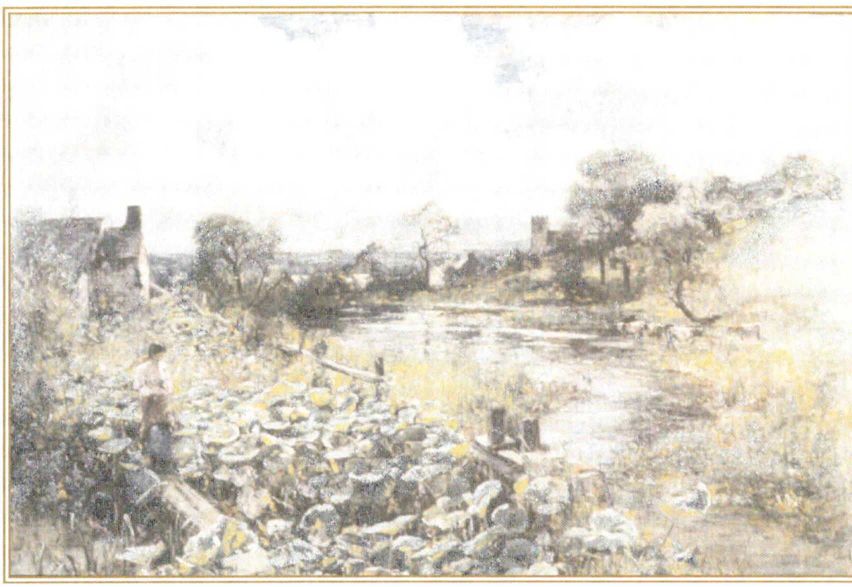

Figure 45. Joshua Anderson Hague, *Spring*
Manchester Art Gallery

Hague often exhibited at the Royal Manchester Institution. In 1873 he became a full member of the Manchester Academy in which he played an extremely active business role for forty three years. In 1889 He had a one man exhibition at the Brasenose Club. Forty five of his paintings were in a retrospective show at Manchester City Art Gallery in 1908.

He also exhibited at the Royal Academy, and was awarded the Silver Medal at the International Exhibition in Paris.

24 Manchester Herald Aug-Sept 1899, Anderson Hague by Maxwell Bennoch.

Hague was one of the group of young Manchester School painters, who gathered at Joseph Knight's studio on Friday and Saturday evenings (1870-72). His picture at the Royal Academy entitled "Bathers" attracted the notice of the artists Watts and Burne Jones, and he showed again at the Academy in 1874 and 1876. He had a number of sponsors, W. E. Hamer, C. J. Galloway, Sam Barlow and William Caver.

In 1875 the group had an exhibition with the London dealer, Durand Ruel. Hague had two works on display. One named, "Moorland Scene" was described as: "an eminently political study, exquisite in its sentiment, and thoroughly harmonious in its parts," and was purchased as soon as it was seen by Don Jose de Murietta, a collector of noted taste. He furthered his reputation in London by showing at the New English Art Club, where his pictures were received with great appreciation.

It is quite astonishing how his work, over the years, actually fits into three distinct categories. His first and probably most well known, grey green, Corot like period lasted around four years, 1876-1880. One critic wrote: **We fear that Mr. Hague is crippled by convention. Perchance his eye for colour has offended him and he has plucked it out, but if he would dare to be himself he has the ability to do good work. A wise man has said "that imitation is suicide." Insist on yourself; never imitate. Your own gift you can present every moment with the cumulative force of a whole life's cultivation; but of the adopted talent of another you have only an extemporaneous half possession.**

With reference to Anderson Hague - Why should nature be looked at through a smoked glass? And then, as to choice of subject and mode of treatment. Art is capable of being didactic, but the painter misses his purpose if, by his method of presenting his lesson, he repels and disgusts. This Mr. Hague does in 'Hard Times'. The ticket upon it leads us to hope that it never may be finished. There are several members of the Academy who delight apparently, in painting poverty, gloom

and desolation, squalid abodes, dirty and penury - smitten neighbourhoods. [25]

He then changed his technique and subject matter, still keeping with his grey tones, he introduced some colour making his paintings warmer. He concentrated upon his colours continually building them up, so that in 1876 one critic wrote: Mr. Hague may be regarded as the English representative of a school which goes in Paris by the title of the Impressionalisties. He does not affect to present the full reality of nature: he does not lay claim to the credit due to a patient interpretation of detail. What he seeks is merely to record the relation of things in nature, and to reduce the variety of incident which an actual scene possess to a brief and general expression represented by balanced masses of colour. Thus in the large landscape with a willow tree over hanging a silent pool there is no pretence of exact local colouring in any part of the composition. [26]

In 1884 the critic for the Manchester Examiner and Times wrote: Anderson Hague still shows increased strength. His Hayfield at Tywyn, of which a water colour drawing was exhibited in the Autumn Exhibition is a work of very high quality. The sky is beautifully painted, atmospheric and breezy, and the clouds seem full of movement and coming rain. The landscape and figures are in entire harmony, and the execution is satisfactory throughout. The sky is beautifully painted, atmospheric and breezy, and the clouds seem full of movement and coming rain.

By the late 1880's Hague had achieved a brilliancy of tone, and his paintings had changed completely over a matter of ten years.

Hague married Sarah Henshall of Heaton Norris in 1875, and they had four sons and two daughters. One of his sons, Anderson (Dick) Hague exhibited at the RA, RCA, MAFA and Walker Art Gallery. They left their home in Heaton Lane, Stockport in 1877 and went to live in Tywyn, near Conwy in North Wales. Here Hague founded, with Edward Norbury, at Plas Mawr, the Royal Cambrian Academy in 1881 and became its Vice President. In 1889

---

25 City News, 15th February 1879.

26 Manchester Guardian, 1876, Mr Anderson Hague's Two Sad and Sombre Impressions of Nature.

he moved to Deganwy where he spent the rest of his life. He still kept his ties with Manchester, his friends would go and stay with him and they would have wonderful musical evenings.

Frederick W. Jackson - 1859-1918

"The chief merits of F. Jackson's work were: fresh, pure, beautiful colour and a vivid interpretation of open-air life."

Walter Butterworth. 27

A former student of Jackson, Laura Knight, recounted how: **He would frequently work in cold and very exposed places in order to paint scenes from nature as they happened. He would paint out of doors in any weather. Under the mittens he wore his hands were swollen, stiff and chapped, as were the edges of his ears and the wings of his nostrils. His commitment to working out of doors eventually affected his health, particularly following his painting trip to Russia in 1914."** 28

Painting at many degrees below zero in Russia may have affected Jackson's health, but at the same time it seemed to work some kind of magic upon him. His travelling companion, Walter Butterworth, said "Russia had a profound effect on Jackson he brought virile, glowing work back with him and added to his store of knowledge, energy and enthusiasm. From that time there was an added dash and boldness in his style." 29 He must have been extremely brave and totally resolute in visiting this somewhat hostile country to paint; since the authorities were not too willing to help him. In fact they considered him a great nuisance.

Jackson was fiercely proud of his Lancashire roots. He was not just a landscape painter. He was also a genre and portrait painter, designer and illustrator.

---

27 City News, March 2nd 1918.

28 Peter Phillips, 1993, The Staithes Group, (Oldham Art Gallery)

29 Manchester Evening News, 2nd March 1918, in Rochdale Art Gallery Catalogue, 1978, F. W. Jackson 1859-1918, by Michael Cross.

As an illustrator he produced a number of drawings for the well known dialect writer Ben Brierley's [30] "Ab-o'th-Yate" Sketches. One of his sketches "The Hand-Loom Weaver" appears as the Frontispiece for Vol.111.

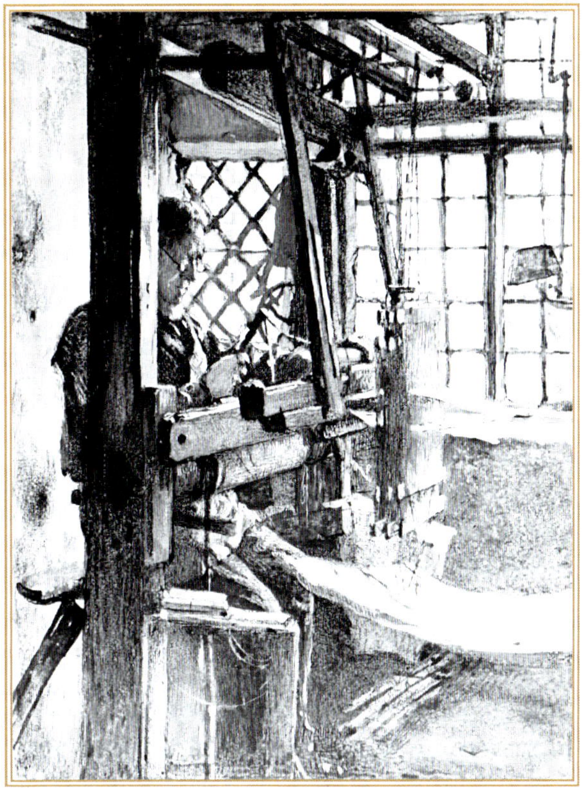

Figure 46. F. W. Jackson, *The Hand-Loom Weaver*
Manchester Art Gallery.

It portrays one man sat weaving at his loom with daylight streaming in from a large leaded window. This is such a valuable piece of art history - superbly depicting the worker's loom in minute detail. James Dronsfield [31] writes: Many of Brierley's characters were drawn from the old hand-loom weavers of the neighbourhood a class of honest hard working men to which he

30 Ben Brierley (1825-1896) A Lancashire writer and expert on the Lancashire dialect.
31 All information on Ben Brierley has been taken from - James Dronsfield, 1896, Ab-o'th-Yates, Sketches by Ben Brierley (Oldham: W.E. Clegg).

himself belonged. Having been born and reared amongst the rattle of shuttles and buzzing of bobbin wheels he had every opportunity of studying the weavers' characteristics.

"Ab-o'th-Yate" was a mythical character of the author's own creation, and when he was asked who "Ab-o'th'-Yate" really was? He answered "that he was as anxious to know as his readers, and was often at a loss to distinguish in his own works what to believe."

The following appears in the preface of "Ab-o'th'-Yate Sketches: **The illustrating of the three volumes has been entrusted to Mr. Fred W. Jackson, whose intimate acquaintance with Lancashire Life in the districts from whence the author found most of his material has been of much service in finding and drawing characters suitable to the text. Mr. Jackson has drawn nine good pictures, all of which have been most carefully reproduced by the "Collotype" process, and add considerably to the interest of this edition.**

Born at Middleton Junction, Oldham in 1859 he was the son of an art dealer and photographer. His brother, Charles Jackson was also an art dealer in Police Street, Manchester. After school he went to evening classes at the Oldham Lyceum where John Houghton Hague was one of the teachers, and when the school was demolished he transferred to the Manchester School of Art where he attended life classes for six months. He also learnt a little from J. D. Watson and Mark Fisher.

Jackson said "Nature was his greatest teacher." The free fields, the open sky, the wandering waste of pearly foam creaming beneath the Yorkshire cliffs were halcyon to him. He was adamant that his artistic talent all came down to "the art of seeing," and that seeing required just as much study for the understanding of art as did that of hearing for the appreciation of music. In his opinion artists were seldom taught in the art schools to see correctly.

It was at Whitby in the late seventies early eighties Jackson came under the influence of Anderson Hague, a member of the Manchester School. A critic made the following remark: **Jackson certainly belonged to the school, although he did not join in until after they had passed through the Valley of the Shadow, and so escaped the imputation of blackness. Jackson came to work alongside Anderson Hague after he had struggled out into**

the daylight, so to speak, and his triumph tonality scaled up to God's own sunshine. 32

He first exhibited at the Royal Academy in 1880, and was a frequent exhibitor at the Manchester Academy of Fine Arts and Yorkshire Union of Artists. He was a member of the Arts Club in 1879, the Limners Club in 1880 and the Manchester Academy of Fine Arts 1881. He was a founder member of the Staithes Group and Art Club. He was also a founder member of the New English Art Club in 1886 and later in 1894 was elected to the RBA. Whilst in Paris he enrolled as a student at the Academie Julian under the tutors, Lefebvre and Boulanger, and in 1884 and 1885 he was accepted at the Paris Salon. He would meet up with his artist friends William and Edward Stott, La Thangue and James Charles who were also studying in Paris.

Jackson travelled at length, painting in Russia, North Africa and various parts of Europe. After a spell of painting in Italy one critic wrote: **Mr. F. W. Jackson - most conspicuous and largest exhibitor who, by rapid strokes, has in a very few years emerged from the dull depths of the school into what seems to be his natural element, the brilliant effulgence that blazes from Italian skies.**

Mr. Jackson's productions give undoubted tone and character to the exhibition, so strongly and freely painted, laid in with such assurance and knowledge, that they might be the outcome of a veteran experience. 33

He finally settled in Hinderwell marrying a local girl in 1907. They bought a place called Ivy Cottage, and Jackson had a huge wooden studio built at the back where he worked and received his fellow painters. He died in Middleton on the 25th February 1918, in his fifty-ninth year. Soon after his death, in December 1918, a large Memorial Exhibition was held at the Manchester City Art Gallery, and a letter of appreciation of his life and work, by Sir George Clausen was read out at the Opening Ceremony. 34

---

32 City News, 2nd March 1918.

33 F. W. Jackson on Seeing, Manchester Guardian, November 21st 1907.

34 Peter Phillips, 1993, The Staithes Group Oldham Art Gallery.

Joseph Knight - 1837-1909

This Manchester born artist was a landscape, genre painter, mezzotint engraver and etcher. At the age of seven he had a tragic accident with a machine, losing an arm in the process. He left school at thirteen, learned to paint and became a professional photographer. For forty years he was a member of the Manchester Academy of Fine Arts and served on its Council. Joining in 1868 he withdrew in 1879 and was re-elected in 1883: Mr. Joseph Knight after a lapse of years has resumed his membership of the local Academy in such his principles and his example have never ceased to be a power.

It is now many years since the appearance of Mr. Knight's early works shocked the sense of propriety amongst the class of art critics whose ideas were all regulated by traditions based on a weakly and quite artificial method of landscape painting. [35]

Within Manchester's art circles he was known as the founder member of the Manchester School of painters. He certainly had a huge influence on these young artists. In 1859 he married Elizabeth Radford of Manchester. He moved to London in 1871 for a spell and then finally settled permanently in North Wales. He was always drawn to North Wales and its beautiful landscape, but he also painted further a field in France, Holland and Italy.

Elias Bancroft one of his oldest friends and fellow artist wrote about Knight in the following way: He set up as a professional photographer in Market Street, Manchester, and it was there he began to paint street Arabs. Henry Crowley, [36] a man of means and a generous lover of art, saw him at work and when he asked Knight "whether he liked painting?" the young artist replied, "yes, I wish I could stick to it." "Do so and I will help you." This was done, and Mr. Knight went for a time to Deganwy."

During the sixties Knight lived and worked in a succession of places, Upper Moss Lane, Union Street (Ardwick), South King Street, Walmer Place and finally in York Place, behind the

35 Manchester Examiner & Times, 19th February 1884.

36 Henry Crowley helped Knight and became an important patron.

Union Chapel in Oxford Road. It was at York Place he and the members of the Manchester School would paint and socialise.

He returned to London for a time and then finally settled down at Bryn Glas, near Conwy. During the time that our life classes were held at the Royal Institution building in Mosley Street, now the City Art Gallery, Mr. Knight was a constant and vital member – a devoted worker himself and a source of inspiration to his fellows. After his removal to London we missed his stimulating influence, and this told upon the classes. To our Spring Exhibition he was a regular contributor to the end with but a slight break. [37]

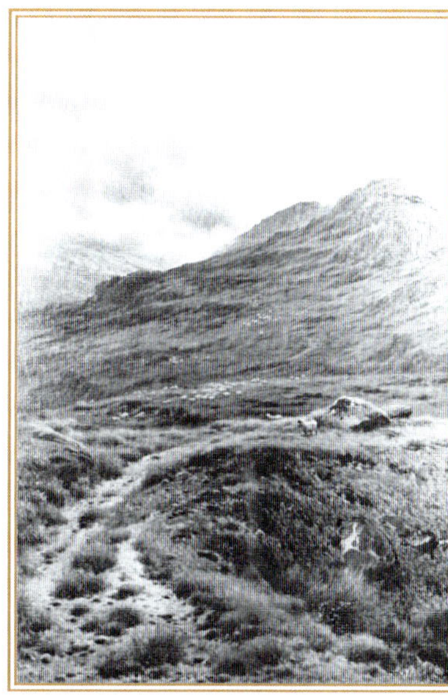

Figure 47. Joseph Knight, ***Lifting Mists***
Manchester Art Gallery

A writer for the City News wanted to add just a little more to what he described as "Mr. Bancroft's homely narrative - so interesting for its intimate knowledge both of the artist and friend." He desired to comment on Mr. Knight's temperament and its influence upon his work: You may discern it in "Lifting Mists" in our own permanent collection at Mosely Street.

Mr. Knight's moods were embodied in his landscapes. He imparted to them a feeling of gloom. Some times the mood is a quiet half-pleasant melancholy, but generally there is a sadness about the work. At his best an indefinable charm is never absent.

Mr. Knight painted from his heart, it may be averred, and so his message goes straight home to those who have eyes to see and heart to feel. This it is that has made him so widely esteemed.

---

37 City News, January 9th 1909, Manchester's Artist's Career: The Late Joseph Knight.

Knight was elected a member of the Dudley Gallery, the Royal Institute of Water Colour Painters, the Royal Etchers, the Royal Cambrian Academy, Limners Club and Art-Min-Afon, Betws-y-Coed. At the Royal Academy his works were frequently hung on the line. His work is in their permanent collection as well as the Victoria & Albert, the Tate Gallery, The Manchester City Art Gallery, Walker Art Gallery, Liverpool and other provincial galleries. In 1874 he was a RMI prize-winner, and in 1891 he won a bronze medal at the Paris Exhibition.

The Manchester Courier wrote: **As a painter he had almost a magical power of investing an oft-treated subject with new beauty, or with a touch of solemnity and mystery that revealed unsuspected resources. Of evening with its melancholy' of mountain grandeur softened by the play of subdued light, of wide sweeping estuaries yielding far-reaching, lovely vistas, of moonlight and dawn, he knew the secret, and he was able to interpret it to his fellow-men.**

His chief guerdon was joy in his art and the knowledge that it was appreciated by an ever growing circle of admirers.

William Meredith - 1851-1916

Meredith was described as a thorough Bohemian and most entertaining conversationalist. He went on to be well known for his black and white pictures. His work was much after the style of George Sheffield and some thought that he even excelled his old master.

This Manchester born artist [38] at the age of twelve attended evening classes at the School of Art in the Royal Institution and then entered the Manchester Academy where he was elected a Sociate in 1872 and a Member two years later. Here he made friends with a number of the younger artists, enjoying their company and admiring their techniques so much so he became a member of the Manchester School of Painters. He was also a member of the Brasenose Club.

His subjects, mainly seaside and country landscapes were

38 Information: Momus, March 10 1881, W. Meredith.

graceful, well balanced, often on a large scale and entirely painted out-of-doors. North Wales, Surrey, Brittany and Normandy were his favourites.

His work went through strongly marked phases. At first sketches, in which grey overhung low-toned landscapes. These were succeeded by oil paintings with heavy impasto in which greenish skies and dense masses of immense foliage were the most characteristic features. Next came a time of brilliant light, and the use of brighter colour throughout his work. Most of his Normandy studies belong to this period.

He had been accused of being almost contemptuously regardless of detail by some critics and that he contented himself with fidelity to the general aspects of a scene, sacrificing much to breadth of effect. This was highly disputed by an art critic for Momus, who had been to an exhibition at the Manchester Academy, and using one of Meredith's paintings: "Tramps On The Portsmouth Road" as an example, declared "this painting was living proof that Meredith could paint details with accuracy, and without detriment to the more important qualities of a picture."

The truth was Meredith had his own particular views on his landscape art and was full of faith in his principles of art and was uncompromising in rejecting all traditions which he regarded as detracting from the truth of landscape. He knew exactly what he was doing and would not be harassed by the Manchester press.

Momus's critic allows us an insight into Meredith's character:

He was enviously boyish in the possession of inexhaustible animal spirits. He sings a good song to his own accompaniment; he tells a good story; he is a wonderful mimic, and generous to a fault. No one will begrudge his bright and prosperous future, for success will not spoil him. He is free from the two great hindrances to development - self conceit and self contemplation.

Throughout his artistic career Meredith receive a good number of conflicting press reports. Ironically, this did not stop when he died. There were two totally conflicting reports on his death in 1916. The Manchester City News [39] stated: The funeral took place on Tuesday

39 Manchester City News, February 8th 1916, Mr. William Meredith.

at the Southern Cemetery, and was attended by many of Mr. Meredith's friends. Whereas the Manchester Evening News [40] stated: **Late in December, Meredith who had been in needy circumstances for some time, entered a local hospital, and it was there that his death occurred a few days ago. He had, apparently, no relatives or friends, and the funeral has been deferred in order that some endeavour might be made to save a talented artist from a pauper's grave.**

William Percy - 1820-1903

Percy was a native of Manchester. He died in Ashton on Mersey in 1903. He started his artistic career at a very early age, exhibiting his first picture in the Autumn Exhibition of the Royal Institution 1833. Three years later he went to London as pupil and assistant to William Bradley who then enjoyed a wide reputation as a portrait painter. He remained in London until 1839 and then returned to his family home.

The following are a chosen few of Percy's artistic recollections: **As a lad I began by painting my father and mother at home. Then there was the excise man, a quaint looking old man - I painted him - painted market people in Shudehill at seven o'clock in the morning. Here is an example for rising - early rising - young artists.**

I used to buy my colours, grind them, burn them - umber, sienna, ochre - and they would dry and use well. I put them into bladders squeezing the moisture out. This was before Rand's tubes were invented. Some times the bladders would burst, and there would be an awful mess.

Aged fourteen I painted Mr. Titley's portrait, a plumber and glazier whose place was opposite the Crown Inn, where artists sometimes resort - I exhibited this painting –"Portrait of a Gentleman." A man looked at it, referred to his catalogue and remarked "Portrait of a Gentleman! Looks a d----d sight more

40 Manchester Evening News, January 28th 1916, Manchester Artist's Death.

like old Titley" and passed on. After that I gave the names of my sitters.

At sixteen I went to London outside the coach, Peveril of the Peak. There was a strap put over us to keep us on the coach. We left Manchester at ten o'clock in the morning and reached the Saracen's Head, Snow Hill at ten o'clock next morning. I became a pupil of William Bradley. He usually charged one hundred guineas for training a pupil. I wrote to my father asking him to send the money, and he replied that he could not whereupon Bradley said that he would take me without a premium if my father would pay for my lodgings. My father was not able to do this, so Bradley took me as a pupil without premium and paid the cost of my living as well.

When I left Bradley I came to Manchester took a garret in King Street and turned it into a studio. There I painted portraits, landscape, or anything that came in my way. I got a commission to paint Landseer's "Hawking in the Olden Times." I procured an engraving, drew it in, then for colour went to the painting, which was being exhibited in Manchester. I received fifteen guineas for my copy.

Percy was a founder member of the Manchester Academy.

The old Manchester Academy had its premises in St. Ann's Street. We got into debt to the extent of about £200, and at a meeting we held it was decided that in order to liquidate the debt every member must paint a picture and sell it, if possible - £5 of the sum received and ten per cent of the remainder-if any-to go to the liquidation fund. I painted two Italian organ grinders – one old and one young. I posed them and painted them under a strong Italian sunlight, derived from the gas overhead and painted a landscape background, with sunny effect. To our soldier models we usually paid eighteen pence for the first hour, and one shilling for each succeeding hour. The picture was bought at the sale by auction by Mr. John Hick of Bolton for fifteen guineas. [41]

41 William Percy, Recollections of a Manchester Artist, City News, 12th October 1895.

He was also a member of the Manchester Literary Club, and Limners' Club for many years.

Richard Gay Somerset - 1848-1928

"Art does not consist in recording the phenomenal, but in interpreting the beautiful, and as far as in him lies that is what he tries to do."

R. G. Somerset.

Described as a delicate and sensitive youth, and a well known classical scholar, Somerset was the son of the sub-editor and sometimes art critic of the old Manchester Courier. He was educated at the Manchester School of Art, studying under Mr. Buckley. He left in the company of Anderson Hague, J Partington, J. H. Davies, Elias Bancroft and F. A. Winkfield. He and Anderson Hague had known each other since their school days and naturally started to paint together.

They were much impressed and influenced by the works of the French painter, Corot. This resulted in a period of painting in low tones with grey greens as the dominant note. In 1872 J. H. Davies joined them and together they made a number of trips to Brittany. [42] All three worked in a similar way, and with each expedition their work became brighter.

Somerset enjoyed travelling and he made over sixteen trips up and down the Mediterranean in coasting steamers, and had a strong knowledge of the countless number of ports on both sides of the sea. On his journeys he preferred to paint subjects with an archaeological interest.

He was an eminent member of the Manchester School of Painters, an original member of the Royal Cambrian Academy becoming its vice-president in 1919, and one of the oldest members of the Manchester Academy of Fine Arts, which said of him: **There is no one better deserving of recognition than Mr. R. G. Somerset. For something like a quarter of a century he has been a strenuous and consistent contributor, sending us the best work that it is in him to do; and his healthy, breezy, essentially**

42 See Chapter 8.

manly outlook on the simple facts of country life, imparts an air of personal friendliness, so to speak to his pictures. 43

When reporting on the R.M.I's exhibition on Modern Art the Courier's critic 44 proclaimed it was the work of R. G. Somerset which was the most prominent and important work on show in the landscape art section: His fine landscape representing a view near Milford in Surrey is one of the most complete and satisfactory landscapes in the collection.

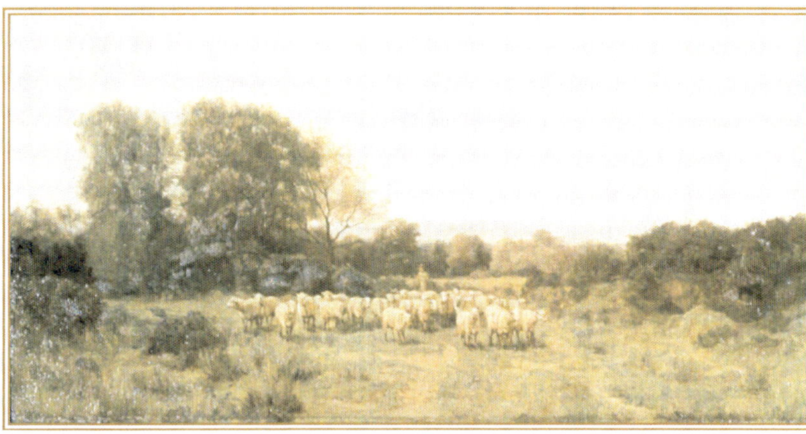

Figure 48. Richard Gay Somerset, *A Surrey Pastoral*
Manchester Art Gallery

It is remarkable for its agreeable tone and rich pearly quality of colour; some passages are remarkably fine, such as the middle distance, the tree work on the left of the canvas, and the beautiful turflike quality of the foreground.

The whole canvas is full of light and atmosphere, and the general result in the picture is highly satisfactory and full of bright promise for the future.

W. Maxwell Reekie 45 questioned whether there was within the four walls of the Manchester Academy of Fine Arts a more modest and unassuming man than Richard Gay Somerset. He declared: In

43 Pictures at the Academy of Art, Manchester City News, January, 1897.
44 Courier, October 16th 1877.
45 W. Maxwell Reekie, 1920 MAFA Cuttings Book, 1V-R.G. Somerset.

the ranks of pure landscape painters R. G. Somerset had attained a high place, but not without long and careful study and much searching among the hidden secrets of Nature.

On his eightieth birthday Somerset reflected on the changes that had taken place during his eighty years and declared he was full of joy to note the improvements socially, morally and intellectually taking place around him. It is invariably those who have failed to make the best of the present who lament over those good-old times. For myself I am glad they are left behind for I know the difference between then and now.

There are more schools, institutions and facilities for improvement. There is less crime and poverty today than formerly. I remember when the courts used to sit until four and five o'clock , and often after, with a population half its present size. Now with a population of 750,000, it rarely sits after two o'clock. Does this not speak for itself?

I am an incurable optimist. Croakers of the present day who are continually calling it bad make me wish for their own personal enlightenment that they could have a taste of the conditions of life that existed when I was a boy. [46]

He died at the age of eighty one, and had been painting in the open air up to two months before his death.

Henry Clarence Whaite - 1828-1912

When Whaite decided to give up his studio in London at the age of eighty two a sale was held at Willis's Rooms. Here more that one hundred and twenty pictures representing his art in many of its periods and phases was sold.

En masse these paintings made a spectacular splash of colour. What a treat, here were some of his finest Welsh landscapes and delicate watercolour drawings beautifully set out for all to see. The sale included some of his most excellent exhibition pictures, many of which had already been seen in Manchester where Whaite was very well known and highly respected as a professional artist. The highest price of the sale, £210 was given for his large picture "The Strength of the Hills," an excellent example of his handling of the

46 Manchester City News, Obituary, December, 1928.

rocks of his well loved North Wales. Apparently the Chancellor of the Exchequer, who was an early visitor to the showroom, bought several of Mr. Whaite's pictures and so too, Judge Parry. 47

"He is a cheery old boy, bright eyed, and hopeful in his outlook on life, and still full to the brim with love and enthusiasm for his appointed mission - painting nature." 48

This was a description of Whaite when he was eighty years old and the president of the Manchester Academy of Fine Arts. From the beginning of his career as an artist Whaite had been a constant and close student of nature, and for years lived almost out of doors, spending the whole of the winter painting in a hut which he was able to move about from place to place on the hills.

Whaite was a native of Manchester born in Bridge Street, Deansgate on 27th January 1828. 49 His father, Henry Whaite established in the same street a fancy bazaar which included artistic productions. He founded the annual German Fair on these premises.

Educated at the Manchester Grammar School he received his artistic education at the Manchester School of Art, then housed in the Old Assembly Rooms in Brown Street and afterwards in the rooms of the Royal Institution. His tutors were Mr. Zephaniah Bell and Mr. J. A. Hammersley.

He left Manchester for London with a view to becoming a decorative painter. First he attended Leigh's School in Newman Street, and then the Schools of the Royal Academy. On his return to Manchester he was brimming with enthusiasm and offered gratuitously to decorate the Reception Rooms of the new Town Hall. His offer was not accepted. It must have been a sickening blow, and it certainly made him think twice about a career in decorative painting. On account of ill health he went to stay in Switzerland in the company of Mr. Hammersley. Here he fell in love with the scenery and moved over to the ranks of the landscape painters.

---

47 Guardian, 13th January, 1911.

48 Manchester City News, January 1980.

49 Biography taken from: Manchester City News, January 1980, Fifty Years of Art in the City.

He won the Heywood silver medal in 1851, and two gold Heywood medals in 1862 and 1882 (these were awarded by the Council of the Royal Manchester Institution.) Whaite exhibited regularly at the Manchester Royal Institution and never missed an exhibition after his first picture was hung there. Whaite was one of the first members of the Manchester Academy of Fine Arts and in due course became its president. He was also the President of the Royal Cambrian Academy and a member of the Royal Water Colour Society.

Whaite had an intense feeling for subtle effects of light and colour and greatly admired Turner, spending hours studying his pictures in the National Gallery. In the same way Turner had, he loved to present his landscape under striking if not unusual conditions.

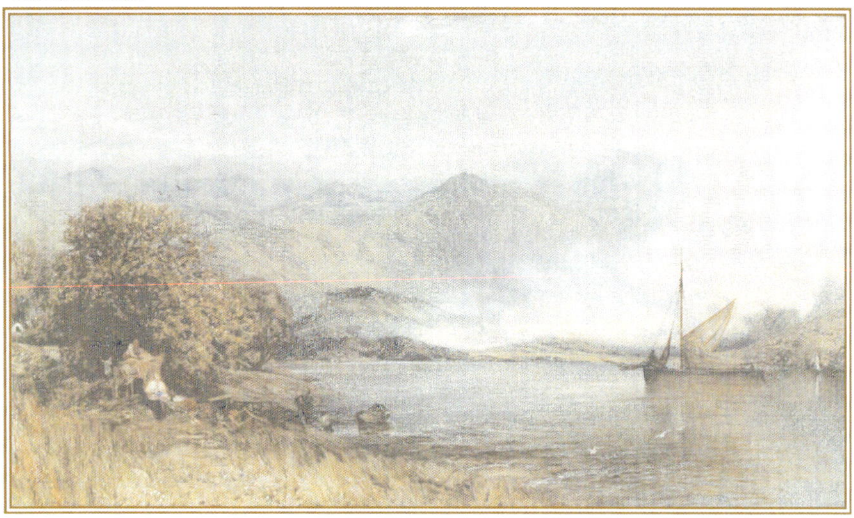

Figure 49. Clarence Whaite, *Just Arrived By The Sloop In Conway Valley, North Wales*
Manchester Art Gallery

One critic [50] wrote of Whaite: **He sometimes attempted more than art could compass, that he endeavoured to express in one picture so much thought and emotion that its unity was endangered if not destroyed. His reach often exceeded his grasp, therefore his art was not always perfect. But his failures**

50 Manchester Guardian, June 1912, Mr. Clarence Whaite.

were better than many men's successes, and we owe him more than we owe to others whose art has been perfect as far as it has gone. When reach and grasp were one, then his work was extremely fine, and our enjoyment of it, of its high appeal to us, has no reservations.

Mr. Whaite was seen as a gentleman of much personal charm, and was fond of telling how at the opening of the Liverpool and Manchester Railway he was taken in hand by the Duke of Wellington.

He was greatly appreciated in Manchester especially amongst his colleagues who held him in high esteem. The sculptor, John Cassidy made a bust of Whaite in bronze which was presented to the City Art Gallery on behalf of his numerous friends and admirers.

CHAPTER 13

VICTORIAN FEMALE ARTISTS MAKING THEIR MARK ON MANCHESTER'S ART SCENE

By 1861 Manchester boasted one hundred and eighty one professional painters the largest number in any provincial town. Of these, forty were talented professional women artists who were not afraid to experiment and produce exciting works. Portraits, still life, landscapes, fairy paintings etc., were all handled with great aplomb and placed on display for everyone to appreciate.

The public enjoyed their works, along with the Manchester Press, who actually seemed to go out of their way to praise a good number of these artists. They definitely had their favourites, and could be slightly patronising at times, but on the whole they were usually most complimentary and gave credit where it was due.

It is only now some of these excellent artists are becoming more well known. They had a great deal in common, they produced good art, had professional backgrounds and throughout their lives worked and exhibited in Manchester. Of course, their personalities were totally different.

Louisa Mary Bancroft - 1864-1938

Bancroft was the daughter of William and Mary Heald of Mere School House, Mere, Cheshire. The census for 1881 lists her as a pupil teacher aged seventeen.

In 1887 she married the landscape painter, Elias Bancroft at St Paul's in Over Tabley, Cheshire. In 1871 their address was 18 York Place, Chorlton-on-Medlock and they moved to 9 Buckingham Crescent South Manchester in 1901.[1] They had a studio in Acomb Street, Greenheys which was used by classes of Manchester Academy students from 1922.

Louisa studied at the Warrington School of Art under John Christmas Thompson, [2] where she became a flower and miniature painter. She worked her way up the Manchester Academy of Fine Arts

1 Warrington Library, Museum and Archives Service.
2 J. C. Thompson 1824-1906. Head of the Warrington School of Art 1855-1906.

ladder becoming a member in 1895, a Council member in 1899 and secretary from 1924-38 when she left Manchester to live in Whitby. In 1927 she became an associate of the RCA and a Fellow of the RSA.

In 1928 she received a letter from the City Art Gallery's curator, Mr. Haward, informing her that her painting "Wallflowers" had been purchased by the Art Gallery Committee for the sum of fifteen guineas. In this letter he asked her if she would be good enough to tell him the year in which the work was painted and also let him know anything about the painting which might be of use to the gallery in the future if ever the picture were damaged or had to be cleaned.

Bancroft wrote to Mr. Haward: **I can hardly tell you when I commenced the painting, but it was completed last Spring, occasionally the flowers pass out of season before I have finished with them – absence from home, or illness may have taken up my time, so I put the study on one side until I can get the mass of bloom again.**

I am most particular to use only permanent colours generally the Cambridge Colours manufactured by Messrs. Madderton, and their pure poppy oil and copal varnish. I work on linen canvas, (generally with a chalk foundation.)

It was indeed an accolade to have a painting purchased by the gallery, but this was not the end of her dealings with the gallery. Seven years later the gallery purchased a second flower painting "Old Fashioned Flowers." They purchased the oil painting for £20 including copyright. Mr. Haward said, "I should like to add on my own behalf that I am delighted that the painting is to find a permanent home in this collection." She wrote from Acomb Street, Manchester: **Thank you for your communication of March 7th. I greatly appreciate your kind expression of opinion on my picture "Old Fashioned Flowers." It was painted in Whitby during the month of July 1934. The subject was suggested to me by seeing the flowers on the gardener's well-worn potting shed table, with background of rough discoloured whitewashed wall. I used Belgian canvas and Madderton's colours.**

At this particular time, flower painting was often seen by some art critics as a rather unsophisticated genre with nuances of being a lady-like and pleasant art, without any definite historical underpinning, and most definitely inferior to the great genres of portraiture and history painting - but nothing could have been more wide of the mark. It had an exceptional art history with its past thoroughly entrenched within a Still Life genre once known as "natura morta" - dead nature. Religious, scientific and allegorical in content, with herbal and botanical links, it was held in very high esteem throughout Europe.

Countless messages could be conveyed to a viewer by selecting certain flowers, which in most cases were allegories for a vast range of subjects: sexual, political even deadly connotations were depicted by these gorgeous blooms. Each flower had its own language and if its viewer was a connoisseur (and many were) they would indeed know exactly what was being portrayed under those subtle layers of paint.

Louisa, in her own way, became tangled up in this particular genre's Victorian history and helped to immortalise it within the Manchester Art Gallery's walls.

Louisa must have been a collector of fine textiles. As a patron, she presented the Gallery with an impressive collection of 18th and early 19th century dresses and other articles of attire.

Dress, lemon taffeta brocade, with terracotta stripes; 1780
Bodice, white muslin, with braided embroidery; early 19th century
Collar, white muslin, embroidered; early 19th century
Gown, white muslin, hand embroidered hem and yoke, Empire period
Gown, white muslin; Empire period
Bonnet, white muslin; early 19th century
Child's sun bonnet, brown silk; early 19th century
Pair of Mittens, grey cotton, mid 19th century
Ribbon, three pieces, woven silk with floral pattern
French, late 18th century Fan, ivory, with gold and silver inlay; early Victorian

She was cordially thanked for her very interesting addition to the gallery's small but gradually increasing collection of dresses in a letter dated 16th February 1933.

Mary Louise Breakell - Exhibited 1876-1912

Mary Breakell was born in Manchester and started her artistic career as a pupil at the Manchester School of Art. She then attended the Slade School, London, under Professor Legros.Whilst there she exhibited her first picture "A Forest Maid," at the Academy.

Deciding that the opportunities for studying in the Metropolis did not compare with Paris she went to study at Rodolphe Julian's Academy in Paris [3] under the direction of Tony Robert Flurey. Breakell said "The women of the Passage des Panoramas - a Bohemian, barn sort of place - prided themselves on their seriousness of purpose, as opposed to the more "dilettante demoiselles" of Julian's rue Vivienne studio." [4]

At this time Marie Bashkirtseff was numbered amongst Julian's pupils. Bashkirtseff with her Russian aristocratic background was quite a coup for the Academy. Breakell described her as arrogant, always turning up late and disrupting the class with her chambermaid chaperone and little Roman Wolf dog in tow. She wore fine corseted dresses and furs and was obsessed with her own beauty. [5]

Apparently Bashkirtseff took great delight in telling all the other students how much Robert Fleury adored her as a pupil and Julian too. Although her presence was a large feather in Julian's cap, and he certainly did play up to her, Bashkirtseff was extremely talented. Unfortunately, she had a very short career dying of tuberculosis in 1884.

Being in Paris and attending the Rodolphe Julian's Academy in the late nineteenth century conjured up all kinds of enviable thoughts, especially with those female artists whose circumstances did not allow them to study abroad, and who were continually fighting against the male authorities where life drawing classes were concerned. Enviable because it was well known in artistic circles that Julian was a great believer in his female students being educated in the same manner as

---

3 The Academie Julian was an art school in Paris, established in 1868 by Rodolphe Julian at the Passage des Panoramas, as a studio school for art students with an academic tradition. For young women, the Academie Julian was an important alternative training centre to the Ecole des Beaux-Arts the official art school of France, which barred women from studying there until1897. Female students were allowed to paint from nude male models at the Academie.

4 All the information on Mary Breakell at the Academie Julian has been taken from: Jane R. Becker, Nothing Like A Rival To Spur One on: Overcoming All Obstacles The Women of the Academie Julian.

5 Marie Bashkirtseff 1858-1884 was a Ukrainian born Russian diarist, painter, sculptor. She was also a feminist and in 1881, using the nom de plume "Pauline Orrel," she wrote several articles for Hubertine Auclert's feminist newspaper, La Citoyenne. See her journal: I am the most interesting book of all.

his male students, thus enabling them to have a career when they left the Academy.

But, it was not quite so rosy as it sounded. Breakell wrote: **We English girls worked the hardest in the deepest earnest. We rose before it was light, and dressed with frozen fingers. We breakfasted with the worthy working folk of Paris in their blue blouses at the marble tables, trudging bravely for an hour through the snowy streets and leafless Elysian Fields and boulevards (for it was bitter cold in Paris that winter of 1882).**

Leaving Paris for health reasons she went to Barbizon near Fontainbleau to paint. Here she became good friends with Robert Louis Stevenson and his wife who were residing in the same village.

Breakell exhibited a number of pictures at the Royal Academy, 1879 "The Forest Maid," 1883 "A Garden in France," and 1890 "A Garden in Larkspur, Brittany," which was considered to be one of her more successful pictures, along with a painting exhibited at Burlington House in 1896, of a Breton garden, overgrown and deserted, with children playing among the flowers. [6]

The Manchester critics usually gave Breakell a good review: **One of the most competent of our local lady artists has been exhibiting in a studio in Brazenose Street.**

Few ladies have undergone so thorough a training, and few can show more satisfactory results. Instead of the wilted bunches of flowers, and the washed out landscape in water colour, and the large-eyed women with carmine lips and abnormally chubby babies, which we have been accustomed to accept with as much resignation as we could summon from the average young woman painter.

Miss Breakell paints with a strength and knowledge which we can only characterize as masculine, and her work challenges, and has little reason to fear, comparison with that of most of her male competitors. It may almost be said that this quality of virility is in some instances overdone, and becomes an affection and a blemish. In aiming at the display of force, the artist sometimes sacrifices

6 Hearth and Home, Women in the World of Art, No xxv, Miss Mary L. Breakell.

delicacy. Miss Breakell has done so well already that she must expect in the future to be judged by a very high standard. [7]

Not only was she appreciated in her native city: she became popular with the London Press, who were quite happy to name-drop: Mary Breakell was "At Home" at 20 Campden Hill Square on the 10th and 13th inst., when a large and distinguished circle of friends and connoisseurs came to view her pictures and portraits for the Victorian Exhibition at Earls Court.

The portraits are all remarkable for breadth and vigour of treatment and life-like expression. While at the same time most careful manipulation of all the minute details of women's dress. Among her visitors was Countess Anne Kearney.

Miss Susan Isabel Dacre - 1844-1933

Susan Isabel Dacre played a very significant role in promoting Manchester's Victorian art scene, and now receives the acclaim she deserves.

Born in Leamington she came to Manchester in her infancy, and was educated at a convent in Salford. Her childhood was not an easy one, but it did improve when in 1857 her widowed mother became the landlady of the Stamford Arms, Altrincham.

One of her mother's more famous customers was Anthony Trollope who stayed with them whilst visiting the Art Treasures Exhibition in Manchester. Apparently all morning he would sit in the deep bay of the snug writing. He would then stop and have some lunch, after which we are told "he would beautify himself, having a great taste in waistcoats and spats." This done he would then make off to the exhibition. He was finishing the manuscript of "Barchester Towers" at the time, and lent it to the family to read and consequently it became one of Dacre's favourites.

Dacre lived in Paris between 1858-68, first as a pupil then as a governess. In 1869 she spent the winter in Italy and then returned to Paris, but with the outbreak of the Franco-Prussian War she was sent home. On returning too soon, she and her brother were caught up in the

---

7 City News, December 31st 1887, <u>Some Recent Work by Manchester Artists</u>, Miss M.L.Breakell.

Commune and were forced to build barricades. They were, with great difficulty, helped to escape back to England in 1871. On her return to Manchester she continued her artistic career and attended classes at the School of Art, Cavendish Street, under the direction of Mr. W. Muckley. Her mother was now the landlady of the Ducie Arms, Strangeways.

In 1874 she went to Rome for two years with her lifelong friend Miss Robinson, afterwards Mrs. A. L. Swynnerton. From 1877-1880 she was again in Paris, a fellow-pupil with Marie Bashkirtseff, and bracketed with her as first in the concourse mentioned in the famous Diary.

She lived in London for a time then returned to Manchester in 1883 and shared a studio in 10 South King Street with Mary Florence Monkhouse. She founded the Manchester Women Painters' Society with Miss Robinson and became its president.

Dacre became an active member of the Manchester Academy of Fine Arts. She had her work on display at the Royal Jubilee Exhibition in 1887, and assisted Ford Madox Brown with the decoration of the exhibition's dome.

In 1897 she began an artistic partnership with the artist, Francis Dodd, which lasted over fourteen years. Dodd had attended classes at the Glasgow School of Art under the tutors Archibald Kay and Francis Newbery. On being awarded the Haladane travelling scholarship in 1893 he was able to study at Aman-Jean's Atelier in Paris.

Settling in Manchester in 1895 he held a series of one-man shows at Dacre's studio in South King Street and another studio in Acomb Street, Greenheys. Dacre was the subject of a number of paintings and prints by Dodd. One was entitled "Signora Lotto."

In a letter dated 5th November 1940 Dodd wrote the following to Lawrence Haward, the Curator of the City Art Gallery: **Signora Lotto was so called because we were both engaged in tracking Lotto and his work through books of Italian Art and Illustration. I began it in Hammersmith in 1905 and finished it in Fitzroy Street in 1907: I say that at a guess, but the date is probably on it.** [8]

[8] Letter taken from a file in the Manchester Art Gallery.

The date was on it - 1906. There was also two documents with the painting, the top one had inscribed on it: "To Susy from Francis. In remembrance." The bottom one had inscribed on it: "To all rascally picture cleaners and, other evil destroyers of fair work etc.. This Picture is painted VARNISH and its surface is therefore extremely delicate. Curst be any man Jack of you who attempts to clean it otherwise than by the friction of silk WASTE."

Dacre was interested in the Women's Suffrage movement and sat on the local committee. She was an intimate friend of Miss Lydia Becker. One of Dacre's relevant Manchester paintings is a portrait of Lydia Ernestine Becker (1827-1890).

This oil painting now hangs in the C.I. S. Manchester Gallery part of the Manchester Art Gallery. It portrays a confident woman: with no-nonsense eyes and an immaculately straight hair parting.

But there seems a softer side also vies for the viewer's attention – subtly represented by her necklace, soft white lace trim and rather striking large red petaled corsage.

Becker played a key role within Manchester's suffragette history. She was born in Cooper Street in central Manchester on 24th February 1827, and was the eldest of fifteen children.

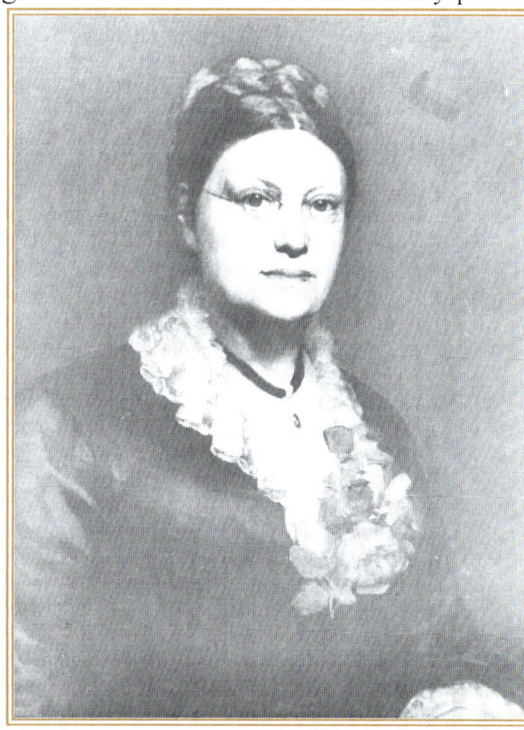

Figure 50. Susan I. Dacre, *Lydia Becker*
Manchester Art Gallery

She was an early Manchester suffragist who campaigned vigorously for the "Cause" of votes for women, a generation before the Pankhursts and the suffragettes. By addressing meetings, establishing the first periodical exclusively devoted to women's suffrage and in coordinating a nationwide campaign, she did much to prepare the ground for the final onslaught of the militants in the Edwardian era." [9]

Momus summed her up in the following manner: **Usually when ladies rush in to print they make the "novel" the medium of their outpourings, but Miss Becker, like Harriet Martinean and other strong minded females, boldly attacks political economy, and is always ready to lead our wives and daughters to that goal which some husbands and fathers look upon with so much dread.**

As a rule we admit the home virtues; but we cannot withhold our admiration from those who have boldly stood forward in defence of their sex, and who advocate, that even in mental culture, they are not inferior to us. Such women as George Eliot, Harriet Martineau, Charlotte Bronte, George Sand, Rosa Bonheur would be amongst the brightest ornaments in any group of nineteenth century celebrities. [10]

Mr. L. Haward, the curator of the Manchester City Art Gallery in 1919, very nearly did not accept this painting for the gallery. It would seem Mrs. Conway, a representative of the Manchester Branch of the The National Union of Women's Suffrage, had approached Mr. Haward with regard to loaning the portrait of "Lydia Becker" painted by Isabel S. Dacre to the Gallery. On March 7th 1919 Mr. Haward sent the following letter to Mrs. Conway:

Dear Mrs. Conway,

I have been in bed with a temperature ever since I saw you the day of Mr. Trevelyan's meeting, otherwise I should have written to you officially to repeat what I told you when I saw you, namely, that after carefully looking at the portrait of Lydia Becker by Miss Dacre and realising its interest as a document, I nevertheless consider that its merit as a painting is not sufficiently high to justify our hanging it in this Gallery if your Society offered it on loan, as I understand it has thought of doing.

The head is, of course, well painted but the hands and wrists are very weak, and the picture as a whole has suffered from want of attention. I cannot help thinking that it might be worth while to get in touch with Miss Dacre and ask her if she would not undertake to work on it again. It is a pity clearly that it should remain as it is for it certainly does not do justice to it.

---

9 Audrey Kelly, Lydia Becker and The Cause.
10 Momus, Temple of Fame Lydia Becker 1878.

If it was not possible to re-work the painting. What would be the next best thing? Apparently reduce its size.

It was Councillor Caroline Herford, O.B.E., who played the main role in obtaining the picture for the Gallery. In a letter written to her on the 27th November 1919, Haward describes how he would like to alter the painting's size, thus getting rid of its weak points "wrists and hands."

Dear Miss Herford,

I was sorry to miss you to-day as I should have had a word about Miss Dacre's portrait with you.

I have had a diagram made to show the old the present and the possible future size of the canvas, and I am of opinion that the suggestion of reducing it from 25 x 21 is the best. At the same time when I saw the portrait here in Manchester, I felt that the picture would gain very much by being converted into an oval instead of being left rectangular.

All this is rather a difficult subject to propose either through you, or directly by letter with Miss Dacre, and what I would like to do is that when I am in London again with my Chairman, which will be sometime between now and Christmas, we should go over to Blackheath to see Miss Dacre and discuss the final shape of the canvas with her while the picture is in front of us. Perhaps if you are writing to her you will be good enough to let her know what I have suggested.

As to the frame both Mr. Todd and I think it would be better for us to have the framing done here at the expense of my Committee. Of course, if Miss Dacre has any suggestion as to what she would consider the best type of frame, I shall be very happy to hear what she has to say, but this again is a point which I think we could better discuss together at Blackheath rather than by letter. 11

Councillor Herford duly wrote to Dacre, who replied: **I would prefer the portrait to be sent to Messrs. Harwell & Co., 17 Lamb's Conduit Street, London. I will examine it there and tell you what I think ought to be done to it.**

This portrait has a label next to it in the Manchester Gallery - entitled "Attitude." This of course refers to Lydia Becker and the Manchester suffragettes and their campaign for Votes for Women. The picture has been cut down (hands and wrists removed). However, the portrait is still in a rectangular frame.

In April 1913 the suffragettes, with great attitude, made their mark upon the gallery. It was reported in all the Manchester newspapers

11 Letters taken from MAG file.

with titles such as: Manchester City Art Gallery Outrage - Glass of Many Pictures Smashed - Three Women Arrested. The story was as follows:

Just before nine o'clock last night when the Manchester City Art Gallery was due to close and there were few people about, an attendant heard repeated cracking of glass. Rushing into the room he found three women making a rush round the room cracking the glass of the biggest and most valuable pictures in the collection. Nowhere in the Gallery are hung so many famous pictures in so short a space.

The outrage was quickly and neatly carried through; two attendants rushed to arrest the women, but as there were three to two one of the women escaped from the room. They called to the doorkeeper, and immediately the big doors were closed and retreat cut off.

The Town Hall was informed. The Chief Constable and a Superintendent at once went across, and took the women to the Town Hall. There they questioned them, and after charging them allowed them out on bail until the morning; when they would appear before the Stipendiary Magistrate.

The names of the women are given as Annie Briggs, Housekeeper, Alexandra Road, Castleton, Rochdale, Lillian Forrester, Married Woman, Grosvenor Road, Whalley Range, Evelyn Manesta, Governess, Grosvenor Road, Whalley Range. They were charged with committing unlawful, wilful and malicious damage to property of the Manchester Corporation consisting of thirteen pictures.

The nature of the damage: The glasses of the pictures were in all cases cracked, in some cases smashed in more than one place, and several times the hammer heads went right through the glass. The cost of the damage to the glass alone was put at £170 by Mr. Pickford at the police court proceedings. Broken glass was lying all over the room, and in some cases, it is stated, had been actually driven into the canvas, and its extraction may cause further damage. In some cases parts of the figures and landscapes seem to have been blurred or torn away.

A hammer and a steel bolt were found in the room by the police. The hammer was a small one tied round with ribbons in the colours of the Women's Social and Political Union, with a card attached to them. On one side of the card were the words, "Parliament for dishonourable men; prison for honourable women;" and on the other side, "Stop forcible feeding." Elsewhere in Manchester women about this time were pouring ink in street letter boxes, as a protest by the militant suffragists against the sentence on Mrs. Pankhurst.

When charged with malicious damage Briggs said "I object to the word "Malicious," as it was done for political reasons." Mrs Forrester said "With respect to the thirteen pictures I cannot see how the damage to the glass came to £170." (It was eventually priced at £85.00.)

They were released on bail provided they would give an undertaking not to do any further damage in the meantime. This undertaking was given, and bail was allowed to each defendant in her own recognisances in the sum of £100 and one surety of £100. The Reverend A. E. Cornibeer, rector of Sacred Trinity, Salford, was accepted as surety for each defendant.

The public galleries of the court contained many women, and when the defendants came into the dock there was some clapping of hands. The Stipendiary Magistrate said "that if anything of that kind occurred again he would be compelled to ask the women to go out."

With the exception of a solitary "hear, hear" at a remark of one of the defendants, and a voice towards the end asking "Can anyone speak on their behalf?" the case ran smoothly. At the close, however three women in the gallery unfurled a short flag or scroll with the words on it "Votes for Women," and this was taken possession of by the police.

Perhaps Mr. Haward brought a little of this to mind when he was making his decision about Dacre's painting.

Dacre was not afraid to experiment. She was an extremely successful painter of children, and her Italian landscapes which she began to produce in 1899 were serene with an intimate beauty.

The City Gallery own a number of Dacre's Italian paintings, including "Italian Women In Church." This was a gift from a group of subscribers.

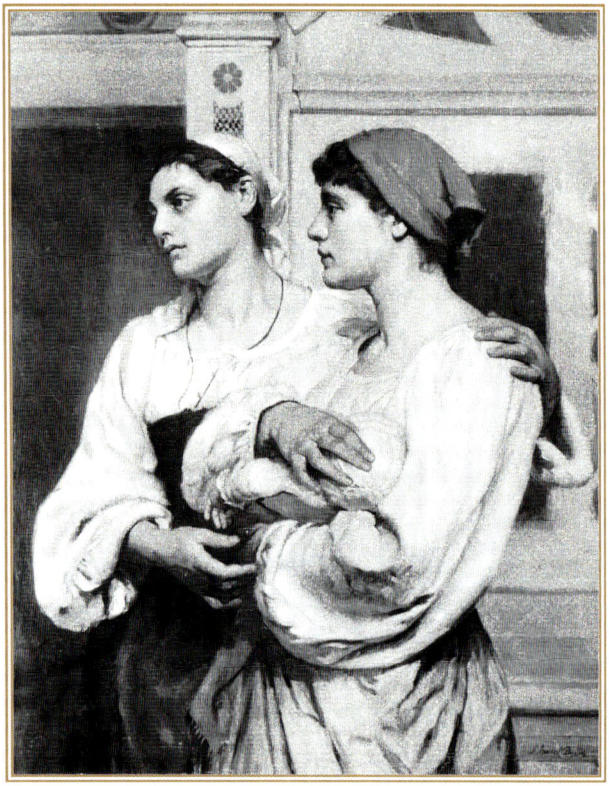

Figure 51. S. I. Dacre, *Italian Women In Church*
Manchester Art Gallery

The Gallery received the following Post Office telegram from Dodd sent on 22nd February 1927 and were very pleased to receive the painting.

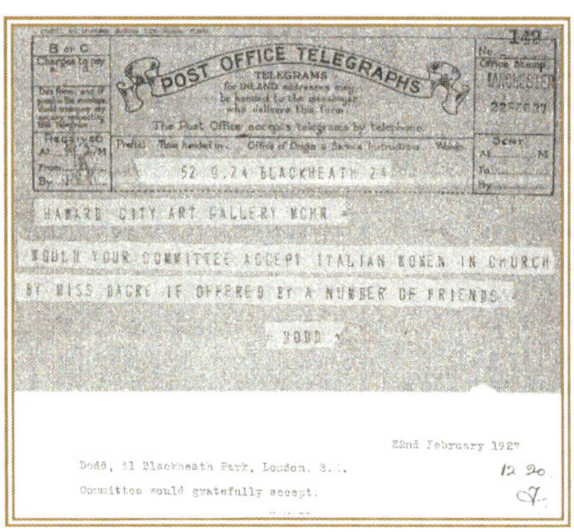

POST OFFICE TELEGRAPHS

TELEGRAMS for INLAND addresses may be handed to the messenger who delivers this form.

The Post Office accepts telegrams by telephone.

142

52 9.24 BLACKHEATH 24

HAWARD CITY ART GALLERY MCHR =

WOULD YOUR COMMITTEE ACCEPT ITALIAN WOMEN IN CHURCH BY MISS DACRE IF OFFERED BY A NUMBER OF FRIENDS

DODD +

22nd February 1927

Dodd, 51 Blackheath Park, London, S.E.

Committee would gratefully accept.

12.20

Figure 52. *Post Office Telegram re: S. I. Dacre*
Manchester Art Gallery

Dacre also turned to Spain for inspiration and exhibited some of her paintings at the Grundy and Smith Galleries in Exchange Street. The Manchester City News wrote: **Spanish landscapes painted in Ronda and Granada by Miss Dacre can be seen at Messrs. Grundy and Smith's galleries in Exchange Street. These Spanish scenes show this accomplished artist in her best and happiest mood.**

Miss Dacre as a landscape painter is a modern of the moderns: she seeks to give only a general impression of a scene to express broadly and simply the effects of colour and light that she observes at a particular time and place, avoiding all topographical details that are unessential to her purpose. Those who care about art will always be divided in opinion as to the Impressionist method, which satisfies some and leaves others discontented with what they feel to be vagueness and lack of reality.

Yet everyone who has the decorative sense and loves fine colour will admire Miss Dacre's latest works. Particularly, "Ronda From The West: Afternoon," which Mr. Whistler would call a harmony of purple and gold. [12]

The writer congratulated Dacre on one of the most attractive and successful little exhibitions of its kind that have been held in Manchester for a long time past.

Her Italian landscapes were exhibited in the Walker Gallery, 118 New Bond Street, London in 1912, and were very much appreciated by one art critic: **The artist, one would say, had stood up to the colour of Italy rather than given way to its hectic and barley-sugar glories, which since Turner magnified them with the 1,000-power reflector of his art have so dazzled the eyes of our painters. Miss Dacre has seen Italy very definitely in shape, and has chosen the freshness and keenness of its complexion.**

The drawing varies a deal and at times tends to weakness, but in the Perugia Square, in a view of the roofs of Perugia, and in the "Convent at Parioli, Rome" where it is most needed it takes grip and reveals undeniable strength. he roofs especially have rhythmic

12 Spanish Landscapes by Miss Dacre, Manchester City News, Sept-October 1900.

style that many of our young Michelangelo's might take off their hat to.

This was a laudable write up for Dacre and would do her ever growing artistic reputation as "an extremely talented female artist" no harm at all. In his column the critic decides that this was a notable little collection, expressive of an artist of unusual temperament and a skill that works finely within its limits. He did however feel that there was not a pot-boiler in the exhibition.

He then came to the following conclusion: **In the humbler restaurants in Rome there is usually an entry near the end of the menu "dolce ingenere" which has been interpreted by tourists as "sweetness in general." Here it is not sweetness in general nor Italy in general, but such work is a particular communication about Italy, something that appealed clemently to the artist and could not be denied expression.**

Dacre left Manchester for London in 1904 along with Francis Dodd, who married Mary Arabella Ingle, the daughter of a London solicitor, in 1911. She died three days after entering her ninetieth year at Blackheath.

The following appeared in her obituary: **She knew all the vicissitudes of fortune, but in every circumstance she remained the same large-minded, sympathetic, humorous, and generous woman.**

Louise Jopling - 1843-1933

"Mrs. Louise Jopling-Rowe was a great social figure in her day, and her life was as full as it was long." 13

Louise Jopling nee Louise Goode was born in Manchester the fifth child of T. S. Goode, a railway contractor. She was a painter of portraits, genre and landscape. "I was married in 1861, at the age of seventeen, to Frank Romer who was in the Civil Service."

---

13 Times, 20th November 1933, Mrs Jopling-Rowe - Artist And Lecturer.

"We lived in London had two children; and no thought of an art career entered my head. 14 In 1865, Frank returned home one day and said: "How would you like to live in Paris?" He had been offered the position of private secretary to Baron Nathaniel de Rothschild." Louise jumped at the chance, little did she realise this would be the beginning of her career as an artist.

On seeing some of Jopling's drawings, Baroness Rothschild recognised her artistic potential and helped her to take lessons with a Monsieur Charles Chaplin. Described by Jopling as follows: **I went to Monsieur Charles Chaplin, whose studio for women students was the fashion just then. I found the great man in his studio palette in hand, before one of his decorative subjects - probably intended for the Tuileries. Monsieur Chaplin was tall and elegant. His fair hair and blue eyes showed his English origin.**

Jopling found studio life a strange experience since she had never been to a school of any sort, having always learnt with a governess at home. But she soon became acclimatised: **My companions were charming and the fact of my being a foreigner, and the mother of the two pretty little boys, who with their nurse, used to fetch me from the studio made the other students take an affectionate interest in me.**

She could not believe she could run her working and domestic life together so easily: **Only in France one is expected to cultivate what little talent one possesses. How my relations in England would have stared - fancy entertaining the idea of becoming a professional - I, a married woman!**

I had sixteen delightful months of study. I was able to see the great man at work and this was my best lesson. Whilst at the studio I did two heads in sanguine. Monsieur said "They must go to the Salon." To my joy my drawings were accepted and hung on the line.

And then it all went disastrously wrong. Her husband committed a behind the scenes crime and they had to leave Paris putting an immediate end to her studies: **This put an end to my art studies, as**

14 The following information has been taken from Louise Jopling, Twenty Years Of My Life,

never after this did I have the leisure, or money to continue them. I had to become my own instructor. We left Paris with literally only the clothes we wore and lived at Greville Place with my husband's parents.

Slowly getting back on her feet again she became acquainted with the artist, William Frith, who took a good look at her portfolio and advised her not to study at the Royal Academy Schools lest she should lose her individuality. So instead she went to study at Leigh's School of Art in Newman Street, where she had as fellow-students Sir Johnston Forbes-Robertson and Samuel Butler, the author of "Erewhon."

Her artistic life might have been getting back on track, but her private life was in a shambles and she eventually left her husband, who had acquired a large amount of gambling debts. Still reeling from this, the most appalling thing happened: her beloved son Geoffrey died. She threw herself into her art.

Having already, at the age of 18, exhibited drawings at the Paris Salon, she turned to the Royal Academy and in 1871 entered her first picture: It was a self portrait entitled "Bud and Bloom." Thereafter she continued to exhibit regularly at the Academy, the Grosvenor Gallery, and the Paris Salon. She was the first woman to be elected a member of the Royal Society of British Artists.

In 1874, she married Joseph Middleton Jopling a watercolour painter. After he died in 1884, she set up a school of art and lectured and published several books including "Tête-à-Tête Bridge" and "Hints to Students and Amateurs," she also contributed poems, short stories and articles to various periodicals. She said of her school: **My school began to be noticed in the daily papers: The Pall Mall Gazette in November had an illustrated page. The Theme of my discourse to my interviewer was "That there is no sex in art." I found teaching intensely interesting. I learned so much myself. I was continually correcting faults not only in my pupil's work but in my own.**

Jopling must have thought it all worth while when she received a letter stating: "English women and girls, dear Mrs. Jopling owe you such a debt of gratitude, as can never be repaid!"

She was married for a third time to George Rowe, a lawyer. They settled in Buckinghamshire, where she became president of the Chiltern Club of Arts and Handicrafts as well as the Buckinghamshire Art Guild. She also wrote a number of plays and became an enthusiastic gardener.

The Times described Mrs. Jopling-Rowe as follows: She was an extremely handsome and vivacious woman, and her jesting tribute to herself, in a "parlour game," to the effect that "He who is in love with Mrs. Jopling, can neither be a fool nor a fopling," was a fair comment on the effect she made.

Millais painted her portrait, which is now in the Tate Gallery, and she was immensely popular in the artistic London of her prime. [15]

Louise had an extremely long and successful life, she died at the age of ninety.

Rose Magnus - 1859-1900

Rose was the second daughter of Hermann Magnus of Fallowfield. They were an extremely artistic family. Her father was a connoisseur of art and her mother was a successful portraitist in charcoal and chalks. Her brother Herman was an artist as was her sister Emma, who painted portraits, figures and stills mainly in oil. Both sisters studied at the Manchester School of Art, and attended the Slade School, University College, London. Here Rose attracted the special notice of Professor Legros with her drawings from the figure.

In December 1881 she became a student of the Manchester Academy of Art, and exhibited in the Spring Exhibition of 1882. She was elected an associate of the Academy in March 1884 and advanced to full membership in the March of 1885.

Rose was a considerable and constant contributor to London and leading provincial exhibitions. She began as a painter of small landscapes in low tone, in the manner of what was then known as the Manchester School and her name was often linked with this group of artists.

---

15 Times, 20th November, 1933. Mrs. Jopling-Rowe - Artist And Lecturer. A list of her best known pictures is given in E.C. Clayton, English Female Artists, Published in 1876.

At the Jubilee Exhibition at Old Trafford in 1887 she was represented by her painting "Lamp Light." One of her works is in the permanent collection of the gallery in Whitworth Park and another in the Mappin Art Gallery Sheffield. Her musical gifts were considerable and she was a fairly accomplished violinist.

Tragically, Rose died suddenly of pneumonia on June 7th 1900 at Llanfairfechan, near Bangor. She had been in Manchester the week previously in perfect health. [16]

Fanny Sugars -1856-1933

Sugars painted flowers and wildlife. She lived in Elm Grove Didsbury for a time and studied at the Manchester School of Art in 1874. She continued her studies in Paris at the Academie Julian where she was a pupil of Lefebvre.

On her return to Manchester she shared a studio in King Street with a number of other female artists. She first exhibited in Manchester in 1880, and in 1881 she joined the Manchester Society of Women Artists. She also exhibited at the R.A. between 1889-1901. She was elected a full member of the Manchester Academy of Fine Arts in 1897. Sugars helped Ford Madox Brown to decorate the dome of the Royal Jubilee Exhibition in 1887. She later lived in Huyton, Lancs around 1903 and exhibited many works in Liverpool.

---

16 This biography has been taken from: Manchester City News, Rose Magnus, June 1900.

CHAPTER 14

EMILY GERTRUDE THOMSON 1850-1929

Emily Gertrude Thomson was a very versatile artist and highly praised within Manchester's Art circles.

The following article appeared in Momus:

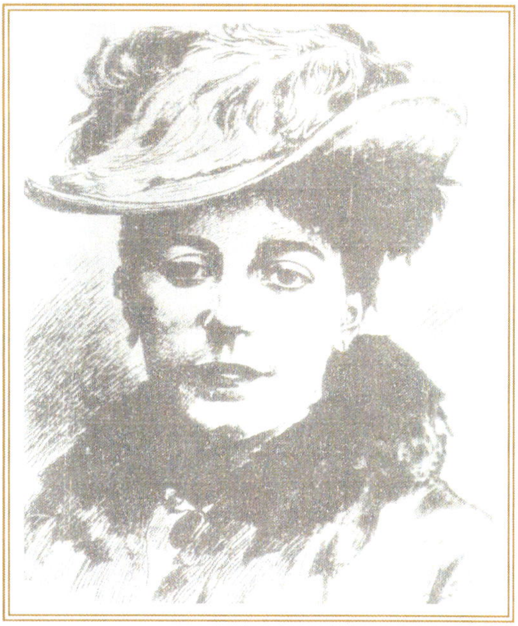

Figure 53. ***Portrait of E. G. Thomson, Momus 1880***
Manchester Central Library

The portrait of a young lady so well and favourably known in the Art World will no doubt be welcomed by that numerous class of readers who delight in seeing modest and unassuming merit take its proper place among the celebrities.

Miss Thomson's Art productions are widely known, and Manchester always feels a special interest in those protégées whose instruction has been entirely local, and whose celebrity reflects honour on the city which is proud of processing an individuality that makes itself felt, not only in the School of Politics but in the domain of Art.

She went to the School of Art and remained under Mr. Muckley's tuition for several years, becoming one of his favourite pupils; after which she attended the studio of Mr. F. J. Shields, who intimated her strength lay in design. She studied for some time at Messrs. Wedgwood's Works at Etruria in Staffordshire painting on china. Her designs found ready purchase.

Miss Thomson has ambition, and with chances equal to her desires there is no knowing what she may achieve. The bent of her genius inclines towards Mural painting, and with youth and genius on her side, there is no knowing what fortune may have in store. Those who have a future can afford to wait. 1

Obviously Thomson was appreciated and respected within Manchester's art circles. Two years before this article appeared in Momus a critic for the Manchester City News wrote: 2 **Miss Gertrude Thomson contributes an important work on a somewhat larger scale than most of the charming drawings she has hitherto exhibited. Her subject is again taken from fairyland. A group of water elves are watching with sad and anxious eyes the dead child.**

He was referring to one of her illustrations for "The Fairies - A Child's Song" written by William Allingham. 3 In this book Thomson illustrates how the fairies steal little Bridget away and cause her to die of sorrow.

They stole little Bridget
For seven years long;
When she came down again
Her friends were all gone.

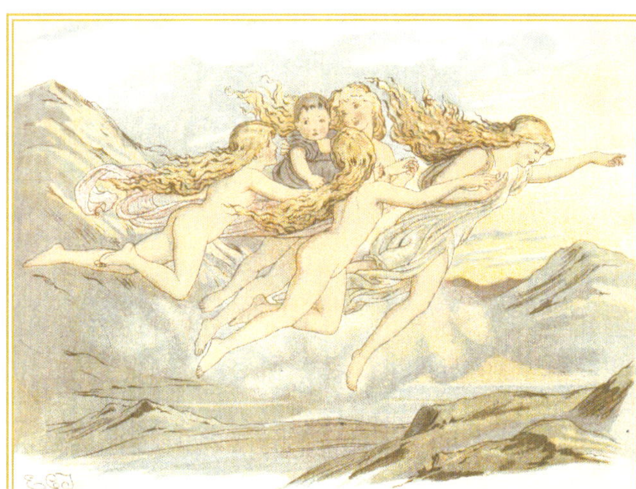

Figure 54. E. G. Thomson, *Bridget and the Fairies*

1 Momus, Thursday February 19th 1880, p195.
2 Manchester City News, 14th March 1878 Manchester Academy of Arts Exhibition.
3 William Allingham was an Irish man of letters and a poet. He was born in 1824, (sometimes disputed for 1829) and died in 1889. He was part of the Rossetti Circle. Three illustrations have been taken from his book.

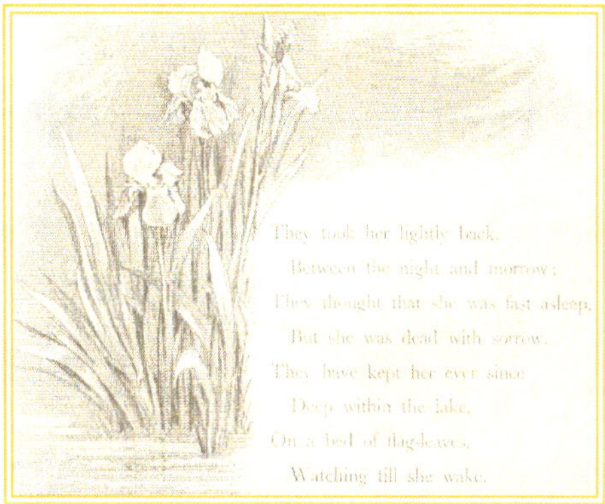

Figure 55. E. G. Thomson, *Flag.*

"Bridget Deep Below The Lake" is the picture the critic from the Manchester City news referred to. Thomson captures the sad fairy tale in this poignant watery scene.

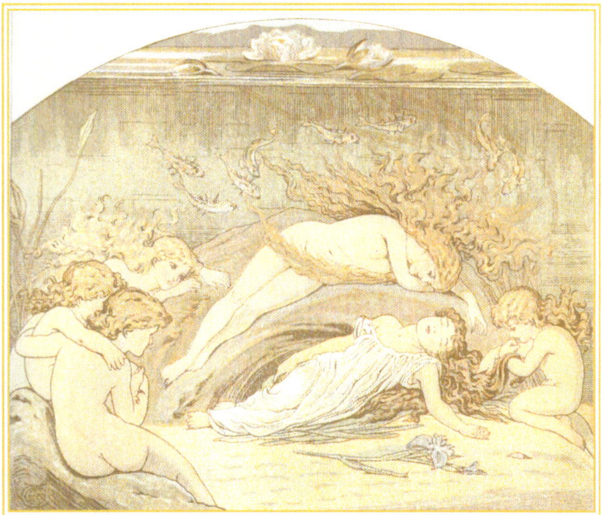

Figure 56. E. G. Thomson, *Bridget Deep Below The Lake*

All the fairies sit around little Bridget waiting for her to wake. Their long tresses sway with the gentle movement of the water and one small fairy caresses Bridget's hair. Tiny fish dart around and almost become tangled up in one fairy's long floating locks.

The scene is tranquil, nearly as tranquil as the water lilies lying on the surface of the lake. In some ways Thomson has made this picture romantic, and far from the truth. An optimist may think Bridget might wake up. But the truth is this is a depiction of a dark Victorian fairy tale with no happy ending. The blue iris, so prominently lying next to Bridget, reflects the whole message. It is a symbol of death: a symbol which reaches back to Homer and the Greek Goddess Iris. 4

Five days later the Manchester Guardian was also brimming over with praise for her painting using the words "elegance" and "refinement" to describe her work. It was quite an accolade to have such praise from two influential newspapers. The words elegance and refinement not only portray her artistic techniques, they also help to describe her artistic temperament, a temperament that was very much entwined around her delicate fairy depictions.

Her father, Alexander Thomson was a Professor of Greek and Hebrew at Lancashire Independent College. Thomson studied at the Manchester School of Art, won a number of Queen's Prizes, and became a member of the Royal Society of Miniature Painters. At various points in her career, she painted portraits, illustrated books, and designed stained-glass windows; she exhibited in Manchester, Liverpool, Brussels and Canada. 5

Works by her are in the permanent collection of the Manchester Art Gallery and the Victoria and Albert Museum. Her stained glass windows can be seen at Cheltenham College and at the church of St. John the Divine, Brooklands, Cheshire.

Thomson exhibited one of her designs, "Britomart Defending the Red Cross Knight," for Cheltenham Ladies' College, and received the following praise: **Some excellent work is contributed by Miss E. G. Thomson. Her design "Britomart Defending The Red Cross Knight" is finely drawn, and as spirited as the purpose of the design would allow.** 6

4 Iris was thought to lead the souls of dead women to the Elysian Fields and the Greeks would plant purple iris on the graves of women.
flowers.org.uk/Flowers/facts/e-j/iris.htm

5 Information from Manchester Art Gallery.

6 The City News.

These stained glass windows echoed by the stone tracery on the grand staircase at Cheltenham Ladies' College are splendid. Named the Britomart Windows they are based upon six pictures taken from Spencer's allegory of the "Faery Queene." They were produced by Heaton, Butler and Bayne.

Thomson designed four of the windows and her tutor and good friend Frederic Shields designed two - the first and the fifth. The first window was given by Patrick Smith, in memory of his daughter, Teena Smith 1883, and the second is in memory of Mrs. Francis Mary Owen 1883. 7

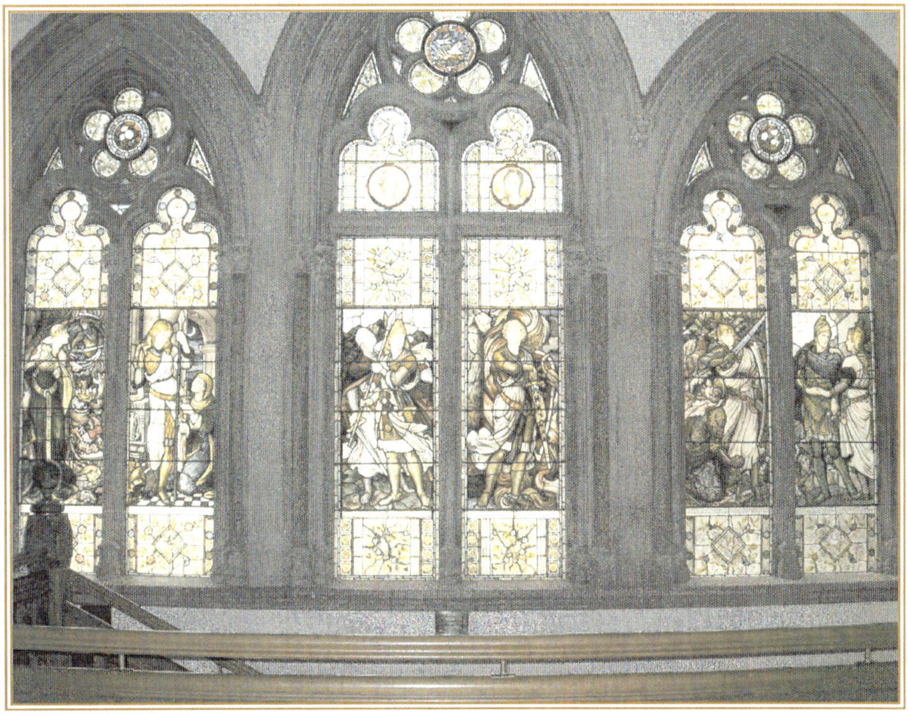

Figure 57. E. G. Thomson and Frederic Shields, *The Britomart Windows*
Cheltenham Ladies' College

The Pre-Raphaelite designer, Robert Turnill Bayne, must have been delighted with this commission. Each window is a permanent monument to the Pre-Raphaelite movement.

7 Guide to the Cheltenham Ladies' College, 1931.

Take for example the second window from the left designed by Thomson depicting the Lady Knight with her nurse Glauce. The script under the window reads:

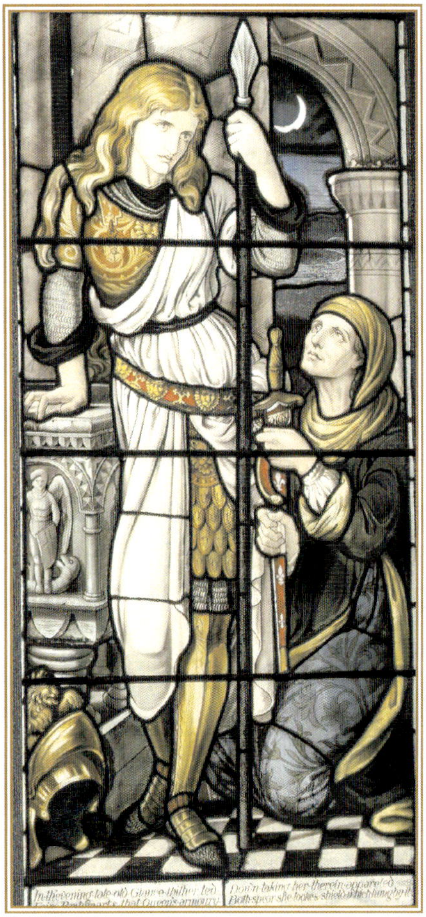

Figure 58. E. G. Thomson,
Britomart Window
Cheltenham Ladies' College

In.the.evening.late.old.Glauce.thither.led.Faire.Bridmart.&.that.
Queen's.armoury.
Down.taking.her.therein.appareled.
Both.spear.she.tooke.&.shield.which.hung.by.it.

The Lady Knight and her nurse Glauce are in the church putting on the armour of Queen Angela, so that they may start to seek guidance from Merlin.

Similarly to the Pre-Raphaelite painters Thomson relies strongly on narrative sources for her designs. She bonds her images with the text and in so doing she manipulates time. The depictions in this window will always relate to Spenser and his late sixteenth century poem, but they have been artistically translated by using the Pre-Raphaelite techniques of the nineteenth century. The dark poem becomes a heroic Romantic Fairy Tale.

But it does not end there. In fact, this is just the beginning. Between them Thomson and Bayne have managed to conjure up a perfect Pre-Raphaelite image. Britomart is a classic symbol for the movement. She is slender with a long neck and beautiful large eyes. Her long golden tresses are parted and fall in immaculate curls over her shoulders. She is indeed stunning. She stands completely static with her eyes transfixed. Who knows what she is thinking? Perhaps she is thinking of Arthegal, whose image she has just seen in a magic mirror given to her by Merlin. She has fallen deeply almost, obsessively, in love with this image.

This window is brimming with symbolism. The new crescent moon is ambivalent with both solar and lunar - good and evil. Here it is the light of the night depicting new beginnings: growing energy, newness and hope. It is also the symbol for a maiden Goddess, in this case, Britomart our Warrior Queen. She is fully aware that she is about to face both good and evil, but once she triumphs over evil she knows she will have a new beginning full of energy and hope.

The church's sturdy Romanesque arch, with its deep cut pattern, forms a strong and stable back ground. It is repeated on the tomb where she rests her hand so obviously drawing the viewer's eye to a carving of George and the Dragon depicting good over evil: the dragon being the devil and St. George, England's patron saint slaying it.

Her armour, spear, visa and sword all play an important role within Spenser's poem, but they too have their own symbolism. The lion heads on her belt and armour are depictions of a virgin warrior Goddess. The fleur-de-lis on her sword is a stylised lotus or lily – the flower of light and life. It vies with the lion heads. When it resembles a spearhead it is phallic and represents masculine and military power.

Both depictions are pertinent to Britomart. She is a virgin warrior Goddess about to go into battle. She will wield her sword and kill her enemy disguised as a male knight.

Glauce her nurse represents a crone Goddess and her superior wisdom has stepped in. She has tried no end of potions and spells to awake her Lady from the enchanted spell cast upon her by Merlin's mirror, but all have failed. Experience tells her there is only one person who can help them now, Merlin. Dutifully she kneels behind her Lady clutching her sword.

In a minute she will take her down to Merlin's cave where he will predict Britomart's future with Arthegal.

But for the time being she has a far away look in her eyes. Perhaps she knows she will die.

But Scudamour for passing great despight
Staid not to answer, scarcely did refraine,
But that in all those knights and ladies sight,
He for revenge had guiltlesse Glauce slaine.
E. Spencer - Faery Queene.

Spenser's poem is a unique tale and in her own way Thomson has captured this uniqueness and skilfully romanticised it into a series of splendid coloured glass windows.

Throughout her artistic career Thomson always stayed in touch with her friends and colleagues in Manchester. For example in a letter written to Mr. Haward, the curator of the Manchester City Art Gallery in 1925 she requests if it would be possible to donate one of her fairy paintings to the gallery: **An idea came to me and I'm wondering if it would be presumptuous to suggest it? It was the people of Manchester who gave me a girl of twenty or so, my first encouragement. My fairy drawings pleased them: they bought all I did. They drifted to London, and sold well. Mr. Ackerman gave me over £100 for the set of six Xmas Cards. It would have been well if I had kept it up. But Mr. Shields drew me away to designing for stained glass.**

So, my idea is, I would like, so much, for my first love, my Fairy work, to be associated with my name in Manchester. Would it be too great a presumption, do you think, for me to offer as a gift to the Committee one of my Fairy drawings? There are three now, framed, at Mr. Bateman's Gallery in Mount Street. They have

never been published and the copyright would be included. The Gallery was delighted to receive a piece of her work.

It was due to her fairy paintings she and Charles Lutwidge Dodgson (Lewis Carroll) became very good friends and working partners.

What happens when an artistic, highly intelligent, gentleman meets an artistic, elegant, refined, young lady? They get on like a house on fire.

Thomson wrote the following about Dodgson. **I always had a mysterious feeling, when looking at him and hearing him speak, that he was not exactly an ordinary human being of flesh and blood.**

Rather did he seem as some delicate, ethereal spirit, enveloped for the moment in a semblance of common humanity...His head was small, and beautifully formed, the brow rather low, broad, white, and finely modelled. Dreamy grey eyes, a sensitive mouth, slightly compressed when in repose, but softening into the most beautiful smile when he spoke.

He had a slight hesitancy sometimes, when speaking... but though Mr. Dodgson deplored it himself, it added a certain piquancy, especially if he was uttering any whimsicality. [8]

Their friendship began in 1879 and finished in 1897. She last saw Dodgson on November 20th 1897 when he visited her Addison Hall studio in London to sketch Isy Watson, a thirteen year old model. They had lunched together and went to see a play. Thomson said "He was exceptionally brilliant that day at lunch, full of repartee and anecdote. He looked extremely well, and as if many years of work still lay before him." He said "If you have nothing special to do come and have tea with me at Paddington and see me off." After their tea at the door of the compartment he turned to shake hands. "Good-bye, I have had such a happy day," he said simply. "I hope you have." Two months later Dodgson died.

Thomson described his funeral in the following way:

> **A steep, stony, country road, with hedges close on either side, fast quickening with the breath of a premature spring. Between the withered leaves of the dead summer a pure white daisy here and there shone out like a little star.**

---

8 "Lewis Carroll: "A Sketch by an Artist-Friend," Gentlewoman, January 1898.

A few mourners slowly climbed the hill in silence, while borne before them on a simple hand-brier was the coffin, half hid in flowers.

Under an old yew, round whose gnarled trunk the green ivy twined, in the pure white chalk earth his body was laid to rest, while the slow bell tolled the passing –

"Of the sweetest soul,
That ever looked with human eyes."

Their relationship began when he noticed some of her "Fairyland" drawings published by Messrs Ackerman of London. These so aroused his interest that he wrote to the publishers for her address. No doubt suitably impressed by Dodgson's reputation as a writer and artist they willingly forwarded his letter on to her. Once he had her address he sent her a barrage of questions - for example: "What forms of drawing, such as oil, body-colour, chalk, pen and ink, pencil, have you tried? Have you done any larger, or more highly finished pictures?" He was also keen to know if she drew from life, or out of her own head? He also enquired as to whether he might purchase one of her paintings (say for a few pounds) which might fall within the limits which he felt he ought to observe when indulging himself in such luxuries. 9

She must have been pleasantly shocked to receive Dodgson's letter out of the blue. She described his letter in the following way: It was at the end of December 1878 that a letter, written in a singularly legible and rather boyish-looking hand came to me ... signed C. L. Dodgson. He had come across some fairy designs of mine, and he should like to see some more of my work. This was the beginning of a frequent and delightful correspondence.

They agreed to meet on 27th June, at the Victoria and Albert Museum: A little before twelve, on the 27th June, I was at the rendezvous and then the humour of the situation suddenly struck

---

9 Morton N. Cohen, assisted by Roger Lancelyn Green, 1997, The Letters Of Lewis Carroll, vol 1, ca 1837-1885.

me, that I had not the ghost of an idea what he was like, nor would he have any better chance of discovering me!

Just as the big clock...clanged out twelve...a gentleman entered, two little girls clinging to his hands, and as I caught sight of the tall slim figure, with the clean shaven, delicate, refined face, I said to myself, "That's Lewis Carroll." He stood for a moment, head erect, glancing swiftly over the room, then bending down, whispered something to one of the children; she, after a moment's pause, pointed straight at me.

Dropping their hands he came forward, and with that winning smile of his that utterly banished the oppressive sense of the Oxford don, said simply, "I am Mr. Dodgson; I was to meet you, I think?" To which I as frankly smiled and said, "How did you know me so soon?" "My little friend found you." I told her I had come to meet a young lady who knew fairies, and she fixed on you at once. But I knew you before she spoke. [10]

Dodgson writes about this event in his diary - June 27th 1879: Took Beatrice and Maud Fearon to see the Macdonalds, and then to the South Kensington Museum, to meet (by appointment) Miss E. G. Thomson, whom I had not met before. She had her sketchbook with her, and showed us some lovely bits she had done from antiques. [11]

This was an immediate friendship. On the 1st July Dodgson met Thomson at the High Street Station where upon they went to the Hulls, and spent about three hours sketching their children.

The writer Morton Cohen [12] points out that there were a good many fairies romping through Charles's verse and letters; and that one of his favourite gift books was William Allingham's "Fairies." Thomson drew twenty three illustrations for this book. Dodgson was infatuated by her fairies, so much so, when he engaged her to work on two of his books he made it perfectly clear he only wanted fairy depictions. "But please draw them from real life." He was emphatic they should be

10 Lewis Carroll, Gentlewoman, vol. xvl, January 29 and February 5 1898.
11 Roger Lancelyn Green, 1971, The Diaries Of Lewis Carroll, vol 2.
12 Morton N. Cohen, 1995, Lewis Carroll A Biography.

drawn from real life. "Please give your fairies real faces. Not like those in Allingham's book. They all seem to look alike."

Cohen also points out "Charles was tightly bound up in Victorian values and decidedly class conscious." In a letter to Thomson he severely criticises one of her depictions, complaining the diameter of the knee and ankle of one of her girls was far too thick. "I think your model must have been a country-peasant child, descended from generations of labourers: there is a marked difference between them and the upper classes- specially as to the size of the ankle. Children are my favourite subjects, but *not* peasant-children since I have come to believe in slender ankles as the normal standard of beauty."

In another letter to Thomson he asked "if she knew Mr. Ruskin the great art critic?" If not he would be happy to introduce her to him. In fact, he introduced her to many influential people within his own artistic circle over the years.

Sometimes they would meet in London and visit the latest art exhibitions exchanging notes and ideas. He was an avid play- goer and regularly invited her to see the latest plays. She may well have gone to more productions with him if he had not kept on informing her she was his "second" choice.

They would discuss her drawings in great detail and paint and photograph together in his studio in Oxford. Thomson describes Dodgson's photographic studio, on the roof of the college in Oxford, as: **A big place filled with all sorts of properties, costumes, etc. He dressed up the children in a variety of quaint costumes.**

Intervals for refreshment and play were frequent. The magic cupboards were opened and mechanical toys spilled out.

We would group together on the floor, Lewis Carroll, the fairies, the beasts and myself, and gay indeed were the hours we spent. How his laugh would ring out like a child's! And the exquisite nonsense he talked! It was like pages out of the Alice's, only more delightful, for there was his own voice and smile to give the true charm to it all. I used to try to recall and record it.

It was impossible - as impossible as to catch the gleam of colour on sunlit water, or to grasp a drifting rainbow. It was a mystic, intangible, gossamer-like thing, that, to chain it down in the words

with which we should have translated it would have been to crush out all life and grace - to destroy it altogether.

For many years there was a delightful interchange of visits. I would go down to Oxford for the day to photograph or draw portraits of his child-friends. The children would return home, sometimes after lunch; in the afternoon Mr Dodgson and I would each bury ourselves in a luxurious armchair and talk, or look over sketches I had bought for him to see, or go through past photographs of famous people.

Then he would make the afternoon tea himself, all in his deft and dainty fashion, and this would bring the happy visit to its close. [13]

One of Dodgson's biographers, Anne Clark, [14] suggests that he was not interested in Thomson's art work and that he really used her to smooth the way for him apropos photographing his naked young female models. Also, she thought Thomson was in love with Dodgson, whom she clearly idolized. Did Dodgson really use Thomson to smooth the way? Maybe he did at the beginning of their relationship. Dodgson was indeed obsessed with drawing and photographing young girl models in the nude, and right from the start he informed Thomson he wanted her to draw all his fairy commissions naked from real life and they must only be girls. She had no qualms about this.

She could well have been besotted with Dodgson, but at the same time she was a grown woman and knew her own mind. If she did not want to accompany Dodgson during his life sessions she would have made it very clear. She probably did know she was paving the way for Dodgson's obsession but did not care. From a female artist's point of view she may well have thought Dodgson was heaven sent. He opened a door for her.

Suddenly she had an articulate and witty escort, all the models she needed, and extremely comfortable surrounds to draw them in. Also

---

13 "Lewis Carroll: A Sketch By An Artist-Friend" From Gentlewoman, January 29 and February 5, 1898.
14 Anne Clark 1997, Lewis Carroll – A biography.

she was safe with the thought that if there was any backlash Dodgson would have to handle it not her. All in all she had an extremely good set up - so if she did have any misgivings about helping him with his indelicate obsession she kept them well hidden.

What ever their initial set up was by the end of their relationship they had formed an extraordinary artistic bond bringing them very close together, and it became obvious that Dodgson really did appreciate her art work.

He had commissioned her to carry out a number of illustrations for his two books, "Serious Poems" and "Games and Puzzles." These books and their illustrations were slightly problematical and did regularly crop up in their correspondence. Basically he could not get Thomson to produce any drawings for them.

When they were discussing her fee for a drawing, he slipped the following comment into his letter: **And while we are on the subject, we had better agree on a scale of charges for "Serious Poems," for which I suppose you will *some* day be beginning to draw. I wonder if you have any idea how long my two books have been on hand? The "Serious Poems" came first: your letter, agreeing to illustrate them, came July 24th 1885: so that I have been waiting just over 8 years for the pictures, of which I have not, as yet seen *one*. The "Games and Puzzles" you undertook in March 1886, more than 7 years ago. The "Serious Poems" have been ready all the time, and could have been published, any Christmas from 1885 onwards, if the pictures had been done.** [15]

Was Thomson aware how frustrated he was with her prevarications?

Could it be she was manipulating Dodgson? So long as he needed her for her drawings their friendship would continue. He did once hint at someone else doing the illustrations, but it never came about. He waited for her drawings right up to his death.

How Dodgson felt about Thomson is debateable. They certainly did have a strong artistic relationship, and she accepted a good deal of criticism. Dodgson thought nothing of constantly criticising Thomson's drawings, in fact he would pester on and on, usually on

---

15 Morton N. Cohen & Edward Wakeling Lewis Carroll & His Illustrators.

the same old subject wrists and ankles. He was fixated with them. However, it was not wrists and ankles he was complaining about in a letter dated, 19th June, 1894. It was clothed fairies.

My Dear Miss Thomson,

I find it so hard to explain, to a lady, why I cannot use this picture, that I *hope* you will excuse anything that seems offensively plain-spoken, as being quite contrary to my *intention*. When this business began, I told you I could have no *clothed* fairies at all. My feeling is this. I object to all *partly* clothed figures, altogether, as being unpleasantly suggestive of impropriety. So I will have none but *wholly* clothed, nude (which to my mind, are not improper *at all*).

This figure is partly clothed; i.e. her hair is utilised, in a way artists often do utilise it and other things, as a partial concession to propriety, and to the principle, maintained by some, that a *wholly* nude figure is improper." The presence of this picture in my book would make all the others look improper. I have two other objections to the picture: but, without them, what I have said is enough by itself to prevent my using it. The other two are, first that the head is too large for the feet: she looks *top-heavy*. Secondly, I don't like the smiling and beckoning to supposed spectators. Even in a *draped* figure, such an expression would look a *little* too bold': in an *undraped* one, it is, to me, unpleasantly so. I am afraid all this is unpleasant reading: but I don't see how I can avoid that result.

Thomson's fairies were, therefore, always naked in all her commissions for Dodgson. When she drew a number of illustrations for Dodgson's "Serious Poems" (Three Sunsets) Cohen wrote: These pictures by Thomson are antiseptic nudes that have nothing to do with the poems, simply pleasant art works conforming to Charles's taste.

It is hard to gauge how the Victorians felt about such nude depictions. The artist and poetess, Christina Rossetti, was shocked by Thomson's naked fairy paintings. One evening her good friend the artist Frederic Shields proudly showed her some of his favourite student's fairy pictures. These particular designs were for Christmas cards.

She wrote to him the following day: I do admire the grace and beauty of the designs, but I do not think that to call a figure a "fairy" settles the right and wrong of such figures. You (as far as I know) are no dealer in such wares. Therefore I think it possible you will agree with me in thinking that all do well to forbear such delineations, and that most of all women artists should lead the way. I ought not now I fear – to be having to say awkwardly what would not have been so totally ignored in my tone last night, but last night's blunder must not make me the slave of false shame this morning. [16]

Frederic Shields must have been mortified at this letter; a deeply pious man he definitely did not believe in painting nudity for the nude's sake. Quite naively he had taken a great delight in showing Christina Rossetti (what he thought to be) the most exquisite paintings of child fairies with their dainty tinted butterfly wings.

As times and attitudes changed Thomson began to question whether she should drape her fairies, or indeed paint them at all, because she ended up writing to Frederic Shields on the subject, and he replied:

What shall you do other than sea fairies? I don't know – doing them so beautifully, what you might achieve in other subjects, but hitherto I look on most of your work as the playful sport of a kitten with a worsted ball. It knows not its power. It shall toss mice soon, yea rats mayhap – with teeth, and count that play then....And to find subjects that you feel a heat about, or that will get up a heat in you when, you must seek them, in books, in your memories, in your hopes and fears, in the streets and the house, seek them diligently, and you shall find them subjects that will *fit you like a good glove*- and you will know as soon as you try them on, which they are.

Drapery! This strikes me -you will have to meet that difficulty some day- when people who live above water will have to be dealt with. Its conception by different artists and nature is very expressive. And as soon as you undertake any other, or almost any other, subjects but water babies, you will find yourself strangled by calicoes and flannels, or burnt by them like the shirt of Nessus, till you wish the whole race had remained in Admite innocence, if only for the cost to your brains of dressing them with propriety. [17]

Thomson did seem to be in a turmoil as to whether, just for propriety's sake, she should clad her nude paintings. Interestingly, the more well known fairy painters such as Dadd, Doyle and the Scots Pre-

---

16 Ernestine Mills, The Life and Letters of Frederic Shields.
17 Ernestine Mills, The Life and Letters of Frederic Shields.

Raphaelite painter, Joseph Noel Paton had no qualms about leaving their fairies naked.

Christopher Wood [18] said of Paton's "The Reconciliation of Oberon and Titania:" The presence of quite so many naked females generated a highly erotic charge, and it seemed amazing that mid-Victorian prudery did not condemn Paton for this. Instead it was shown at the Royal Scottish Academy, and entered for the Westminster Hall Competitions, where it won a £300 prize. The critics were unanimous in praising what seemed an astonishing *tour de force* for such a young artist, then only twenty six.

Encouraged by his success Paton went to even more audacious lengths with his next fairy picture, "The Quarrel of Oberon and Titania," completed in 1849. Wood describes the picture as being full of naked fairies, both male, and female, with numerous amorous incidents and fairy couplings taking place. Dodgson saw the picture in 1857, and counted 165 fairies, but neither he nor the critics remarked on the number of naked female fairies, nor their amorous couplings.

Was Thomson worried about her drawings unnecessarily? Something must have been gnawing away at her, because she changed direction and began to concentrate on designing, especially stained glass windows. This may have been partly connected to Dodgson.

In the late eighties he decided to issue an edition of Alice for the use of children of ages "from nought to five" called "The Nursery Alice" and he commissioned Thomson to draw a design for the cover. She kept promising to send him the illustration but in the end the book went to press without it. The book contained twenty illustrations by John Tenniel (enlarged and coloured from the drawings by Gertrude Thomson). [19] Eventually she designed and coloured the cover and all went well, but in 1895 there seemed to be a disagreement over the drawings for "Three Sunsets" and their friendship became fraught. In essence, Dodgson said "the drawings did not suit the size of the book to be illustrated." Thomson said "the size of the book did not suit the size of her drawings."

---

18 Christopher Wood, 2000, Fairies in Victorian Art.
19 Ricochet-jeunes.org/eng/biblio/books/alice

He wrote to Thomson declaring he was adamant that the size of the book had been fixed first, and the fact that most of the drawings were too large to be reduced without losing much of their beauty, had come to her consciousness too late. He therefore no longer thought them suitable for his book. He suggested he should return the copyright on these drawings, and she repay him the £50.8.0. he had paid for it. "If you cannot see your way to adopting this plan, I think I might perhaps use them for the "Serious Poems." In that case I should not want any of the pictures which we planned more than 10 years ago. This might bring in some of the £50, but if there were maybe eight more woodcuts it could cost £100 for illustrations."

There was a long silence with no response to his letter. So he wrote "having had no answer to my letter I presume you do not see your way to repurchasing the copyright of the 12 drawings. My plan is therefore to publish your drawings in my "Serious Poems' (Three Sunsets). They will do very well as "illustrations," though not perhaps showing any very distinct connection with the text!... The book will not pay its expenses: but I don't mind that. The public must have the pictures, in their full beauty."

Thomson may have taken endless criticism from Dodgson but when she received some from a Manchester critic in 1885 - she was furious.

Pictures at the Manchester Academy - Figures & Portraits: The Women Painters

Every visitor must observe that the most obvious figure paintings exhibited at the Manchester academy this year are the work of the ladies.

Rosa Bonier and the painter of the Roll Call long since proved conclusively that the gentle sex is not a disqualification for the effective treatment of masculine subjects and that the female mind has abundant sympathy with wild activity and material incident.

The ladies who have been admitted as members of the Manchester Academy do not soar as high, but they have fully justified their right to the position they have won." [20]

20 The City News 1885.

The critic then goes on to praise several of their paintings. Alas when he comes to Gertrude Thomson's he is not so kind. He goes out of his way to criticise her work.

Miss Gertrude Thomson seems to have carried her art as far as it is possible to go in the direction she has chosen for herself.

Her neatly-outlined Christmas cards and designs are very pretty, but they are deficient in vivacity and freshness. Her style would be immensely improved if some of the subtlety and tenderness of Stothard [21] could be engrafted upon it, and she would do well to seek a fresh field for her fancy to work in.

How did she feel about this? At first she was humiliated, but her humiliation soon turned to outrage and, seething with anger, she reached for her pen. In an excellent analogy she enlikens the critic to a serpent. She then concludes her letter in the following way: I made a mistake possibly in sending these things, but then people "are mostly fools," and I cannot expect to be exempt from the general failing. But let me tell the critic that the most of these drawings which he regards with such scorn were done to while away hours of pain and weariness during months of close confinement, and I defy even the critic himself to present his "freshness and vivacity" under such circumstances.

My fault was in letting such things be seen.

As to having the tenderness and subtlety of Stoddard engrafted upon me, though I have the greatest admiration for these qualities, and with your critics kind leave, I would prefer to be myself with all my sins and weaknesses.

21 Thomas Stothard 1755-1834, Neoclassical Painter, Engraver and Illustrator.

Thomson was an excellent portrait painter and a member of the Miniature Portrait Society.

Amongst her commissions she drew a number of Russian refugees for illustrations in Charles Rowley's book "Fifty Years of Work Without Wages." One of these illustrations was a portrait of Prince Kropotkin.

Rowley was a great admirer of Prince Kropotkin describing him as follows:

Kropotkin is a true noble, who has thrown off mere rank, riches, Court life, great possessions on account of his profound and pure love of his fellow-creatures and his dislike of wasteful artificialities.

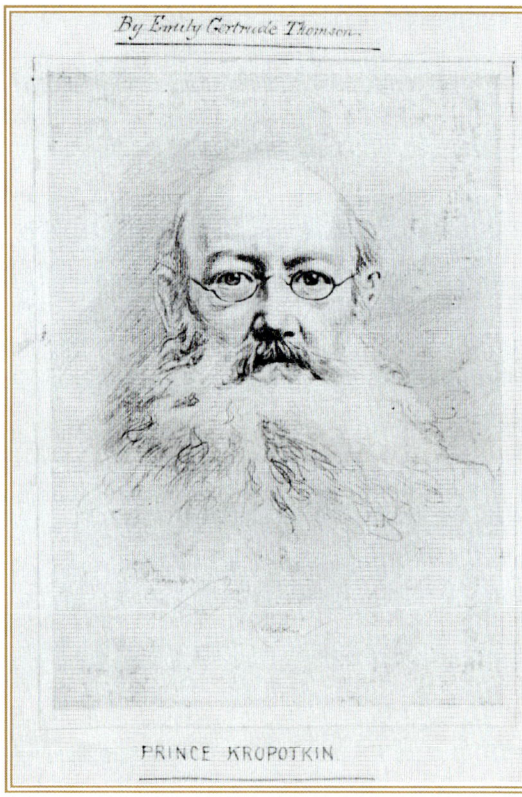

Figure 59. E. G. Thomson,
Prince Kropotkin
Manchester Central Library

Julius Soskice's portrait by Thomson also appears in this book. "One of the finest of the escaped refugees is my friend Dr. Soskice," writes Rowley. "He married a ward of mine, Juliet Hueffer, whose father was musical critic of the Times, her grandfather being Ford Madox Brown. Soskice is a lawyer and a profound student of international economics. He is a rare example of the man whose country is not worthy of him, though he would love to serve her."

Thomson also drew Father Gapon's portrait. She and he were good friends. Rowley tells how Father Gapon had a tragic ending to his life. When Father Gapon was in England I met him several times and was much impressed by him. A Russian friend interpreted for us. There is no doubt that Gapon was murdered by Government spies. He had done what to me seems to be unwise. While doing democratic work among the people he had received money help from Government sources. He thought he was loyal to the cause of emancipation, but his double dealings brought their dread reward.

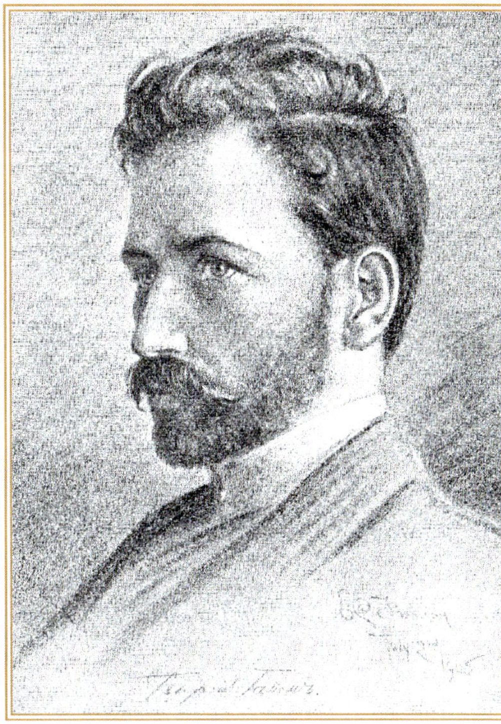

Figure 60. E. G. Thomson,
Father Gapon
Manchester Central Library

This Lancashire character by Thomson for Rowley's book portrays a typical forthright no-nonsense Lancashire man. The caption says:

A Lancashire Habit: "I'm not arguing. I'm telling thee!"

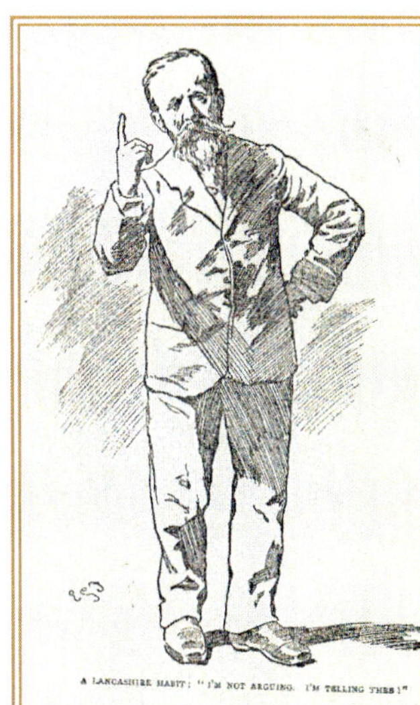

Figure 61. E. G. Thomson,
A Lancashire Habit
Manchester Central Library

In 1889 The Ancoats Brotherhood sprang from a number of Sunday meetings which had taken place during the winter months. These were extremely successful with audiences ranging from a thousand to four hundred. Rowley decided to extend these meetings into the summer and formed The Ancoats Brotherhood.

Thomson represented the Brotherhood with a depiction of George and the Dragon.

She designed and illustrated a variety of different images for her Manchester clients from concert hall tickets to illustrations for the Burgons Calendar of Lancashire Artists for 1889. Her concert hall tickets, in aid of the Ancoats Recreation fund, were very popular and became collectors' items.

Towards the end of her life, she found it necessary to dispose of the numerous mementoes Dodgson had given her, many of which she had kept for over fifty years. She died before completing the sale of one of her most prized possessions – a miniature she had made of Dodgson.

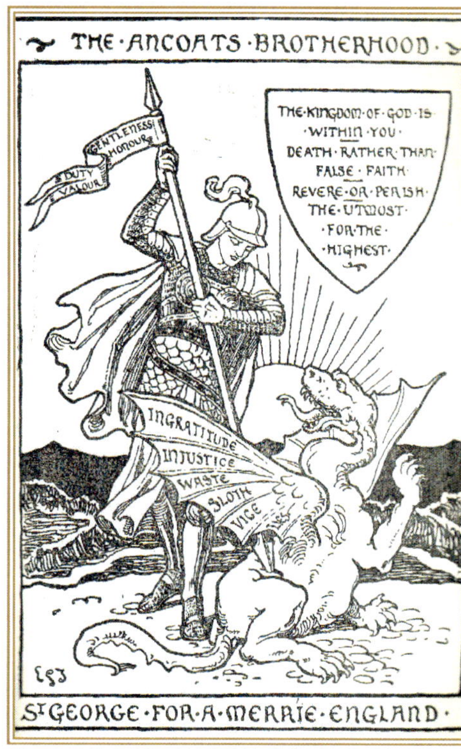

Figure 62. E. G. Thomson,
The Ancoats Brotherhood
Manchester Central Library

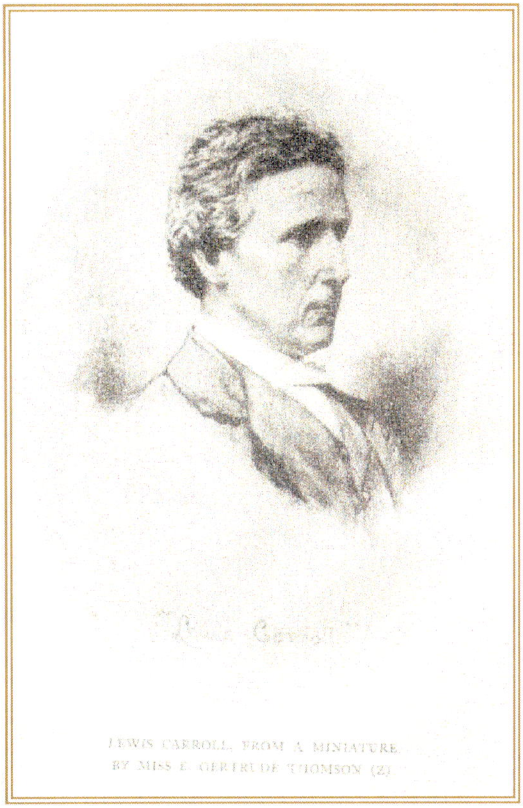

Figure 63. E. G. Thomson,
Portrait of Lewis Carroll
Columbia University Press

This miniature together with a large water colour portrait, was acquired by Professor J Enrique Zanetti, Columbia University and were displayed in an exhibition commemorating "The Hundredth Anniversary Of The Birth Of Lewis Carroll" 1932. In this catalogue Thomson merits a whole chapter to herself.

Thomson always kept in touch with Manchester and the friends she had made there. She also remained a good friend of Frederic Shields and visited him regularly right up to his death.

CHAPTER 15

ANNIE LOUISA SWYNNERTON 1844-1933

Swynnerton was born in Kersal, near Manchester. Her father was a solicitor and she had seven sisters. She and two of her sisters trained at the Manchester School of Art under W. J. Muckley, and then the Academy Julian in Paris. At the outset she painted still life, but soon began to practise in portraiture.

She first exhibited at the Royal Academy in 1879 and continued to exhibit a good number of portraits during the early part of the twentieth century. Three of her works were purchased for the nation under the terms of the Chantrey Bequest, [1] in 1924, 1929 and in 1930, the last one being a portrait of Dame Millicent Fawcett, G.B.E., LL.D (1847-1929), suffragist and educational reformer. All were included in the Chantrey Collection Winter Exhibition, R.A., 1949. [2] She also had work purchased by the French Government for the Luxembourg Gallery, Paris.

She was a member of the Society of Women Artists (1887), The Royal Society of Portrait Painters (1891) and the New English Club (1909). In 1922, at the age of seventy six, to her great credit, she was elected an Associate of the Royal Academy, the first woman to achieve this status since Mary Moser and Angelica Kauffman became founder members in 1768. She was invited to exhibit at the International Society of Sculptors Painters and Engravers and also exhibited in London at the Grosvenor and New Galleries.

In 1893 Swynnerton exhibited three paintings for the World's Columbian Exposition in Chicago. She received the following comment: **Mrs. Swynnerton's "Mater Triumphalis" at the Art Palace wins almost as much commendation as Lady Butler's famous picture, "The Roll Call."**

---

1 Sir Francis Leggatt Chantrey (1781-1841), Sculptor. Made his name with the naturalistic bust of the radical John Horne Tooke. He left his fortune to the promotion of contemporary British Art.
2 Paragraph taken from Four Centuries Of Lancashire Art.

Her paintings in the east vestibule of the Woman's Building were commented on as follows:

> The east vestibule of the Woman's Building is decorated by two large mural paintings. The one by Mrs. Swynnerton represents three different phases of nursing, the care of the young, the sick, and the aged. The decoration is in the form of a triptych.
>
> The central panel represents the Crimean Hospital at Scutari, with the sick and wounded soldiers lying on their pallet beds, their faces turned toward the single gracious figure of Florence Nightingale standing in their midst, a figure full of dignity and of pathos. It was in this hospital that the dying boy kissed the shadow of Florence Nightingale as it fell upon the wall by his bed.
>
> In one of the smaller panels we have a handsome robust young mother with a lusty child upon her knee, while the remaining one shows us the figure of an aged woman beside her sits her young granddaughter. One feels here that the situation is reversed; the young girl is repaying something of the care and love which in her infancy were lavished upon her. There is a wealth of sentiment and tenderness in this three-fold presentation of woman's great duty and prerogative, the care of the weak and helpless. [3]

In 1895 Swynnerton became the second woman, after Henrietta Rae to be elected a member of the Hanging Committee of the Liverpool Autumn Exhibition held at the Walker Art Gallery, Liverpool.

Swynnerton became a good friend of the Manchester painter Susan Isabel Dacre, and in 1884 they were both, on the same day, elected to full membership of the Manchester Academy. They were the first female artists to be accorded this honour. Jointly they formed the Manchester Society of Women Painters.

---

3 E. Crawford, <u>A Celebration of Women Writers,</u>
dig.tal.library.upenn.edu/women/elliott/art/235.html

They travelled round Italy together and whilst in Rome Annie met her future husband the sculptor Joseph Swynnerton, who was born in Douglas, Isle-of-Man. [4] He had arrived in Rome in 1869 and entered the Academy of St. Luke, where in his first year he won Pope Pius IX's second (silver) medal, and in his second year the first (gold) medal for sculpture,- the silver medal being probably the last that bore that Pope's effigy.

It was his half-size statue of "Cain," highly commended by the art critic John Ruskin, that earned him his name in Manchester. On exhibiting this statue in Manchester he received numerous orders from Manchester's magnates. He was elected a member of the Literary Society and the Manchester Academy of Fine Arts.

He was always happiest in his studio in Rome. For several years this was in the Piazza Trinita de Monti, and afterwards on the ground floor of the house he built himself, in the new part of the city - No. 2 Via Montebello, overlooking the British Embassy's garden. He and Annie married in 1883 and lived in Rome until his death in 1910.

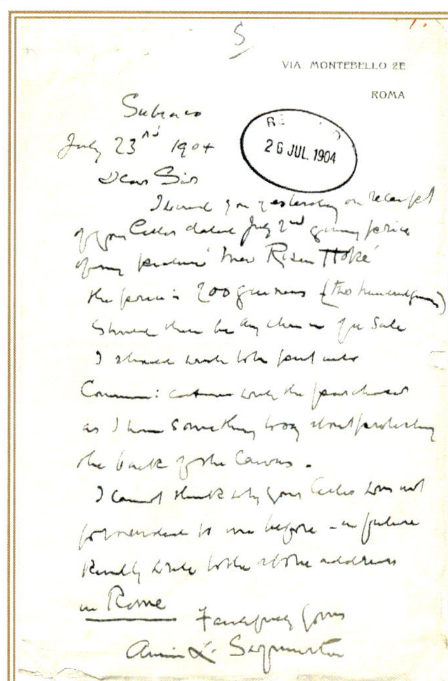
VIA MONTEBELLO 2E
ROMA
Subiaco
July 23rd 1904
26 JUL. 1904
Dear Sir
[illegible]
[illegible] 'New Risen Hope'
the price is 200 guineas (two hundred guineas)
[illegible]
[illegible]
in Rome
Faithfully yours
Annie L. Swynnerton

Figure 64. ***Letter written by Annie L. Swynnerton***

According to this letter they were still living at Via Montebello 2E in July 1904. This letter is a valuable piece of history allowing an insight into how much Swynnerton charged for one of her paintings. Here she quotes a price of 200 guineas for her painting "New Risen Hope."

After her husband died she returned to Manchester and the art critic for the City News, just to name one, was very pleased to see her back.

He wrote: **In her earlier days she had been a frequent exhibitor in Mosley Street,**

4 A Manx Sculptor and His Work, Isle-of-man.com/manxnotebook/mannin.

but before the Jubilee Exhibition of the Manchester Academy last year we had long missed her work from these walls.

Her contributions to the present exhibition are not only a delight, but a revelation to most of us. We would not willingly forego a single example she has here.

Her virility, her many-sidedness, her sustained power are surprising. The assured mastery of her drawing; the roundness of the modelling, and the tangibility of her classical nude figures, the tenderness of the flesh painting of her symbolic female forms, the Titianesque richness of her colour; these are matters to note and give thanks for.

He also waxes lyrical about her painting "Oreads," consisting of five cave-goddesses, hand fast and singing on a rock by the sea: [5]

How nobly the lines of the figures fall. You might call them sculpturesque but for the sense of instantaneous motion and bounding vitality. And they are not women, but goddesses confessed.

This picture is a typical illustration of the distinction between the nude and the undressed. Look at it! Does the absence of drapery strike you at all except as an afterthought? Would not the imposition of clothing on any of these majestic forms be an outrage nay, an indelicacy? [6]

5 In mythology Oreads were nymphs of the mountains, and Oceanids were nymphs of the sea.

6 Autumn Exhibition, City News, 15th October, 1910.

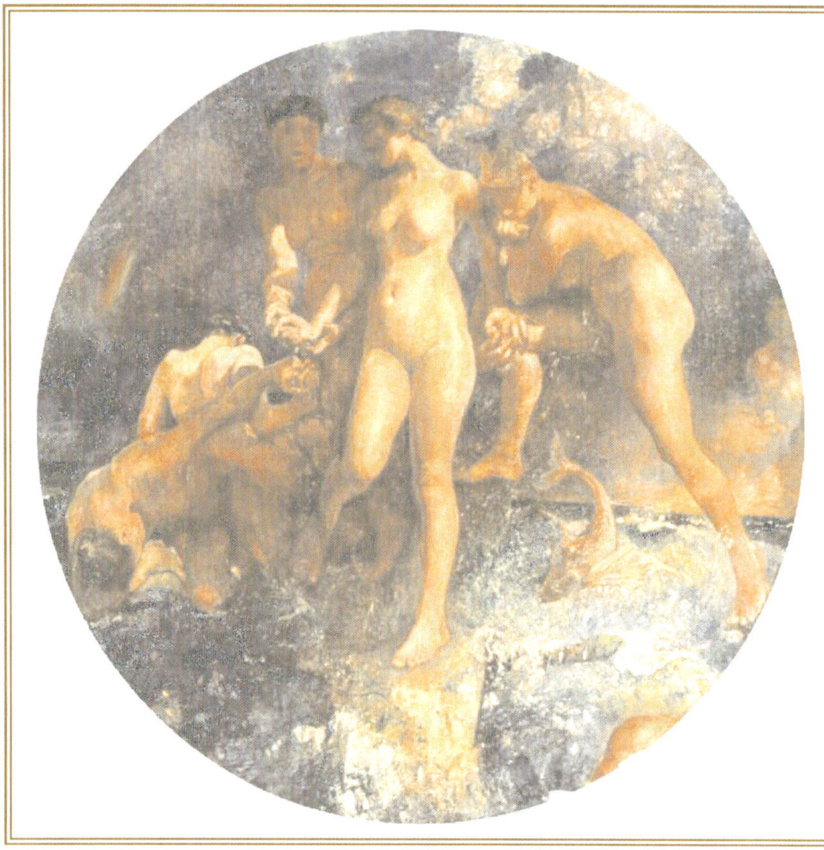

Figure. 65. A. L. Swynnerton, *Oreads*
Tate, London 2005

The critic from the Evening News declared that one of the great features of the exhibition was the beauty and strength of this Manchester born painter. He had a slightly different slant on Swynnerton's "Oreads" he thought they were: **wild creatures splendid in animal strength and beauty, whose voices are the sounds of the mountain winds. And in light and brilliant, nay burning colour, the picture is like triumphant organ-music calling upon us to rejoice in the glorious manifested powers of nature.** 7

He makes no reference to the absence of drapery. Once again, this substantiates that a piece of art can be interpreted in a number of diverse ways, especially when it contains a nude, or in this case several nudes.

7 Evening News, 9th September, 1910.

The Tate presented an exhibition in 2002 named "Exposed: The Victorian Nude." Partly described as follows: This exhibition charts the precarious development of subject matter which was both prestigious and dangerous, highlighting concerns about sexuality, desire and censorship that are still relevant today.

A number of Swynnerton's paintings were included in this exhibition. When this same exhibition reached the Brooklyn Museum, New York, Paulanne Simmons [8] stated: If the nude, alternately interpreted as a sign of aesthetic advancement or moral decay, reflects a society's attitudes on sexuality, public health, social welfare, racial attitudes, suffragist issues, religion and censorship, as this exhibition proposes, then Exposed: The Victorian Nude is definitely ... well ... revealing.

Astutely, Simmons describes one of Swynnerton's paintings in the exhibition as a symbol of female emancipation, and in doing so, she immediately hits the nail on the head. Perhaps female emancipation should have been added to Simmon's list. Ludicrously, Swynnerton actually had to fight to paint her nudes. It was only because she stood up to her male colleagues, and took no notice of Victorian tittle-tattle based upon "nice ladies not standing next to men in life drawing classes," she managed to produce any nude paintings at all.Swynnerton was raised on an artistic rhetoric with its roots firmly planted way back in time. Perfectly summed up by the German artist Johann Zoffany during the late eighteenth century when he painted his famous group portrait "The Academicians of the Royal Academy."

In this famous painting the Academy's members are shown gathered around a nude male model at a time when women were excluded from such training in order to protect their modesty. Zoffany, determined to include the female artists Mary Moser and Angelica Kauffman, added them as portraits hanging on the wall.

These archaic rules still persisted in Manchester during the nineteenth century and in her own particular way Swynnerton helped to bring them to a standstill. Not only did she and a number of other female artists form their own life drawing classes, they also managed to break down the masculine walls of the Manchester Academy of Fine

---

8 Curator's Choice: There's More To The Victorians Than Meets The Eye, nymuseums.com/ps0210it.hm

Arts and in so doing it was no longer seen as unladylike for a female artist to produce a painting of a nude person.

On her return from Italy she began to exhibit again at the Royal Academy and her work was much sought after, especially by Sir George Clausen who purchased "New-Risen Hope," depicting the figure of a naked child in 1906. He later presented this painting to the National Gallery of Victoria in Melbourne. John Singer Sargent bought "Oreads" in 1907 and gave it to the Tate Gallery, London in 1922, and it was in 1922, with the help of Clausen and Sargent, Swynnerton became the first woman to be elected an Associate of the Royal Academy. This was quite a feat since the only previous women to rank as Academicians were Angelica Kauffman and Mary Moser in 1768, and they were made members without election.

At eighty four Swynnerton received the following praise: **Among the contributions made by North Country artists to the Royal Academy Summer Exhibition none is more outstanding than the work of Mrs Annie Swynnerton of Manchester, who despite her eighty four years confounds the critics by submitting one of the best pictures seen in the show. Mrs Swynnerton's energy is marvellous. She refrains undiminished her ability to paint in a simple, beautiful and appealing way, and it is a crowning achievement that at this time of the day the Senior Associate should continue to hold the highest honours among the women artists. "The Convalescent" is a delicious piece of work. The study of the girl sealed in a landscape has a pathos and charm of its own.** [9]

At eighty seven Swynnerton received the following praise from Lady Alexander Haig: **Mrs Annie Swynnerton paints for long hours in her studio by the sea at her bungalow on Hayling Island, Hampshire. She has a magnetic vivid personality and her memory is remarkable – she recites poetry for hours at a time.** [10]

---

9 Daily Despatch, 6th March 1929, Mrs A Swynnerton's Academy Marvel.

10 Lady Alexander Haig, Woman Artist – Eighty Seven: Long Hours in Studio.

CHAPTER 16

EXHIBITIONS

Victoria's reign is almost at an end and when it finally passes Manchester is blessed with an extremely healthy art scene; a scene which will continue to grow and gather in a new generation of art lovers and entrepreneurs. This chapter could be seen as a conclusion, but really it is just an excuse for a short peep into a number of the city's exhibitions to see how Manchester's Victorian Art Scene had evolved.

Manchester was now well known for its fine art exhibitions, especially those held within the City Art Gallery. The preview was definitely the highlight for every exhibition. It was an exciting occasion and was always well attended by a variety of people connected with the arts. There was great kudos to be had if one was seen at this kind of function. Business deals were made and a huge amount of gossip exchanged. It was also a regular fashion show between both sexes.

Whereas the preview stayed much the same with music, speeches, and refreshments, over a period of time, the Gallery's exhibitions changed. They evolved from the displaying of invariable fine arts to a more diverse range of arts. This phase took some time and caused many groans and temper tantrums from all walks of life before a light could be seen at the end of the tunnel.

The Arts Committee certainly had their hands full. Each exhibition had to appeal to a large percentage of its miscellaneous visitors or it would be seen as a failure, and too many failures meant jobs axed and reputations lost. Manchester's art scene was jealously guarded and extremely competitive: a position within the arts was always coveted, so with this in mind a lot of hard thought went into each exhibition. The Committee supervised a mixture of exhibitions during the Victorian period, and the following are just a chosen few along with some of the effects they had on their viewers.

Having been accused of a certain amount of neglect towards local artists the Art Committee decided to promote their Manchester artists through an exhibition. They invited four of the leading members of the Manchester Academy each to fill a room at Mosley Street with representations of their work. These artists were: Clarence Whaite, Anderson Hague, F. W. Jackson and Tom Mostyn. Joseph Knight had originally been approached, but was unable to exhibit so Tom Mostyn stood in for him.

It was hoped that as an outcome of the exhibition public interest in local art, as represented by the Manchester Academy in particular, would be stimulated. It was also hoped that the well-to-do citizens who attended the opening function would take the hint conveyed by the Lord Mayor a little later on in the proceedings.

There was a large representative gathering at the ceremony including members of the City Council, artists and friends of art. Among them was the Mayor of Salford (Mrs. Frankenburg) and Councillor Walter Butterworth, Chairman of the Art Gallery Committee.

The Lord Mayor expressly hoped that the exhibition would prove such a success that the Art Gallery Committee would be well rewarded in its effort to make known to everyone the works of the various artists who were connected with Manchester. **Personally I have always felt strongly that those artists were not supported as they ought to be. It was all very well for Manchester people to take their money to London and elsewhere, but if it were found that the same value could be got here, as was often the case, it was their duty to spend their money where it was made.**

This exhibition was centred around four prominent Manchester artists, and the Lord Mayor had added a certain amount of prestige and support for the Committee. On the whole it was well received and all its visitors were delighted to see their local artists receiving praise and attention.

Twelve months later, in December 1907, the Gallery Committee staged a completely different kind of exhibition with links further afield than Manchester. It was entitled: "Modern French Paintings At The City Art Gallery." The bulk of the works belonged to the Durand-Ruel and Staats Forbes [1] collections, the former was a famous Parisian Art Dealer, the latter an English Railway Director. The collections were bravely created at a time when the official directors of art, and

1 James Staats Forbes, 1823-1904, General Manager of the London Chatham and Dover Railway. He was an art connoisseur, and uncle of Stanhope Alexander Forbes.

the public at large, were blind to the merits of such revolutionary work. The Committee knew they were going out on a limb exhibiting these paintings, but it was vital Manchester should be seen as a forward thinking city especially where the arts were concerned.

This exhibition consisted of two major movements in nineteenth century art, the Barbizon and the Impressionist Movements. All the leaders of their respective schools were represented enabling the viewer to see how these movements evolved.

The Manchester Guardian 2 congratulated the Committee on the way they had brought all these paintings together, but its critic did have one regret: My only criticism with regard to this exhibition is perhaps Whistler who was so powerful an influence in the art of the latter half of the last century should have been included in the exhibition.

With regard to the pictures he continued: We may admire them or not, and it is certainly permissible not to admire them all, but they are serious productions which deserve and will repay study, and their existence must be faced as part of the natural development of modern art.

Then he gave his own opinion on the exhibits, declaring that it was impossible to run the old with the new and that all the traditional techniques had been sacrificed for the more modern ones: The first sensation we receive from the exhibition is one of a shock of contact with virulent, quivering light and air, and it is to express just these things that the old traditions of painting have one by one been sacrificed.

The critic from the Yorkshire Post also referred to older techniques, but was far more lenient: Whereas the old realism was mainly devoted to the study of detail in things themselves, the new impressionism is chiefly concerned with the phenomena of light vibrating through the living air directly, or reflected from the surface of rippled water. Never have I seen the particular effect more perfectly conveyed than it is in "Vetheuil" one of Monet's more recent paintings, in which the painted ripples almost have the hypnotising effect of the reality. 3

---

2 Manchester Guardian, 10th December 1907, Modern French Paintings At The City Art Gallery. First Notice.

3 Yorkshire Post, 11th December 1907, French Art At Manchester.

At last, here was a critic just enjoying the paintings. He had allowed himself to wallow in them and had become mesmerised with their play on light and colour. He did not see the Impressionists as some dire tribe of uncivilised French artists. He knew they were part of the old school with a history not only deep rooted in French artistic traditions but English ones too and with this in mind he advised visitors to the exhibition to linger for a while in the entrance room: **Visitors to this admirably arranged collection should linger a while in the entrance room, and dwell upon the examples of Constable, Turner and Boddington the three Englishmen whose children the modern French Impressionists are. In addition to these Englishmen the early French naturalists of the Barbizon School - Corot, Millet, Diaz, Daubigny, Tryon and others - are represented upon the walls of the first room.**

This French Impressionist Exhibition did not go down very well with the Manchester landscape artist, Frederick Jackson. He was not at all enamoured with it. He issued a warning to all students of art in a lecture at the Municipal School of Art on "Methods of Training In Landscape"[4] not to copy the Impressionists. During this lecture he referred to the exhibition in Manchester of the work of the French Impressionists which he scathingly said "had borne fruit among the young painters in Manchester." He continued: **It was safe for the student to leave the modern alone for the present and fall back upon the recognised masters such as Michelangelo, Leonardo, Titian, whose works the tide of fashion had long since ceased to trouble, than listen to the eulogy and damnation of opposing critics.**

Jackson painted out of doors, even when it was freezing and his hands were numb and blue, but he had his own theories on this: "Artists were apt to forget that they were working in a light much stronger than in which their pictures would be viewed." And, while he was on the subject of light he went on to warn his students not to fall into the trap of making their pictures too dark, stating: **They might**

---

4 Manchester Guardian, Impressionist Painting – Mr. F. W. Jackson's Warning to Students, 17th September, 1908.

easily fall into the error of making their pictures too dark, especially if they followed too closely the theory of values, as was done by an earnest band of students who left that school about thirty years ago, and became known as the Manchester School of Painters.

Much of the excellent work they did was unfortunately begun in too low a key, and it had since suffered much from bad atmosphere. From their failures much might be learned. No matter how good the work, if it did not fulfil the mission of giving pleasure, it failed.

Ironically, Jackson had joined this group a little later when they were experimenting with colour and became known as one of the Manchester Painters.

From an artistic and personal point of view Jackson did not enjoy this exhibition and definitely did not appreciate the way its producers worked. Whether he managed to convince his students these new methods (in his opinion) were wrong is another matter. History might be moving on, but the same old arguments were still around and it would take more time to change certain attitudes before any major changes could be claimed.

"Let a man of genius use the Daguerreotype as it should be used, and it will rise to heights that none of us can imagine."

Eugene Delacroix 1853.

The next exhibition held in January 1909 caused quite a stir, but it could be seen as a major break through for the Arts Committee. Impressionistic techniques were once again being maligned. But, this was only half the story. The Art Committee had agreed to hold a photographic exhibition. It was open to professional photographers as well as amateurs and was a representative show of the best in photography. Here was something new, exciting and different. The burning question on a number of lips and especially on one critic's pen nib was: 5 "Is Photography a Form of Art?" He wrote: **All sorts of stiff little problems in aesthetics are raised in the Northern**

5 Manchester Guardian, 7th January 1909, Photographic Exhibition - At The Manchester Art Gallery.

Photographic Exhibition, which opened in the Manchester City Art Gallery yesterday.

The lending of our City Art Gallery for an exhibition of photographs in itself seems to imply recognition of the newer claims to photography.

When is a photograph not a photograph but a work of art? According to our critic it would seem this conundrum was easily solved depending on whether you were a plain person or a subtle person, or as he put it: **And that brings one up smartly against the difficulty of whether photography can ever be "art" at all. The plain man says, in the idiom of plain men, that the Impressionistic photograph, if not art, is something uncommonly like it; but the subtle person goes on vexed by doubt. "When is a photograph not a photograph but a work of art?" he asks, and is not satisfied by being told that the question is needless fighting over words.**

Questions were being asked, and not just by plain and subtle individuals. "Should a photographic exhibition be put on show in Manchester's City Art Gallery?" "Was it abusing all the gallery stood for?" This last question puzzled some people, because they were not quite sure what the gallery did stand for. Then the most important question of all was broached, "what was the gallery's stance on art?" The public had become curious and wanted to know if the Arts Committee consider art to be just drawing and painting or did they consider it involved a number of other techniques such as photography?

Councillor Butterworth opened the exhibition and he made it clear the Arts Committee had been criticised for allowing the exhibition to be held within the walls of the gallery. In his speech he said: "The Art Gallery was, of course, the proper place to be the home of the fine arts, but he hoped to see in Manchester a time when there would be ample accommodation for arts and crafts other than those highest forms of the fine arts."

Butterworth was convinced that one of the tragedies of modern civilisation was that, in a city like Manchester, there was such a deep chasm between the works of fine art, which were studied, and the actual life lived by the people in their homes and workshops. He hoped that when the gallery had more room it would be able to adopt a far wider and more sympathetic attitude, and would favour cooperation with all kinds of workers who could produce work good of its kind.

One critic made his feelings clear about the exhibition. He used some very uncomplimentary phrases all aimed at the photographer's techniques: "He cannot box up imagination in his camera." "The photographer cannot escape the restrictions of his medium." "The beauty his mind sees comes out on his plate too often as prettiness."

Basically, he was unable to come to terms with a number of photographers experimenting and trying to make their cameras capture "atmosphere." He was not pleased with, as he put it, Liverpool Docks being etherealised to a grey dream, the dock offices like a dream palace, and the barges in the quiet water as filmy as in a Turner picture.

For all this criticism the Arts Committee stood their ground, not only had they embarked on a new and exciting adventure, they had the Mayor's backing with all its rhetoric. They were making it perfectly clear that they wanted Manchester's citizens to become more aware of the works of the various artists connected with the city, and so did the Daily News. [6] Their correspondent quickly jumped on the band wagon with an article headed "Art Not A Luxury." He was particularly concerned with Manchester's textiles and wanted to know why in a city which was world famous for its textiles were there none on permanent display? Other cities such as Zurich, Cologne, Munich and a dozen other commercial cities of modern growth all had impressive textile collections on display.

It was pointed out that Lyons had a magnificent collection of silk textiles filling a beautiful building as large as the Manchester City Art Gallery. Furthermore, it was regularly studied, not only by the people of Lyons, but by those interested in silk production all over the world. Whereas in Manchester, the chief centre of the textile industry, there was no provision for such an exhibition. The Bock collection acquired by the Art Gallery Committee twenty years ago, had never yet been properly shown.

---

6 Art Not A Luxury, 27th May, 1909.

This article made the Director of the School of Technology, Mr. J. H. Reynolds, wring his hands with despair. Why? Because no matter how he tried, the present facilities at the Museum of Decorative Crafts at the School of Art were not fully taken advantage of. Only students visited the Museum and despite the fact it was open to everyone the general public never came near it even though the collection contained many fine examples of textile design. He had tried to encourage amateurs to attend the classes at the School of Art in order to improve their taste but so far these facilities had not been taken advantage of.

He thought it really came down to educating the public's taste, and in so doing creating a demand for examples of fine craftsmanship. In the city of Manchester there were cotton trade firms able and willing to produce the most beautiful and delightful fabrics, alike in texture and in design, but these were expensive with a very limited market - mainly because they were immediately imitated in inferior low priced materials destroying any market for the original.

The crux of the matter was the textile industry was perfectly capable of producing beautiful artistic materials, but the public's taste was beset with difficulties. The calico printer had in general to print for the million, not only in this country, but abroad. He had to accommodate himself to the taste of Fiji Islanders and the West Africans. The other day when a manufacturer had shown Reynolds a handkerchief which had a huge sale on the West Coast of Africa, he was horrified with it, because it was stamped with a hideous caricature of George the Third.

With all this in mind, plus the aftermath of the recent photographic exhibition, the Committee decided to launch a new experiment. After twenty six years they decided to abandon the customary Autumn Exhibition due to lack of space. A small one of a more adventurous nature was to be held. Described by the Courier 7 as follows: **The Art Gallery Committee of the Manchester Corporation has ventured on a special exhibition of modern oil paintings, watercolour drawings, etchings, lithographs, woodcuts, sculpture and jewellery and it is as interesting as it is instructive. Too little is known locally**

---

7 Special Exhibition at the Municipal Gallery: Art In Manchester, 8th September 1909.

of the work of men who, at more or less of distance, carry on the tradition of William Morris and his friends.

The Committee had made a momentous decision when changing their exhibition schedule. They were now moving further and further away from the repetitive fine art exhibitions and concentrating more on mixed media displays. It was a brave move to make but it certainly paid off in the end. The reason being - now all Manchester's artists and citizens could enjoy its splendid art scene not just the chosen few.

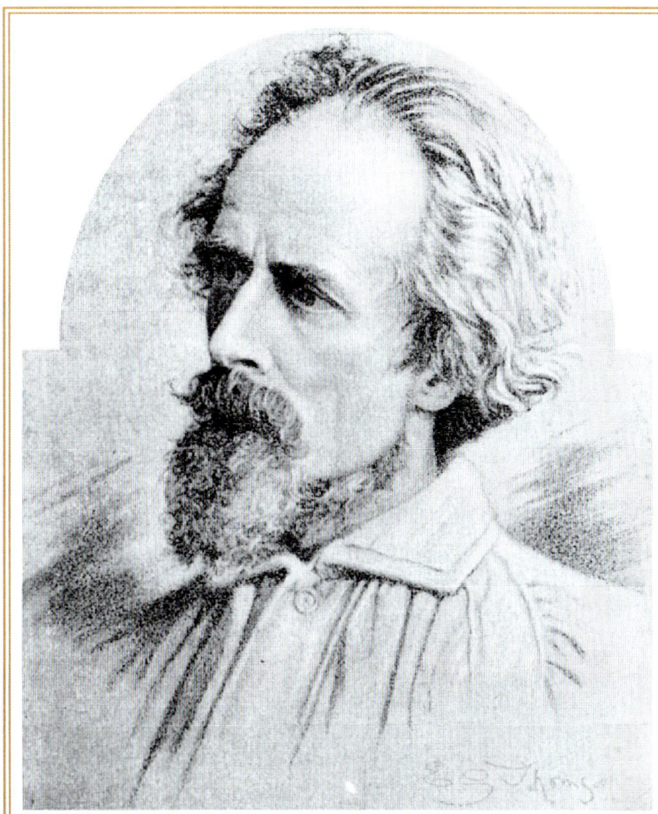

We should thank Manchester's Victorian Artists for leaving us such an incredible legacy to build upon. A legacy which is still rich in pride, excitement, fun and just a touch of angst every now and then. [8]

8 Portrait of Frederic Shields by E. G. Thomson.

BIBLIOGRAPHY

Adams Steven, 1994, *The Barbizon School & The Origins Of Impressionism* London, Phaidon Press Limited.
Allingham William, *The Fairies*, London, Thos.De La Rue & Co.
Archer John H. G., 1985, *Art And Architecture In Victorian Manchester,* Manchester: University Press.
Axon W. E. A., 1886, *The Annals of Manchester*, J. Heywood, Deansgate & Ridgefield.
Bailey Millard, 1924, *History of The San Francisco Bay Region,* San Francisco: American Historical Society.
Bajac Quentin, 2002, *The Invention of Photography: The First Fifty Years,* London: Thames & Hudson.
Becker R. J. and Weisberg G. P., 1999, *Overcoming All Obstacles: The Women of the Academie Julian,* New York: Dahesh Museum.
Billcliffe Roger, 1985, *The Glasgow Boys,* The Glasgow School of Painting 1875- 1895, London: John Murray (P) Limited.
Brierley Ben, 1896, *"Ab-o'th'-Yate" Sketches,* vols. 1,11, 111, Edited by James Dronsfield. Oldham: W. E. Clegg.
Brookes Warwick, 1889, *Pencil Pictures of Child Life,* Manchester Press.
Byrde Penelope, 1992, *Nineteenth Century Fashion,* London: B. T. Batsford.
Child Dennis, 2002, *Painters In The Northern Counties of England And Wales,* Wiltshire: Hilmarton Manor Press.
Clark Anne, 1979, Lewis Carroll A Biography London: J.M. Dent & Sons.
Cleveland S. D., 1931, *The Royal Manchester Institution* Printed by direction of the Council
Clifford Timothy, 1983, *A Guide to Manchester City Art Galleries,* Surrey: South Leigh Press Limited.
Cohen Morton N., 1995, *Lewis Carroll, A Biography*, London: Macmillan.
Cohen Morton N., 1979, *The Letters Of Lewis Carroll,* vol 1, ca. 1837-1885, London: Macmillan.
Cohen Morton N., 1979, *The Letters Of Lewis Carroll,* vol 2, ca. 1886-1898, London: Macmillan.
Cohen Morton N. & Edward Wakeling, 2003, *Lewis Carroll And His Illustrators,* Oxford: Pan Macmillan.
Coombs Trevor, 1990, *Rising From Reality, Art in Oldham from 1820-1890,* Manchester: Snape Partners.
Crust L, 1910, *Eton College Portraits,* p.34, n.91, illustr.pl. XXXV1.
Darbyshire Alfred, 1907, *The Art of the Victorian Stage,* Manchester: Sherratt & Hughes
Dewsbury Sheila, 2003, *The Story So Far: The Manchester Academy of Fine Arts - 1859-2003,* Manchester: Manchester Academy of Fine Arts.
Edwards Jane, Treuherz J. B., 1978, *Concise Catalogue of British Paintings, vol ii, British Artists Born In Or After 1850, Manchester City Art Galleries,* City of Manchester – Manchester Cultural Services.
Fawcett Trevor, 1974, *The Rise of English Provincial Art, Artists, Patrons and Institutions outside London 1800-1830,* Oxford, Clarendon Press.
Foster Charles, 1999, *Arley Hall and Gardens Cheshire,* Norwich, Jarrold Publishing.
Gauge John, 1995, *Colour and Culture*, London: Thames and Hudson.
Green Roger Lancelyn, 1971, *The Diaries Of Lewis Carroll,* vol 2, Connecticut: Greenwood Press Publishers.

Harris Museum and Art Gallery, Preston, 1958, *Four Centuries Of Lancashire Art,* Preston: Corporation.
Haward Lawrence, 1917, *The Manchester Art Gallery Reproductions from the Collection and Catalogue,* Introduction, London: Eyre & Spottiswoode, LDD.
Holland Su and Campion Paul, 2002, *The Parish Church of St. Ann, St. Ann's Square,* Manchester, (Manchester: St. Ann's Church).
Hughes Edan Milton, 1989, *Artists In California 1786-1940,* vol ii, San Francisco: Hughes Publishing Company.
Jopling Louise, 1925, *Twenty Years Of My Life, 1867-1887,* Edinburgh: Morrison & Gibb Limited.
Kelly Audrey, 1992, *Lydia Becker and The Cause,* Centre for North-West Regional Studies, University of Lancaster.
Lockett T. A., 1968, *Three Lives It Happened Round Manchester,* London: University Press Limited.
Lucie-Smith Edward, 1984, *Dictionary Of Art Terms,* London: Thames and Hudson.
Macmillan Publishers Limited, 2000, *The Grove Dictionary of Art.*
Manchester City Art Galleries, *A Century Of Collecting 1882-1982, 1983,* Hampshire: BAS Printers Limited.
Messinger Gary S, 1985, *Manchester In The Victorian Age. The Half Known City,* Manchester: University Press.
Mills Ernestine, *The Life and Letters of Frederic Shields 1833-1911,* Longmans, Green And Co., London.
Murray Peter and Linda, 1989, *The Penguin Dictionary Of Art and Artists,* (London: Penguin Group).
Newton Bill, *Manchester Royal Jubilee Exhibition Old Trafford, 1887,* Manchester: Trafford Leisure Services.
Oldham Art Gallery: *Oldham Art and Artists Represented in the Public Gallery,*
Ormond R, 1973, 2 vols, *Early Victorian Portraits.*
Pach Walter, 1938, *Queer Thing, Painting – Forty Years In The World Of Art,* NewYork: Books For Libraries Press.
Phythian J Ernest, 1903, *Hours At the Manchester City Art Gallery,* Manchester: Sherratt & Hughes.
Pike T. John, 2002, *The Sense Of Pleasure,* A Collection of Still Life Paintings, London: Thames & Hudson.
Pool Phoebe, 1967, *Impressionism,* London: Thames and Hudson.
Puget Catherine, Campbell Julian, 2004, *Peintres britanniques en Bretagne,* Musee de Pont-Aven.
Rossetti William Michael, 1895, *Dante Gabriel Rossetti. His Family-letters with a Memoir vol 1.*
Rowley Charles, 1911, *Fifty Years of Work Without Wages*, London: Hodder & Stoughton.
Sellars Jane, *Dictionary of Women Artists,* vol 11 London: Fitzroy Dearburn.
Smith Alison, 1996, *The Victorian Nude*, Manchester University Press.
Steegman John, 1957, *Portraits in Welsh Houses,* vol I, North Wales, National Museum of Wales.
Swift Anne, *The Story of George Cooper - Stockport's Last Town Crier 1824-1895*. Stockport Reference Library.
Swindells T, 1907, *Manchester Streets and Manchester Men,* 3rd Series, Manchester: J. E. Cornish Limited.
Thomas Donald, 1999, *The Victorian Underworld,* London: John Murray.

Tickner Lisa, 2003, *Dante Gabriel Rossetti,* London: Tate Publishing.
Tozer Jane & Levitt Sarah, 1983, *Fabric of Society - A Century of People and Their Clothes 1770-1870,* Wales: Laura Ashley Limited.
Tracey W. B., and Pike W.T. 1899 *Manchester and Salford At The Close Of The Nineteenth Century,* Pike's New Century Series No.2, (Brighton: W.T. Pike).
Wood Christopher, 2000, *Fairies In Victorian Art,* Suffolk: Antique Collectors Club Limited.

ARTICLES:

Letherbrow Thomas, 1891, *Robert Crozier,* Manchester: J.E. Cornish.
Manchester City News Notes and Queries, v *Robert Crozier*, 1878, p.266-7 (No.582).
Melbrook Geoffrey, Papers of the Manchester Litarary Club, vol 5, 1879.
Morris E. and McKay A, February 1992, Apollo, 135 *British Art Students in Paris 1814-1890*, p.p. 78-84.
Nicholson Francis, and Axon Ernest, Transactions of Lancashire & Cheshire Antiquarian Society - 1910, *The Hatfield Family of Manchester and The Food Riots of 1757 and 1812.*
Nodal J. H., 1884, *Art In Lancashire And Cheshire,* Papers of the Manchester Literary Club p.467.
Redfern B. A., 1911, *St. Pauls Literary and Educational Society Manchester,* vol xxll, 1876.
Treuherz Julian, *Jonathan Hatfield of Manchester and Naples,* Apollo Feb 1983.

CATALOGUES:

Arts Council Exhibition 1978, *Great Victorian Pictures: Their Path to Fame.*
Aspland P.P., *Brasenose Club, Manchester Catalogue of the Exhibition of Works of J.H.E. Partington,* Illustrated by Sketches, 1879, Ashton-Under-Lyne: William Brown
Catalogue of an Exhibition to commemorate The One Hundredth Anniversary of the Birth Of Lewis Carroll, 1832 – 1898, New York: Columbia University Press.
The Oldham Collection: *Later Oldham Artists, November 1990-Ocober 1991.*

NEWSPAPERS:

Bolton Chronicle.
Clarion.
City Jackdaw.
Manchester City News.
Manchester Guardian.
Manchester Herald.
Observer, Oakland, California.
Oldham Evening Chronicle.
Salford Weekly News.

MAGAZINES

North Of England Magazine.
Odds and Ends A Manuscript Magazine.
The Queen.

INTERNET ARTICLES:

Crawford E, *A Celebration of Women Writers,* dig.tal.library.upenn.edu/women/elliott/art/235.html

Flowers and Plants Association, org.uk/Flowers/facts/e-j/iris.htm

Gordon Dick, 9/19/2002, theconnection.org/shows w002/0919b main.asp

Ricochet-jeunes.org/eng/biblio/books/alice

Ross Sherry Lazarus Ross, 2002, artrenewal.org/articles/2002/ExposedVictorianNude/sherry1.asp

Swynnerton J. W. 2005, *A Manx Sculptor and His Work,* Isle-of-man.com/manxnotebook/mannin.

Simmons Paulanne, 2002, Curator's Choice: *There's More To The Victorians Than Meets The Eye,* nymuseums.com/ps0210it.hm

INDEX

3

07709 001331

MW - 07716 543817